CAMP CENTURY

CAMP CENTURY

THE UNTOLD STORY OF AMERICA'S SECRET ARCTIC MILITARY BASE UNDER THE GREENLAND ICE

KRISTIAN H. NIELSEN AND
HENRY NIELSEN

Columbia University Press
New York

Columbia University Press
Publishers Since 1893
New York   Chichester, West Sussex
cup.columbia.edu

Published with the generous support of the Carlsberg Foundation and the
Aarhus University Research Foundation.

Library of Congress Cataloging-in-Publication Data

Names: Nielsen, Henry, author. | Nielsen, Kristian Hvidtfelt, 1968– author. |
Flegal, Heidi, translator.
Title: Camp Century : the untold story of America's secret Arctic military base
under the Greenland ice / Kristian H. Nielsen, and Henry Nielsen ; translation
by Heidi Flegal.
Other titles: Camp Century. English | Untold story of America's secret Arctic
military base under the Greenland ice
Description: New York : Columbia University Press, [2021] | Includes
bibliographical references and index.
Identifiers: LCCN 2021002517 (print) | LCCN 2021002518 (ebook) |
ISBN 9780231201766 (hardback) | ISBN 9780231201773 (trade paperback) |
ISBN 9780231554251 (ebook)
Subjects: LCSH: Camp Century (Nuclear laboratory : Greenland)—History. |
Nuclear weapons—Greenland—History. | Project Iceworm (U.S.)—History. |
United States—Foreign relations—Denmark. | Denmark—Foreign relations—
United States. | Cold War. | Intercontinental ballistic missiles—United
States—History. | United States. Army.
Classification: LCC U167.5.P6 N5413 2021 (print) | LCC U167.5.P6 (ebook) |
DDC 358.1/754709982—dc23
LC record available at https://lccn.loc.gov/2021002517
LC ebook record available at https://lccn.loc.gov/2021002518

Cover design: Julia Kushnirsky
Cover photo: Getty Images

CONTENTS

PREFACE

This book was first conceived as a byproduct of our involvement in a transatlantic research project entitled "Exploring Greenland: Science and Technology in Cold War Settings." The project was a collaborative effort among ten researchers: seven from the Centre for Science Studies at Aarhus University, Denmark, and three from the History Department at Florida State University. Thanks to funding from the Carlsberg Foundation, which ran from 2010 to 2014, the group's work consisted of nine subprojects, one of which revolved around a U.S. Army facility called Camp Century, a scientific base located under the surface of the ice sheet about 220 km (137 miles) east of Thule Air Base in northwestern Greenland.

While working under the umbrella project we have both published articles and book contributions about Camp Century, in Danish and in English. We are not the first to do this, and we will surely not be the last. For many years, however, we have felt the need for a book in English that provides exhaustive coverage of the place often called "the city under the ice." We were lacking a 360-degree view of its purpose, conception, birth, life, and death, not to mention the thorny issue of its earthly remains, which continue to create problems for the three nations they directly affect: Greenland, Denmark, and the United States. It was against this backdrop that we decided, in 2016, to remedy this deficiency. Our efforts bore fruit, appearing first in Danish in 2017 and then translated into this English version, which allows the material to reach a considerably wider yet equally relevant audience.

During this process we have benefited from help and inspiration from many sides, particularly from our fellow participants in the "Exploring Greenland" project. Heartfelt thanks are therefore owed to Ronald E. Doel, Kristine Harper, Matthias Heymann, Lif Lund Jacobsen, Donald J. Kinney, Henrik Knudsen, Janet Martin-Nielsen, and Christopher Jacob Riis for many years of highly rewarding scientific dialogue and debate. Furthermore, an anonymous peer reviewer read our nearly finished Danish manuscript, offering valuable, constructive criticism and playing an important role in preparing the final manuscript for publication. For this, we are grateful.

We also send sincere thanks to Søren Gregersen, an emeritus geophysicist at GEUS, the Geological Survey of Denmark and Greenland, who graciously gave us permission to quote extensively from the unpublished diary in which he chronicled his stay at Camp Century in 1960–1961; to Tuk Erik Jørgen-Jensen for generously sharing with us his experiences as "the man without a shadow" at Thule Air Base while the main events described in this book unfolded; to the Danish publishing house Praxis–Nyt Teknisk Forlag, which in 2015 published a chapter we wrote about Camp Century in their anthology *Forandringens Vinde* (The winds of change); and to the many librarians and archivists in Denmark, Greenland, and the United States who have helped us access the material on which this book is based. Two among this far-flung support network deserve special mention: Susanne Elisabeth Nørskov, a librarian at Aarhus University Library at our campus in Aarhus, Denmark; and Satu Haase-Webb, an independent researcher and historian based in Washington, DC. Last but not least, we are deeply grateful to the Carlsberg Foundation for supporting the work we conducted during the "Exploring Greenland" project.

The English translation was done by Heidi Flegal, whose craftsmanship and commitment to the project are greatly appreciated, and the book's publication was made possible by funding from the Carlsberg Foundation and Aarhus University Research Foundation.

Aarhus, Denmark

January 2021

CAMP CENTURY

INTRODUCTION

O n August 4, 2016, an international scientific team headed by the Canadian glaciologist William Colgan published an academic paper that was to have far-reaching consequences. The authors stated that in their assessment, the debris left behind in the Greenland ice sheet after the U.S. Army withdrew from its nuclear-powered research base Camp Century—which was shut down in 1966 and which, at the time, everyone believed to be buried in the ice cap for good—would resurface in the foreseeable future as a result of global warming. This news, coming out of the blue, triggered an intense debate that dramatically cooled the relationship between Denmark and Greenland (which, along with the Faroe Islands, make up the Kingdom of Denmark). Greenland, today a largely self-governing part of the kingdom, threatened to bring the case before the UN International Court of Justice if Denmark did not promptly assume responsibility for cleaning up the Camp Century site. The scientists estimated that the camp's remains lay some 35–70 meters (115–230 feet) beneath the surface of the ice. The debris is known to include not only buildings and structural elements but also radioactive, chemical, and biological waste. In February 2017, the Danish and Greenlandic governments signed an agreement establishing a body called the Camp Century Climate Monitoring Programme, headed by GEUS (the Geological Survey of Denmark and Greenland) and featured on a dedicated English-language website (https://www.campcenturyclimate.dk).

The current problems with the Camp Century site triggered the most serious political crisis between Denmark and Greenland in two hundred years—since long before Greenland began home-rule government in 1979. This, however, is by no means the only crisis caused by "the city under the ice," one of the evocative names used during the facility's construction in 1959 and 1960. The camp had also given rise to a minor diplomatic crisis between Denmark and the United States when it became clear, in 1959, that the Americans had no intention of following the sound advice, or "recommendation," they had received from the Danish government the previous year: relocate the project to Alaska. Thanks to high-level negotiations, the crisis was soon resolved. It was a relatively simple process at the time, since back then Denmark was not obliged to consult Greenland. This huge island, which had a population of roughly 30,000 in 1960, had the same status as a Danish county, so it had no say in foreign policy issues. But was it wise to refrain from informing the national council of Greenland about the negotiations that were under way? Subsequent events indicate it was not.

Since its construction, Camp Century has been at the crux of other crises, the most dramatic of which unfolded from 1995 through 1997. At that time a group of Danish historians, part of a government-appointed task force mandated to discover and document the extent of flights over Greenland from 1951 through 1968 of American aircraft carrying nuclear weapons, were able to locate a classified document proving that the United States saw Camp Century as the first step toward a colossal subsurface tunnel system that would enable the U.S. Army to launch a nuclear-missile strike at virtually any target in the Soviet Union. Understandably, the information raised eyebrows and caused a great deal of anxiety in the Danish and Greenlandic governments. But even this explosive news did not end in a long-term crisis or break the two parts of the kingdom apart. Perhaps that was because Denmark was fully as surprised as Greenland at the revelation of the huge and audacious Cold War project, which had been planned in utmost secrecy by

FIGURE 0.1 After slipping through a fissure in the Greenland ice cap, the Danish comic-book hero Kurt Dunder ("Johnny Rumble") is saved by the naturally deep-frozen provisions of long-abandoned Camp Century.

strategists at the Pentagon. Or perhaps it was because by 1997 the Cold War was over. The great castle in the clouds, or rather, the great encampment in the ice, had long since vanished, and the remains of Camp Century—minus the nuclear reactor—now lay buried deep beneath the ice cap's frigid, windswept surface.

Since Camp Century's heyday a few books, now somewhat dated, and a wide array of articles have been written about this remarkable feat of engineering under the snow and ice. These sources speak of the construction, the people who lived there, and the camp's water, heating, and electricity supply; the projects conducted at the camp; the camp's ultimate decommissioning; and the grand plans that originally set the whole undertaking in motion. As part of a Carlsberg Foundation–funded research project entitled "Exploring Greenland: Science and Technology in Cold War Settings" (2010–2014), we too have contributed to this body of literature, with several papers shedding light on various facets of Camp Century's history. Even so, we believe this volume is the most exhaustive and well-documented history to date of what transpired in and around Camp Century and of its aftermath, from 1959 through 2019.

STRUCTURE OF THE BOOK

Chapter 1 outlines the history of the relations between Denmark and Greenland and the United States after the end of World War II and up to 1958, when the Americans made their first tentative inquiries to the Danish Ministry of Foreign Affairs seeking permission to set up Camp Century. We also discuss such topics as the U.S. bid to purchase Greenland in 1946; the Greenland Commission's work of 1948 through 1950; the establishment of Thule Air Base in 1951 through 1953; President Dwight D. Eisenhower's strategic "New Look" and "New New Look" national security policies; and the confidential memo sent from the Danish prime minister, Hans Christian ("H.C.") Hansen, to the American ambassador, Val Peterson, in November 1957.

Chapter 2 describes the state of controlled panic that spread through the Danish Ministry of Foreign Affairs when it became clear that the United States was adamant about moving forward on building Camp Century, even though Denmark had advised against it. We demonstrate that the Danish government would have preferred not to have been forced to take a position on "the concept of atoms" in Greenland (to use its own phraseology), and we trace how the Ministry of Foreign Affairs tackled the situation in Denmark when the first article about Camp Century appeared in the American press.

We begin chapter 3 by going back in time, to the story of how the secret strategic defense plan known as Project Iceworm was conceived as the U.S. Army's proposal for a credible nuclear deterrence project, in fierce competition with the Minuteman project under the U.S. Air Force and the Polaris project under the U.S. Navy. We then move on to the construction of Camp Century, focusing in particular on its water supply, waste management, and energy supply and rounding off with a discussion of the Danish-American negotiations on the approval of the facility's most crucial installation: the PM-2A nuclear reactor.

Chapter 4 details the diverging perceptions in the United States and Denmark of the rules of engagement with representatives of the press, who were keen to cover every aspect of Camp Century. This chapter gives numerous examples of how the American authorities sought to employ Camp Century as a positive public relations story, whereas the Danish authorities for several years sought to control the articles resulting from press visits to "the city under the ice."

In chapter 5 we describe everyday life at Camp Century, partly as rendered in accounts from different journalists but mainly based on the personal diary meticulously kept by the Danish scout Søren Gregersen, who spent almost six months at Camp Century—from October 1960 to March 1961—as a guest of the United States.

During its existence Camp Century hosted a considerable number of scientific research projects, in and around the facility. The vast majority had a distinctly military aim. In chapter 6 we discuss three noteworthy examples of this: whiteout studies, rail transport under the ice, and the stability of tunnels embedded in the ice.

Chapter 7 takes an in-depth look at a project that may have had a military aim but that—especially in posterity—has become a symbol of civilian climate research at the highest level of excellence: ice-core drilling. This is the story of the ice-core project's inception and realization; of how it took scientists five to six years to drill to the very bottom of the Greenland ice cap using equipment installed in Camp Century, within the upper layers of the ice sheet itself; and of how analyses of the ice core thus obtained yielded a significant part of the knowledge we have today about climate change, spanning from the distant past right up to the present.

Chapter 8 describes the final months of Camp Century, which was shut down after Project Iceworm was scrapped in early 1963. Here are details on the growing difficulty of keeping the camp running because of the ice sheet's inexorable deformation of the tunnel systems; the removal of the facility's nuclear reactor, monitored by Danish and American radiation experts; the discharge of radioactive wastewater into the ice sheet; and the ultimate fate of the nuclear reactor in the United States.

The legacy of Camp Century is treated in chapter 9. This military facility, which existed for only six years and today lies buried deep under the surface of Greenland's ice sheet, continued to make headlines long after its demise. One recent example, from a major Danish newspaper, refers to the camp's ability, even today, to create "an ice-cold atmosphere between Denmark and Greenland." We conclude the chapter by focusing on three events from the recent past—in 1980, 1995–1997, and 2016–2018—which even after Camp Century's shutdown have contributed to the negative light in which its existence, aftermath, and legacy are held. We round off the chapter and the book by assessing the historical importance of this controversial yet indisputably fascinating "city under the ice."

1

FORTRESS GREENLAND

"DEEPFREEZE DEFENSE"

Look at any standard map of the world and you will find Greenland at the top, in the Far North. It is a vast, remote land covered by an enormous sheet of ancient ice and spanning almost 2,400 kilometers (1,500 miles) from north to south, roughly the distance from Minneapolis to Miami. But standard maps deceive the eye, distorting the real picture around both poles. Greenland actually holds a central position in the Arctic Ocean, midway between the two continents that dominate the Northern Hemisphere.

In 1947, the reality of Arctic geography became abundantly clear to readers of the January 27 issue of *Time* magazine's Atlantic Overseas Edition, which contained an article entitled "Deepfreeze Defense," featuring a map of the North Pole—and Greenland—at the center.[1] This map was drawn by one of *Time*'s regular cartographers, Robert Macfarlane Chapin Jr., who during World War II had provided readers with illustrative maps that could help them understand the military strategies being employed by the nations involved in the various theaters of war. At this point, hostilities had ceased, and geopolitical circumstances had changed. The biggest conflict on the planet was the mounting tension between the United States and the Soviet Union. The situation universally known to posterity as the Cold War had just begun, and the frigid North looked poised to become a pivotal zone of conflict.

From an American point of view, the headline "Deepfreeze Defense" was a highly evocative albeit ambiguous description of Greenland. Like the phrase "Cold War," coined in American politics on April 16, 1947, by the financier and political consultant Bernard Baruch, the phrase "deepfreeze defense" played on the contradiction between a cool adjective and a militaristic noun. Baruch referred to the way the end of World War II had not brought peace to the world but instead ended in a warlike situation, although without open hostilities taking place between capitalist countries ("the Western bloc") and communist countries ("the Eastern bloc"). By using "Deepfreeze Defense" as a headline, meaning that this phrase was introduced to the American public three months before "Cold War" was, *Time* underscored that—counterintuitively, in terms of standard geography—the Far North was a key arena in the conflict between East and West.

The conclusion was that the United States had to mobilize in the Arctic, preferably in a way that would promote the use of its new and powerful weapon: the nuclear bomb, or "A-bomb," developed during World War II and, at that time, still the exclusive preserve of the Americans. In February 1946, Henry Arnold, a general in the U.S. Army, had described to *National Geographic* magazine how, in the future, a surprise enemy attack would be able to come "from the roof of the world," unless "we are in possession of adequate airbases outflanking such a route of approach."[2] In General Arnold's view, there was a close interplay between military expansion with airbases in the Arctic and the deployment of nuclear weapons: "Air power provides not only the best present means of striking the enemy with atomic bombs," the general concluded, "but also the best available defense against them."

The development during World War II of long-range strategic bombers, including the Boeing B-29 "Superfortress," meant that nuclear weapons could now be conveyed directly from the United States to the Soviet Union, over the Arctic. Consequently, a potential retaliatory attack against the USSR could be launched directly from U.S. facilities in the form of airbases in Alaska and Greenland. These airbases beyond the contiguous United States would serve partly as landing sites for the support aircraft that could refuel the long-range bombers in flight and partly as emergency landing sites and staging airbases for bombers, bombs, and other equipment.[3] The trouble was that major airborne operations in the Arctic were rendered largely impossible by difficult weather conditions, magnetic anomalies, poor communication because of atmospheric disturbances, and the absence of airstrips and ancillary facilities.[4]

General Arnold offered a vision of military mobilization in the Arctic that won support from many other military leaders of his day. It was dubbed "the polar concept."[5] The first attempt to realize the polar concept was made in 1946 by Strategic Air Command (SAC), established that year as a U.S. Air Force Major Command and responsible for the command and control of land-based strategic bomber aircraft and intercontinental ballistic missile (ICBM) components. SAC initiated Operation Nanook, which carried out reconnaissance and mapping in various regions of Alaska, the Aleutian archipelago, Siberia, and northern Greenland. According to an agreement with the Danish government, around that time the U.S. government expanded the existing weather station at Thule, which had been set up during World War II and was operated by Danish personnel until 1946. Under the new agreement, American personnel from the U.S. Weather Bureau were stationed at Thule, where a gravel airstrip was also constructed to accommodate reconnaissance planes and emergency landings. The initial intention was to learn more about the special physical conditions that prevailed in northern Greenland, but it was clear that military operations were the ultimate goal.

The "Deepfreeze Defense" article in *Time* was a popularized version of the polar concept. Indeed, Chapin's map of the Arctic plainly showed that from an American point of view Greenland—like Alaska—was a northern bastion between North America on one side and Europe and the Soviet Union on the other. To eliminate any doubts about how to read the map, the strategic value of Greenland was indicated by a "battle turret" border encircling the island: Greenland was a fortified bastion guarding America against the threat from the Soviets, who would surely advance across the reaches of the Arctic. Alaska was likewise cast as an Arctic fortress against encroachment through Siberia.

GREENLAND FOR SALE?

The *Time* article stated that the United States had shown great forethought in buying Alaska from the Russian Empire in 1867, thereby acquiring "a castellated outpost at the northwest angle."[6] At that time, Secretary of State William H. Seward had put pressure on the government to buy Greenland as well, without success. Many of his contemporaries referred to the purchase of Alaska as "Seward's folly," failing to see any value in this territory in the Far North, unconnected to the other states in the union. Nevertheless, *Time* argued, Seward had been forward-looking, and it was a shame he had been unsuccessful in his efforts to bring about a similar purchase of Greenland. As a result, the United States had a relatively weak presence in Greenland, with "only tenuous base rights, to expire with the peace." The article concluded that "now," meaning 1947, would be a good time for America to acquire Greenland. Obviously, Denmark's national pride might stand in the way of a sale, but certain U.S. military men believed they had an answer to that problem: Denmark already owed American investors more than 70 million U.S. dollars—less than the cost of a good-sized hangar ship and, according to *Time*, "more dollar exchange than Copenhagen can easily raise." Could Denmark afford to decline such an offer?

What *Time* did not tell its readers was that the United States had already made an actual offer to buy Greenland from Denmark. In December 1946, the Danish minister of foreign affairs, Gustav Rasmussen, had been in the United States to attend the UN General Assembly. During this visit he also took the opportunity to meet with the U.S. secretary of state, James F. Byrnes, who had expressed that the Americans wished to purchase Greenland from Denmark. Their offer was one billion U.S.

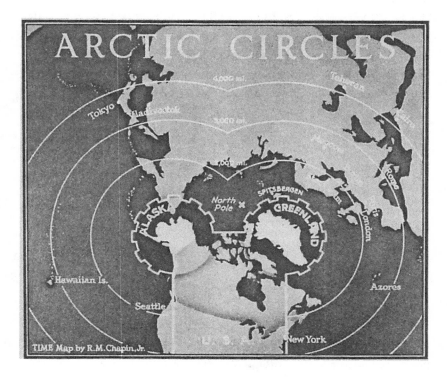

FIGURE 1.1 It was already clear at the end of World War II that Greenland held a crucial geopolitical position, midway between the continents of North America and Eurasia. After the war, the United States launched a "polar strategy" as part of their security policy, the aim of which was to defend the nation by establishing advance military bases in Greenland and Alaska. The illustration of the polar strategy in *Time* magazine leaves no doubt as to how the United States saw Greenland at that time.

dollars, or four times as much as Denmark was receiving in aid from the United States under the Marshall Plan. The size of the U.S. bid was not made known to the public, but it appears in a memo describing an unofficial conversation between Henrik Kauffmann, who was Denmark's ambassador to the United States, and high-level American officials.[7]

If Rasmussen and the rest of the Danish government had accepted the U.S. bid to buy Greenland, it would not have been the first time Denmark sold valuable overseas territories to the Americans. In 1917, it had sold "the Danish West Indies" in the Caribbean (which became the U.S. Virgin Islands) for a sum of 25 million dollars—a sale that came about when the islands gained strategic and national security importance for the Americans following the opening of the Panama Canal and after the outbreak of World War I. At the time, the United States needed the islands to prevent Germany from establishing a naval base there. As for the Danish politicians, they were afraid it would harm Danish neutrality in the war if their country did not accept the U.S. offer and sell. Beyond the purchase price of 25 million, Denmark also received official U.S. acknowledgment of Danish sovereignty over Greenland—meaning that Norway's claim to certain swaths of eastern Greenland had no legitimacy. In 1933, the International Court of Justice in The Hague established Denmark's sovereignty over Greenland in its entirety.[8]

Back in 1920, the United States had informed Denmark that it would not accept a third-party country purchasing Greenland, just in case Denmark had any intention of selling. In other words, if Greenland was not Danish, it would have to be American. However, the new offer to purchase Greenland put Foreign Minister Rasmussen in a difficult situation. His American counterpart had given him three options: (1) to sell Greenland, which America would prefer; (2) to hand over the defense of Greenland to America; or (3) to authorize America to construct military bases in certain areas of Greenland.[9] The second option basically perpetuated the 1941 agreement for Greenland's defense to be handled by the United States. This was an agreement that the serving Danish ambassador, Henrik Kauffmann, had signed—in his self-proclaimed capacity as representative of the Danish government in Greenland, which had been completely cut off from Denmark proper by the German occupation there. This Danish-American agreement was signed on April 9, 1941, precisely one year after the Germans took power in Denmark. According to the 1941 Greenland Agreement, the United States, fully acknowledging Danish sovereignty, had the right to construct and use any installations of a civilian or military nature deemed necessary for the defense of Greenland.[10]

"While we owe much to America, I do not feel we owe them the whole Island of Greenland."[11] Such was the message Foreign Minister Gustav Rasmussen communicated to the U.S. ambassador to Denmark, Josiah Marvel, immediately upon his return to Copenhagen. Neither Rasmussen nor the Danish government had any intention of accepting the American bid for Greenland. In his conversation with Byrnes, Rasmussen had underscored that the decisive factor for Denmark's relationship with Greenland was not pecuniary but based on a shared history. The government and many others in Copenhagen agreed that Denmark ought to expand—not relinquish—its relationship with Greenland, which is why it was best to begin negotiations with the United States for a new agreement on the defense of Greenland.

The Danish government also faced national security challenges that spanned the entire joint kingdom. Not only did it need to consider Greenland's crucial location in the Arctic Ocean, with its then 23,000 or so inhabitants (1947 estimate) lodged between the world's two superpowers. It also had to consider the Faroe Islands in the North Atlantic (population nearly 30,000 in 1947) and the more southerly location of Denmark proper, wedged between the North Sea and the Baltic Sea, with its islands and peninsulas effectively on the physical border between East and West. After World War II, Russian forces had liberated the outlying Danish island of Bornholm in the Baltic Sea (population roughly 47,000 in 1947) from German occupation, remaining there until March 1946. They left the island only after formally agreeing with Denmark that the Danish garrison on the largely rural Bornholm would not exceed a certain size and that "foreign powers" would not be allowed to exert any influence on the island's administration.[12] In this way the USSR had made it clear they did not want to see Denmark become involved in the emerging bloc politics, which was also in tune with Danish policy in 1947. Selling Greenland to the Americans could have undermined Moscow's trust in Denmark, not to mention the insecurity that would have been created among the country's then 4.2 million citizens.

FIGURE 1.2 Gustav Rasmussen (at left) served as Denmark's foreign minister from 1945 to 1953. He harbored certain reservations about Danish membership in NATO, and he supported Hans Hedtoft, who was the Danish prime minister from 1947 to 1950, in his unsuccessful attempt to establish a Scandinavian defense union. As foreign minister, Rasmussen headed the Danish negotiations, which ended with Denmark joining the North Atlantic Treaty, the precursor of NATO, in 1949. Rasmussen is seen here in conversation with U.S. Secretary of State Dean Acheson at the signing of the treaty documents.

In short, in terms of foreign policy and security policy, Denmark was walking a double tightrope stretched out between the United States and the USSR. It could not simply give the U.S. military the right to establish bases in Greenland, out of consideration for the Soviet Union; nor could it unilaterally cancel the 1941 Greenland Agreement, out of consideration for the United States. In this precarious situation, the best thing Denmark could do was to move forward on assuming responsibility for operating the U.S. bases in Greenland, as it was already doing with the weather stations there, and opening parallel negotiations with the Americans to extend the 1941 Greenland Agreement. In

September 1947, just nine months after the American purchase offer, the United States accepted the Danish government's position. And so, having successfully completed this initial tightrope walk, balancing courtesy and determination, Danish diplomacy was able to lay the American bid to rest.[13]

GREENLAND ENTERING THE MODERN AGE

The Danish authorities and prominent voices in Greenland had a very different plan for the island nation's future direction. World War II had brought great change around the globe, and many Greenlanders had become acquainted with the wider world for the first time, coming into contact with American soldiers and American culture. Eske Brun and Aksel Svane, the two Danish administrators who both bore the title of *landsfoged* (literally, "national steward") but effectively served as the wartime governors of Greenland, also sought closer links with the United States to avoid German occupation and to safeguard Greenland so it might resume its links with Denmark after the war, should that prove possible. Until the war began, Greenland had been subject to a Danish trade monopoly, mediated by a state-owned corporation called Den Kongelige Grønlandske Handel (the Royal Greenland Trading Company), and access to Greenland's territory had also been regulated by the Danish authorities. After the war ended, the trade monopoly and partial isolation continued, but leading figures in Denmark and Greenland wanted Greenland to become more open and to have more equal relations with the southern part of the unified realm. In addition, there was a strong international movement toward decolonization, heralding a new order in Denmark's policy on Greenland.[14]

The first step in this process was the appointment of a body called the Greenland Commission, which happened in 1948. The commission was ambitious in its size and its mandate. The 105 members, twelve of whom were Greenlandic, were divided into nine subcommission groups tasked with analyzing all aspects of Greenlandic society, ranging from trade and commerce to politics, administration, culture, religion, education, health care, and much more. The Greenland Commission's report was published in nine volumes, spanning 1,100 pages. This report drew the contours of Greenland as envisioned in the modern era, making it clear that such a step would call for pervasive changes in all walks of Greenlandic life if Greenland were to be more fully integrated with Denmark.[15] The commission concluded that the time was ripe:

> While the policy hitherto followed on the part of Denmark, regardless of its intentions to serve the best interests of the Greenlandic people, has been preconditioned by a certain isolation of the Greenlandic people, we now believe the juncture has been reached at which one can consciously work toward the goal of the Greenlanders becoming equal members of Danish society, while at the same time creating the possibility of opening free access to contact between Greenlanders and other peoples, thereby also helping to strengthen the initiative among the Greenlandic people that will promote Greenland's social, cultural, and economic development.[16]

The Greenland Commission had spoken, and its message was heard. In 1953, Greenland was officially given the status of a Danish *amt* (county) and permanent parliamentary representation, with two seats in the 179-member Folketing in Copenhagen. The decades that followed saw huge changes in Greenlandic society, especially focused on the larger towns and villages on the west coast. Massive financing from the national coffers was used to expand Greenland's school and health-care systems, and new housing and technical infrastructure was built. The fishing industry, especially the cod catch, also grew throughout the 1950s. Much of the modernization effort was managed and carried out by Danish craftsmen, engineers, and civil servants, leading to some disgruntlement among the Greenlanders, who felt pushed aside in the development process. The politicians in the Greenlandic Landsråd (the National Council of Greenland) and the nation's population were especially preoccupied with the issues of equal pay and codetermination in important political decision making.[17]

THE 1951 DEFENSE AGREEMENT
ON GREENLAND

Even before the Greenland Commission was appointed in November 1948, the Cold War had begun to escalate. In the early spring of 1948, the communists had taken power in Czechoslovakia, and the Soviet Union had pressured Finland into signing an "Agreement of Friendship, Cooperation, and Mutual Assistance." Meanwhile, international rumors said that Norway, Denmark, and other countries in Western Europe also risked seeing diplomatic or military offensive action from the Soviet Union. The Danish prime minister at the time, Hans Hedtoft, assured the world that his country did not wish to promote any further bloc affiliation.

At the same time, attempting to signal the country's will to defend itself, should that become necessary, the Danish government was seeking a promise of military aid from the United States, although without Denmark's entering into any mutually binding defense agreement and without any agreement about U.S. military bases in Greenland. The United States, on the other hand, while sympathetic to Denmark's wishes, was not prepared to help Denmark without getting anything in return. Persistent rumors of a Soviet invasion in March 1948, later known in Denmark as *Påskekrisen* (the Easter Crisis), meant that in the following months Denmark felt extremely vulnerable in matters relating to the Soviet Union.[18] At the same time, the Danish government realized that staying outside bloc politics—continuing its tightrope act—was no longer a viable option and that the question of bases in Greenland would have to be resolved within the framework of a Western defense alliance.

Elsewhere in Europe, while the Easter Crisis was building up in Denmark, a number of Western European countries were negotiating

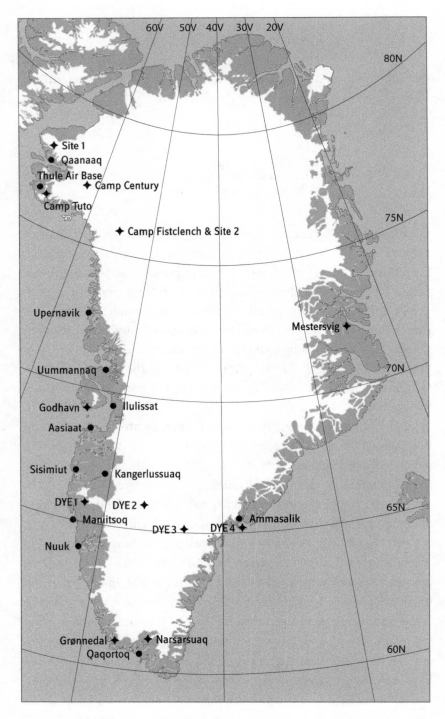

FIGURE 1.3 Map of Greenland showing the ice cap (which covers some 80 percent of the landmass) and ice-free areas (roughly 20 percent). Besides the island's most important towns and settlements (•), the map only shows geographical locations (♦) that play a significant role in this book.

to collaborate more closely on economic, cultural, and security issues. As a result, in March 1948 the United Kingdom, France, Belgium, Luxembourg, and the Netherlands signed the Treaty of Brussels, thereby founding the European military, political, economic, and cultural alliance established among the so-called five powers of Europe. The signatories agreed it would be necessary to enter into a further defense alliance with the United States to counter the Soviet threat and to prevent an upsurge of national militarism throughout Europe. Despite parallel efforts to establish a Scandinavian defense alliance, in which Denmark would also participate, both Norway and Denmark ultimately opted for the North Atlantic model rather than a Scandinavian model (whereas Sweden opted out). Here, Greenland played an important role, in that the United States had made it clear that defending Greenland would have to be an integral part of any Atlantic treaty. Denmark now had to choose between becoming part of the North Atlantic defense alliance, and by this means reaching an equitable agreement on bases with the Americans, or standing outside the alliance, and being forced to negotiate about bases in Greenland with a very large and strongly united defense alliance.[19]

The North Atlantic Treaty (later NATO) became a reality in March 1949, and Denmark was among its twelve founding member states.[20] That very year the United States once again reiterated its request for the right to establish bases in Greenland. Prime Minister Hedtoft was nervous about what this might mean for Denmark's position vis-à-vis the Soviet Union, so first he wanted clarification as to America's willingness to assist Denmark militarily. This was a necessity for Denmark, Hedtoft emphasized at a meeting held on October 27, 1949, in the parliament's Foreign Policy Committee, explaining that "before we played the last card we had, namely Greenland, [we had] to get clarification about what the Americans wanted, and what they could provide in return."[21]

While the Americans regarded Greenland as an Arctic fortress, Prime Minister Hedtoft saw it more as a strategic card, a potential trump in negotiations about what NATO's objectives implied for Denmark. The pressure the Americans were exerting to move forward on building bases in Greenland, as a step in realizing their polar concept, again put Denmark in a sensitive situation relative to the Soviets. From the Danish government's perspective, the logic of this was that if Denmark made Greenlandic territory available to the United States, the strongest military power in NATO, their country would be assuming an extra risk and would therefore be justified in calling for compensation in the form of special requirements that NATO take responsibility for defending Greenland—and the rest of the joint kingdom.[22]

At the same time, the polar concept was winning ground in influential U.S. military circles and evolving into an actual polar strategy for the Arctic region. The Soviet Union had carried out its first nuclear detonation test on August 29, 1949, taking its place as the world's second nuclear power. In this situation, the strategic significance of the Arctic took on a new and more urgent focus. In particular, thanks to a newly developed Boeing aircraft, the B-47 "Stratofortress," SAC was even better equipped to deploy nuclear weapons against the Soviet Union, made possible by in-flight refueling, for instance, over Greenland.[23] But other ideas were also on the table, including the installation of missiles potentially placed beneath the surface of the Greenland ice cap, assuming the technical problems could be solved, and also including the extraction of uranium ("vital strategic materials") in Greenland, as described in a report on the Arctic dated October 1950 and submitted to the U.S. Joint Chiefs of Staff:[24]

> The strategic importance of the Arctic would be considerably increased through the development of sources of vital strategic materials in Arctic areas, guided missiles with ranges of 1200–1500 miles, effective under-the-ice-pack transportation and by the preclusion of an air entry to targets in the USSR from any direction but the north.[25]

The United States was pressed for time. The Korean War erupted in June 1950 when North Korean troops invaded South Korean territory. From the outset, this was a proxy war based on the conflict between the United States, which supported South Korea, and the Soviet Union and China, which supported North Korea. It consequently accelerated the global plan for U.S. airbases, which the Joint Chiefs of Staff had been working on since 1943, to help safeguard American interests not only in Asia but across the globe. These bases were the physical manifestation of the American "perimeter strategy," also referred to as "containment," institutionalized in American foreign policy and security policy with the Truman Doctrine of 1947. The objective of this policy was to enable effective retaliatory action against the Soviet Union from bases around the periphery of the Soviet sphere of influence, such as Western Europe, the Suez Canal area, Pakistan, and Japan, while at the same time containing the spread of communism, which many Americans saw as an aggressive, subversive force on the rise.[26]

Greenland was part of the American plan that revolved around the U.S. military, and when the polar concept gained widespread acceptance in 1946 it brought extra credence to Greenland's important role in U.S. security policy. In February 1951, the Americans contacted the Danish government to inquire about the possibility of constructing a major airbase in the vicinity of Thule, high in northwestern Greenland.[27] This was the first step in Operation Blue Jay, a secret initiative that had been quietly discussed in Washington since October 1950. Denmark had to be forthcoming when considering the American inquiry so as not to position itself unfavorably in light of the imminent negotiations with the United States on strictly military matters. Even so, Denmark was intent on limiting American military presence as much as possible by permitting only minor expansions to existing military facilities and not permitting new facilities. The Danish government was concerned not only about the Soviet Union's reaction but also about the American influence on Greenlandic culture if the U.S. presence brought them into contact with the general population of Greenland.

The negotiations took place in March and April 1951 and resulted in a defense agreement on Greenland that was signed on April 27, 1951. This agreement was part of the NATO collaboration, and it meant that the United States would be permitted to construct and equip special "defense areas" for military use. Initially this would apply to the airbases at Narsarsuaq (originally called Bluie West One, built in 1941), Kangerlussuaq (Bluie West Eight, also built in 1941), and Thule (built in

1951–1953). According to the new agreement, these defense areas could be expanded if specifically agreed between the United States and Denmark. During the negotiations, the Americans had made it clear to the Danes that Thule, being an important part of the polar strategy, had been marked out as a staging base for strategic B-47 bombers or, alternatively, for B-36 "Peacemaker" aircraft, both of which could carry nuclear weapons.[28]

The 1951 Defense Agreement set out the provisional scope and conditions for U.S. military bases in Greenland. It was a compromise between Danish and American interests, even though it "mainly came into being based on American terms."[29] Denmark gained confirmation of its sovereignty over Greenland and also shielded the local population, and the United States got permission to expand its military and geopolitical influence in the Northern Hemisphere. The agreement set out the general rules for U.S. use of such defense areas as the two countries, at any given time, might find to "be necessary for the development of the defense of Greenland and the rest of the North Atlantic Treaty area."[30] Even though here the agreement specifically refers to NATO, and even though in practice the bases in question would be American, the official position was that the bases were joint Danish-American defense areas. A Danish liaison officer was appointed under the existing Danish defense body, Grønlands Kommando (Island Command Greenland, or simply "Greenland Command"), and tasked with sharing operational information with the U.S. commanding officer, to ensure "that the head of Island Command Greenland was in touch with activities."[31]

The United States was also interested in conducting various scientific and technological investigations that were more or less directly relevant to military activities. The 1951 Defense Agreement gave Denmark responsibility for topographic, hydrographic, and geodetic surveys and for making the results of these surveys available to the Americans. Only in cases where the Danes were unable to handle such investigations would the Americans be permitted to conduct them, and even then only with prior permission from Denmark. Other military R&D activities, including basic research, were not covered by the 1951 agreement on Greenland but by generally applicable regulations: the United States would have to apply to the relevant Danish authorities for permission to conduct such activities. The American interest in this work was underscored by the establishment of a special department under the U.S. Army Corps of Engineers called SIPRE—the Snow, Ice, and Permafrost Research Establishment—whose mission was to "conduct basic and applied research in snow, ice and frozen ground."[32] SIPRE was responsible for many of the scientific activities that took place at Thule Air Base and the surrounding research facilities in the following years.

THULE AIR BASE AND NEARBY FACILITIES ON THE ICE CAP

The actual construction of Thule Air Base began in deepest secrecy in the summer of 1951. However, American presence in the Thule area, far to the north on the west coast of Greenland, had begun during World War II, and the Americans had been there ever since. The American weather station Bluie West Six, built during the war, lay just a few kilometers from the indigenous settlement of Pituffik. Just after the war, as part of Operation Nanook, the Americans expanded the existing installation with a gravel landing strip as part of an upgrade to a new and larger weather station. Between 1947 and 1950, American reconnaissance planes thoroughly photographed the area for cartographic purposes. Meanwhile, young university students did surveying and mapping work on the ground.[33] There was little information about the geographical and meteorological conditions in the area, and acquiring this knowledge was an essential precondition for realizing the polar strategy and thus establishing U.S. military supremacy in the Arctic.

Operation Blue Jay was a rare challenge for the army engineers. The aim: to construct a modern airbase in the High Arctic in an area where the existing infrastructure was limited to the tiny landing strip at the

FIGURE 1.4 Operation Blue Jay remained covert until September 1952, when news of the base was released. It appeared, among other places, on the cover of *Life* magazine, which described Thule Air Base as "a modern engineering miracle" and "a strategically priceless arm in the U.S. panoply of defense." According to the *Life* article, the location was first spotted as a good site for an airbase in Greenland by the Greenlandic-Danish explorer Knud Rasmussen and the Norwegian aviator Bernt Balchen. The Norwegian earned renown for his flights across the Arctic during World War II, and after the war he became a colonel in the U.S. Air Force. Balchen was one of the prime movers behind Operation Blue Jay.

weather station near Thule, plus a natural harbor at North Star Bay, a small inlet in Wolstenholme Fjord. In July 1951, an air bridge was established from the United States, and an armada of 120 vessels carrying some 12,000 personnel set out from Norfolk Naval Base, Virginia. The difficulties in constructing a major Arctic airbase were many, but the greatest of all was working in permafrost conditions. If heat from the buildings at the site penetrated the soil, it would disturb the perpetual, solid frost and alter the properties of the ground at the site. For this reason, personnel barracks, workshops, and warehouses were raised up on wooden beams, creating circulation between the floor and the ground surface. Hangars, which were too large to raise on chocks, were equipped with a double floor. The gravel landing strip was redone in asphalt, and the finishing touches included technical installations for electricity, water, heating, and waste management. In just 104 days, all the groundwork for Thule Air Base was done. The following summer, a new workforce was brought in, and the base was completed according to plan.[34]

The U.S. Army Corps of Engineers, which was responsible for constructing Thule Air Base, officially transferred the facility to the U.S. Air Force on November 1, 1952. Several weeks earlier, the first Lockheed F-94B "Starfire" fighter planes had arrived at Thule to provide the area with air defense. In 1953, the American army installed an antiaircraft defense ring around the base, and in connection with this the Danish and American authorities signed an agreement to relocate the local population, which consisted of twenty-seven indigenous Inughuit families, with three weeks' notice. One factor in this was that Danish politicians, taking their cue from Permanent Secretary Eske Brun (the unintentional "governor" of Greenland during World War II), wanted to limit contact between the local Greenlandic population and the visiting Americans at the base. The Danish state constructed homes for the families from Pituffik at a new settlement, Qaanaaq, located 150 km (90 miles) north of Thule Air Base. A year later, the Danish local administration was also relocated, as was the historic trading post built by the polar explorer Knud Rasmussen in 1910. Although at the time the Danish authorities presented the relocation as "voluntary," the Danish Supreme Court established fifty years later that it had, in effect, been a forced resettlement.[35]

From 1953 to 1959, Thule Air Base was an important component in the U.S. polar strategy in more ways than one. Its primary purpose was to serve as an operational and backup base for the B-47s, which around this time were one of the U.S. Air Force's most important strategic bombers. But the B-47 did not have sufficient reach to attack targets in the Soviet Union and return to the United States without refueling—an operation that could conveniently take place in the airspace over Thule. This made it crucial for the Americans to be able to operate B-47s in and out of this airbase, even while maintaining a contingency fleet of auxiliary KC-97 refueling aircraft at the ready.[36] The base was also a landing site for American air-defense jets and reconnaissance planes. As of April 1, 1957, control of Thule Air Base was transferred from the U.S. North Atlantic Command to SAC, and its status was changed from a support base with refueling planes into an actual operational base for strategic bombers. In conjunction with this, the airstrips at Thule were reinforced to accommodate larger bombers. Two major military exercises were held in late 1957, incorporating the new intercontinental B-52 bombers.[37]

Thule Air Base also played a vital role in other aspects of the polar strategy, particularly the question of how best to run military operations on and inside the Greenland ice cap. To investigate this, the American army initiated a major research and development project that called for the construction of several military research facilities not merely *on* the ice but also *within* the ice sheet.[38] While Camp Century, the main topic of this book, was undoubtedly the most spectacular of these, it had a number of important predecessors that merit brief description here.

In 1954, the Americans established two camps with approach ramps that accessed the ice cap: Camp Tuto (short for "Thule Take-Off") and Camp Nuto ("Nunatarssuaq Take-Off," also known as Camp Red Rock). Camp Tuto, with barracks for five hundred men, was by far the larger of the two. It had its own modest airstrip, which could receive small personnel aircraft and slightly larger cargo planes, and an approach ramp of several miles was built nearby, enabling trucks to drive directly up onto the ice sheet. A number of tunnels were also built near Camp Tuto in the ice and the permanently frozen ground to investigate how people could build and live in ice and permafrost and—not least—to study how permanently low temperatures would affect building materials, weapons, fuel, and so forth.[39]

The U.S. military's many scientific activities in Greenland aroused attention in Copenhagen. Naturally, the Danes wanted to find out what

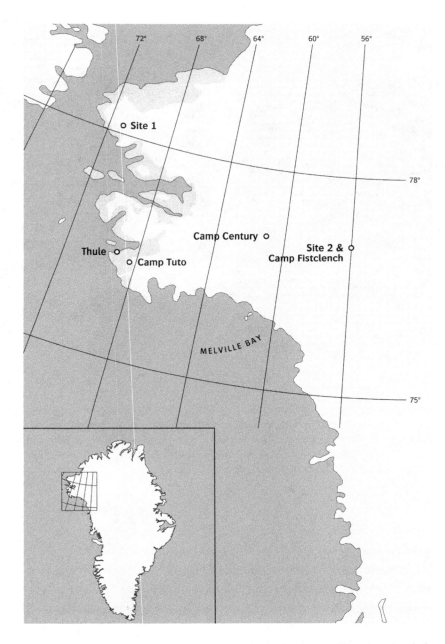

FIGURE 1.5 From 1953 to 1960, the Americans also built a few small bases in the Thule area. With the exception of Camp Nuto, they all appear on the map. The largest of these auxiliary bases was Camp Tuto, which had a ramp road that led directly up onto the ice sheet. Camp Tuto proper was fully decommissioned in 1966, but even today scientific exhibitions in the area use the ramp to gain access to the ice cap. The position of Camp Fistclench and Site 2 in this historic map, taken from DIIS (1997), is slightly inaccurate. See the updated map (figure 1.3).

FIGURE 1.6 Aerial photo of Camp Tuto dated June 4, 1961. This camp was active from 1954 to 1966, serving both as an approach base to the ice cap and as a research station. Until 1966, its facilities included an operational ionosphere station, which was also used by Danish scientists. All equipment and personnel destined for Camp Century (except what little was flown in) was transported by way of Camp Tuto, onto and across the ice sheet.

was really going on, and to do this the Danish liaison officer at Thule Air Base needed help. In the summer of 1954, the base welcomed its first official Danish representative, whose formal status was "adviser on scientific matters" for the Danish liaison officer. The scientific adviser's job was to assist the liaison officer by following and, if possible, personally surveying the scientific activities going on around Thule Air Base and on the ice cap. The adviser would typically work with a Danish research assistant, given the large number and scope of American activities. Because the scientific work chiefly took place in the summer months, the scientific adviser's visits to the base were mainly planned during the summer, and at other times, only as needed. The adviser reported independently to the Danish authorities in Copenhagen and to the *Landshøvding* (national chieftain) for Greenland, who was based in the nation's capital city of Nuuk, then known by its Danish name, Godthåb. In the busy summers of 1954 and 1955, two Danes served as adviser and assistant, respectively: the geologist Johannes Troelsen and the geographer Børge Fristrup.[40]

At this point, military engineers had long since embarked on their efforts to establish bases on the ice sheet. Site 1 and Site 2 were built in 1953 as part of the expansion of Thule Air Base's defense infrastructure, with Site 1 located a good 230 km (140 miles) north of Thule and Site 2 about some 350 km (215 miles) east of the main base. Both sites had radar installations that were part of the Thule Air Base's warning system, and about twenty personnel were stationed at each site for stints of three months. Site 2 lay hidden beneath the surface, housed in large aluminum tubes. Here experiments were performed on various ways to build camps embedded in the ice. This first camp was closed as early as 1956, as the layer of accumulating snow had begun to compress the tube so severely that spending any length of time inside was deemed unsafe. A second, new facility, called Camp Fistclench, was therefore built in close proximity to Site 2. It consisted of tunnels dug directly into the ice using Swiss snow-clearing machines (of which more later) and subsequently covered with curved aluminum sheeting. Near Camp Fistclench the engineers also constructed a tunnel in the ice sheet that was fitted with railroad tracks to test the deformation of the underlying ice when heavy loads of up to five tons were repeatedly driven back and forth on the ice for prolonged periods of time. Camp Fistclench was manned until 1961.[41]

The development of long-range bombers during the 1950s, combined with the superpowers' construction of ICBMs, reduced the role of Thule Air Base as a refueling station. Conversely, the importance of its detection and warning functions in light of potential attacks from the Soviet Union grew. Among other things, this meant that once the keystone in the American polar strategy—the deployment of nuclear weapons using bombers or missiles and crossing the Arctic without landing or refueling—became a military reality, Thule Air Base would no longer be necessary as an advance air base, strictly speaking. In the late 1950s and into the 1960s, the number of flight operations at Thule Air Base was reduced,[42] but that did not mean the base had lost its significance to the U.S. defense strategy. On the contrary. In January 1958, the United States announced it would be setting up a system to detect intercontinental missiles, dubbed the Ballistic Missile Early Warning System (BMEWS) and that Thule Air Base had been designated to host one of the three BMEWS stations. Construction of the massive BMEWS radar array, consisting of four radar dishes each roughly as large as a football field, commenced in 1960. Corresponding facilities were built at Fylingdales Air Base in the United Kingdom and Clear Air Base in Alaska.[43]

THE DANISH NUCLEAR WEAPONS DILEMMA

During the 1950s, nuclear arms became an increasingly important part of the Cold War. At the crux of America's polar strategy was the capability to deploy nuclear warheads using B-52s and other strategic bombers, flying directly from the United States to the USSR across the Arctic and potentially refueling at, or above, Thule Air Base in Greenland. The first Soviet nuclear test in 1949 had demonstrated that in the event of a nuclear war, the most likely outcome would be the utter annihilation of all countries involved. As a direct consequence of this realization, both the NATO agreement from 1949 and the later Warsaw Pact from 1955 were based on an ice-cold logic of deterrence. If the parties involved built up sufficiently large stocks of nuclear weapons, which could be released using semiautomatic detection and warning systems, then every hostile action had the potential to unleash total destruction on the attacker *and* the defender.

Deterrence logic was an integral part of President Dwight D. Eisenhower's "New Look" strategy from 1953, according to which the United States was prepared to respond to all types of attacks using nuclear weapons, even if these were "only" attacks with conventional weapons.

The aim of the New Look strategy was to adjust American defense expenditure relative to the new nuclear reality, which led to dramatic reductions in the funding for the U.S. Army; cuts in U.S. Navy and U.S. Air Force funding were less severe.[44] After 1953, when the Soviet Union began to stockpile hydrogen bombs, the New Look was modified into the "New New Look" strategy, which focused on a selective and flexible response to potential aggression, meaning the armed forces were no longer meant to respond exclusively with nuclear weapons. This was also the strategy John F. Kennedy built on after succeeding Eisenhower as president in 1961. Nevertheless, certain circumstances could lead to "massive retaliation" with nuclear weapons (an expression first used by Secretary of State John Foster Dulles in 1954). This particular expression, alongside the word "deterrence," defined the prevailing thoughts on security policy in the NATO of the 1950s.[45]

NATO's nuclear weapons policy put Denmark back on the tightrope. On the one hand, Danish politicians saw an opportunity to ensure the defense of Denmark in the best possible way through NATO collaboration, which involved adhering to the principle of nuclear deterrence and massive retaliation with atomic weapons, the elements undergirding NATO. "The atom is our friend," as one prominent civil servant from the Danish foreign ministry put it in a 1953 memorandum.[46] On the other hand, Denmark had to be prudent and cautious because of its vulnerable location at the gateway of the Baltic Sea and also because of the American military bases in Greenland, which the Soviet Union obviously perceived as a serious threat. As a result, many Danes, including those in political circles, harbored certain reservations about NATO and its nuclear arms policy. As former prime minister Hans Hedtoft said from the parliamentary rostrum in 1952, speaking that October as chairman of the Social Democratic Party: "NATO collaboration raises complicated problems for our country, which can often be difficult to bring a people to understand when, like ours, that people carries a tradition of neutrality, and also a healthy skepticism of all world powers."[47]

The Danish reluctance to embrace nuclear weapons expressed a political agility that would be put to the test in the years that followed.

This reservation was rooted not only in a matter of principle, namely, the Danish opposition to nuclear arms. It was rooted, in equal measure, in a realistic political analysis that as far as the potential effectiveness of deterrence was concerned, Denmark did not have to explicitly approve nuclear weapons and that it was best for the country to remain nuclear-arms-free in light of its relations with the Soviet Union.[48] In this way Denmark could display its reserved position, accommodating the domestic political voices calling for neutrality and a stand against superpower politics (as Hans Hedtoft had suggested), while at the same time the country could declare that, in principle, it supported NATO's strategy of deterrence and massive retaliation.[49]

In March 1957, the Danish mix of reluctance and flexibility on the issue of nuclear weapons on the kingdom's soil was put to the test for the first time. As early as December 1956, Defense Secretary Charles Wilson of the United States had stated that in the near future America would be offering its NATO allies missiles in the "Nike," "Honest John," and "Matador" classes. All three were built with the capability to deploy nuclear warheads. Then on March 16, 1957, Denmark accepted the American offer to receive a battalion each of Nike and Honest John. Despite Denmark's reassurance that the missiles would not be carrying nuclear devices, the Soviet Union responded swiftly and unambiguously. In an open letter dated March 28, 1957, and addressed to the prime minister, Hans Christian ("H.C.") Hansen, the Soviet premier Nikolai Bulganin warned that "the granting of bases to a foreign state is tantamount to suicide in case atomic war breaks out."[50]

Bulganin mentioned the American bases in Greenland as one of the issues that had given rise to the Soviet warning. "Indeed," he wrote in his open letter, "a vast part of Danish territory, Greenland, has already long been converted into a military base of the United States and is to all intents and purposes outside Danish control."[51] Responding in a letter dated April 26, 1957, Prime Minister Hansen explained that Bulganin's statement about Greenland was not correct:

In your letter, you refer to the position of Greenland. In this connection it is important for me to stress that I can definitely refute your once again. Krag expressed his personal opinion, reiterating that the Danish position on nuclear weapons was unchanged but that there was growing appreciation of the purely defensive nature of small, tactical nuclear weapons that could be used with Nike and Honest John missiles and that these were "almost conventional."[56] Krag supported the view that, at the time, was promoted by the largest party in Denmark's coalition government, the Social Democratic Party: that Denmark could agree to tactical nuclear weapons and that doing so would bolster Denmark's national security. However, it was impossible for him to prevail over the other two coalition parties, the Social Liberals and the Single-Tax Party, which both took a pacifist stance. Consequently, in the situation at hand there was no domestic advantage in trying to change the Danish policy of "no nuclear arms on Danish soil."

After Krag's meeting in Copenhagen with Quarles and Peterson, the Danish Ministry of Foreign Affairs received the monthly report for January from the Danish liaison officer at Thule Air Base, Lieutenant Commander J. M. Stamphøj. As usual, the report was extremely brief. It simply stated that Stamphøj been shown the newly completed batteries of Nike missiles on the base. The margin of the report bears the following handwritten note by the head of the ministry's NATO office, Torben Rønne: "with or without atomic weapons?"[57] This question gave rise to a thorough treatment of the entire course of events in the Danish foreign ministry, resulting in an internal memo dated June 4, 1959, and written by Erik Schram-Nielsen, adviser on foreign affairs and head of the ministry's department for policy and legal affairs. This internal memo stated that the 1951 Defense Agreement contained no requirement that Denmark be informed of how the United States chose to protect the "defense areas" in Greenland and that it was in Denmark's interest, and in the interest of NATO as a whole, to maintain confidentiality about details of the American nuclear weapons program, given that any knowledge divulged about U.S. atomic weapons would make them more vulnerable to attack or sabotage. On the other hand, nothing prevented an investigation into whether any nuclear arms were indeed present at Thule Air Base, since "the Danish authorities have not relinquished their natural right to move about everywhere in

Greenland."[58] Schram-Nielsen concluded that it was in Denmark's best interest *not* to initiate a formal investigation—the same message Prime Minister H. C. Hansen had expressed to the United States in his confidential memo of November 16, 1957. Any other course of action would potentially undermine the entire NATO alliance and its deterrence policy, on which the Danish government had relied so implicitly since 1949, and it would also create domestic problems for the Danish government.

The foreign minister, Jens Otto Krag, agreed, but he still had misgivings about keeping Denmark's actual nuclear weapons policy under wraps. By the spring of 1959, parts of the Danish press had also begun to wonder whether there might already be nuclear weapons on the unified kingdom's territory in Greenland. If it became known that Denmark had been tacitly accepting the deployment of American nuclear warheads to Thule Air Base since November 1957, Denmark would find itself embroiled in a major diplomatic controversy, with the Soviet Union holding the biggest stick. To make matters worse, internal domestic tension about the issue of nuclear weapons would likely bring the Danish government down. As Krag noted in his diary on August 25, 1959:

> Misgivings about H.C. [Hansen]'s and Svenningsen's tacitly giving the green light for storage of US atomic weapons on Greenland in November 1957. They are not backed by any government decision, and the Foreign Policy Committee has had no notification. I have told H.C. that we ought to bring this in order, as concerns government and committee. He said he would consider it. The difficulty lies in these two years past. Perhaps I could seek news in Washington about what has actually gone on, then present the information thereby obtained?[59]

This is where the story of Camp Century begins in earnest.

atomic payloads on Danish soil. Two years later, during the defense negotiations of 1959, new political demands were being made to arm both types of missiles with nuclear warheads. This was a sensitive issue and one that might easily come to the fore if a debate arose about the American nuclear reactor at Camp Century.[11]

At the meeting, Svenningsen voiced concern about the Camp Century situation, stating that the Ministry of Foreign Affairs found the Americans to have acted in an "irregular" manner. Now the ministry wished to see things for itself, to try to get an impression of "how much progress the Americans had made in constructing the reactor." Specifically, the foreign ministry "feared that something about the matter might come up in the press, or in the Foreign Policy Committee, and that the entire question of atomic weapons and that sort of thing in Greenland would be drawn into the affair." Hans Henrik Koch, who was also at this meeting (and chaired the executive committee of the Danish Atomic Energy Commission), said he believed the technical problems relating to the nuclear reactor were manageable, "except for a detail with regard to the disposing of 'waste.'" There was one thing Koch found strange, as well: why did the camp have to be so big, with room for sixty scientists and forty other occupants? Conducting tests on a nuclear reactor could hardly keep sixty scientists busy. Koch concluded that the actual purpose of the camp had not been fully declared and explained, in light of which he was concerned "that there are also military purposes behind the installation."[12]

Captain Otto K. Lind (the meeting's fifth and final participant, from the Ministry of Defense) added that it was also somewhat unclear whether the camp was to be built in conjunction with another camp on the ice sheet, Site 2, which the Americans had already built with Denmark's permission and which therefore had to be counted among the existing U.S. defense areas. At the meeting, it was decided that the Ministry of Defense would ask its liaison officer at Thule Air Base to pay a visit to the location at issue, in order to clarify the camp's position and how far advanced the work was. If necessary, a Danish expert would have to be sent to the United States to investigate further. One of the two written minutes of this meeting focused, in its conclusion, on the American receptiveness to the Danish authorities' apprehension about "the concept of atoms" in Greenland:

> It was also mentioned that there is hardly reason to believe that the Americans would begin to construct the nuclear reactor, even in the defense areas, without asking—given that they are familiar with the misgivings we have in this country about the concept of atoms. When they changed their air defense at Thule from regular cannons to Nike batteries we were also consulted, even though they were certainly not obliged to do so. We have no knowledge of the Nike batteries being equipped with atomic charges. No action is to be taken from this end.[13]

THE CONCEPT OF ATOMS IN LIGHT OF THE *SKATE* AFFAIR

Ambassador Val Peterson's message that the United States had already begun constructing the scientific military base in Greenland and the ancillary nuclear reactor put the Danish government in a difficult position in a number of respects. The camp embedded in the ice was not merely a domestic policy problem related to the ongoing political negotiations about the Danish defense agreement. It also created the potential risk of an emerging public debate about the safety of the nuclear reactor and the possible exposure of the secret agreement between the United States and Prime Minister Hansen about nuclear weapons at Thule. Last but not least, the whole affair laid bare the weaknesses in Denmark's position when it came to administrating and overseeing matters in Greenland.

Although the issue of Camp Century's construction suddenly became extremely urgent for the Danish authorities in August 1959, this was not the first time the topic had been presented to the Danish Ministry of Foreign Affairs. In early November 1958, Ward Allen, the U.S. embassy secretary in Copenhagen, had informed Axel Serup, an office head at the Danish foreign ministry, about the U.S. Army's plans

FIGURE 2.2 Photographed here on August 14, 1958, the nuclear submarine USS *Skate* lies moored near the drifting research station Alpha, positioned on the pack ice in the Arctic Ocean. Just a few days earlier, submerged, the *Skate* had crossed the North Pole. When the submarine was later prohibited from entering the Port of Copenhagen, it sailed instead to Bergen, Norway. In 1959, the *Skate* became the first submarine to surface at the North Pole.

to build a scientific camp under the ice in Greenland. Allen explained to Serup that according to the plan, the camp was to be outfitted with a mobile nuclear reactor to provide electricity and heating and that it would be constructed outside the American defense areas in Greenland. He further let Serup know that the embassy "would like to be informally apprised of any remarks to which the matter gave rise."[14]

On November 19, 1958, after the matter had been discussed at the ministry, Serup had an informal conversation with Allen during which he drew the embassy secretary's attention to the fact that "a potential experiment with an atomic reactor on Greenland would raise a number of problems which, I guess, particularly against the backdrop of the whole *Skate* affair, would be desirable to avoid."[15] Serup was referring to events related to the planned exhibition visit of a nuclear submarine from the U.S. Navy, the USS *Skate*, to the Port of Copenhagen in late August 1958. The occasion was that the *Skate* had just navigated across the North Pole, being only the second vessel in the world to do so, after another American nuclear submarine, the USS *Nautilus*. Following these historic polar achievements in August 1958, the *Nautilus* had planned a stopover visit at Portland in the United Kingdom, while the *Skate* set course for Scandinavia, planning port calls in Norway and Denmark.

Shortly before the *Skate* was scheduled to arrive at the Port of Copenhagen, news broke that the country's Atomic Energy Commission (AEC) had warned Prime Minister Hansen, also acting foreign minister at the time, about the risk of hazardous radiation, which might occur in the event of an accident. "We have not dared to take upon ourselves the responsibility of not underlining the extremely great danger that could be associated with an accident happening to the atomic U-boat, for instance in running aground or colliding with another ship in the heart of the metropolis," an anonymous member of the Danish AEC explained to a *Politiken* newspaper reporter on August 22, 1958.[16] The next day, the front page of this respectable broadsheet bore the headline: "Dramatic Warning from Scientists: 'Half of Denmark Laid Waste.'"[17]

The Danish AEC had not carried out an independent risk analysis but had relied on an American report prepared by the Hanford Laboratory, where much of the U.S. military's research on nuclear energy took place. This report showed that emissions amounting to just 25 percent of the radioactivity in a 50 MW reactor—the presumed size of the submarine's reactor—could potentially emit lethal doses of radiation at a distance of up to 15 miles (25 km, reaching Roskilde to the west), to temporary evacuation within a radius of up to 125 miles (200 km, reaching Fredericia to the west), and to the destruction of crops within a radius of some 300 miles (500 km, or all of the Danish mainland and islands). Hansen took the scientists' warning to heart and called off "the otherwise interesting visit."[18]

The Danish cancelation caused something of a stir elsewhere in the world, since many destinations would receive American nuclear submarines without any major security concerns. There was, however, a spokesman for the British Admiralty who pointed out that it was precisely for security reasons that the *Nautilus* would be calling at the Isle of Portland in the English Channel, rather than in metropolitan London. In response to the cancellation, the U.S. State Department issued a brief statement citing that the *Nautilus* would arrive in New York City the following week, where the crew would be celebrated with a ticker-tape parade. Appearing alongside the Danish AEC report on the *Politiken* front page on August 23, 1958, several excerpts of this statement appeared in Danish. As one translated passage explained: "It is self-evident that the United States would never permit a vessel considered dangerous to put into port in a country that is an ally. . . . The *Nautilus* and the *Skate* have been constructed with due consideration given to the possibility of a collision or other damage."[19]

Because of the buzz outside Denmark, where many saw the Danish cancellation as criticism of U.S. nuclear submarines making port calls, Prime Minister Hansen felt compelled to issue the following statement: "There is not the slightest hint of foreign political pressure or domestic posturing behind the cancellation; neither directly nor indirectly." Here he was referring to the scientific risk assessment from Denmark's own AEC, elaborating on the decision: "Some might make merry or mock excessive wariness and that sort of thing, but I refuse to stand as unenlightened on these problems yet be called upon to act boldly on behalf of science."[20]

The cancelled port call was also brought up during the Danish defense minister Poul Hansen's three-week visit to the United States in November 1959. Newly returned from his trip, on which he had viewed defense weapons and bases and held briefings with high-level military officials at the Pentagon, Poul Hansen refuted claims that the *Skate* affair would create a precedent for the Danish government's view on port calls in Denmark from nuclear submarines and ships. During a press conference held at the U.S. naval base in Norfolk, Virginia, the minister had explained that Denmark's refusal to receive the *Skate* was based on inadequate knowledge about the submarine's security measures and equipment. He also expected the future would bring a greater focus on security issues when nuclear-powered vessels docked in Danish ports.[21]

As it happened, Defense Minister Poul Hansen's press conference statement about the security challenges of port calls by nuclear submarines and warships was delivered the day before the informal conversation between Axel Serup and Ward Allen on November 19, 1958. This was their discussion of the planned military camp and nuclear reactor in Greenland, during which Serup had also mentioned the *Skate* affair. The meeting between these two men resulted in a situation that, to the casual observer, resembled a mutual understanding between the United States and Denmark: the same sort of understanding Poul Hansen's ministerial visit to the United States seemed to have achieved. Serup communicated to the Americans the Danish government's view, namely, that the American nuclear reactor experiments did not necessarily have to take place in Greenland. Why not carry out this testing in Alaska, Serup proposed, "where the same problems would not arise."[22] At any rate, in the Danish government's view the matter did not warrant being raised officially. According to Serup's own notes from the meeting, Allen had indicated that he understood the Danish position and would subsequently report it to Washington. Allen had added, however, that from the American point of view it might also be an option, "on their own, in accordance with the Greenland treaty, to conduct an experiment of this nature in a defense area."[23]

THE CONCEPT OF ATOMS REVISITED

Axel Serup interpreted his meeting with Ward Allen, the embassy secretary, as expressing a certain understanding or receptiveness on the part of the American authorities to the Danes' courteous refusal of the American plans for a scientific, nuclear-powered military camp under the ice in Greenland, which at this point, in the winter of 1958/1959, had not yet been officially named "Camp Century." Danish politicians and officials may well have hoped or believed that the idea of a military camp in the ice sheet, complete with nuclear reactor, had been abandoned or that the plans had been relocated to Alaska. However, any such hopes were soon dashed. As early as February 16, 1959, the Danes received the official U.S. request for permission (in the calendar year 1959) to construct the camp as part of the annual application for permission to conduct scientific activities outside the defense areas in Greenland. Essentially, this was all part of the standard routine. Since the signing of the Danish-American Defense Agreement on Greenland in 1951, the procedure was that each year the Americans applied for—and usually received—permission from the Danish authorities to conduct scientific activities outside the agreed "defense areas." In this sense, the American request from February 1959 resembled all previous requests under the 1951 Defense Agreement. And as usual, this request also invited Danish scientists to participate in the investigations and experiments, likewise offering to make the scientific findings available to the Danish government.[24]

This invitation for scientific collaboration and knowledge sharing was genuine. The American geographer Paul Siple, who was the scientific head of the U.S. Army's science office, visited Copenhagen in November 1958—coinciding with the first informal American request regarding a camp under the ice. While we do not know whether he spoke with any Danes about this camp, we do know that Siple held several meetings with Danish scientists about their potential participation in the U.S. Army's research program in Greenland. Among the Danes he met were Helge Larsen (the head of the Arctic Institute), Børge Fristrup (a geographer specializing in Greenland and amanuensis at the University of Copenhagen), and Aksel Nørvang (an assistant professor at the University of Copenhagen and scientific adviser to the Danish liaison officers at Thule Air Base in the summers of 1956 through 1958).[25]

While the 1959 application from the United States to conduct scientific activities outside the defense areas was fairly routine, it was exceptional in one respect. There was a passage mentioning the "Construction of a sub-surface camp to test engineering techniques and

methods."[26] The Danish authorities subsequently asked for further details about this camp, which they received just a few days later, on February 20, 1959.[27] The explanatory document indicated that the camp, referred to as "Under Snow Camp," was to be seen as an extension of the U.S. Army's scientific investigation projects, which were already underway at an existing camp built on and partially within the ice sheet. This facility was Camp Fistclench, described earlier, which had been constructed in the summer of 1957 near Site 2, one of the U.S. early-warning radar installations in the area, built in 1955 some 350 km east of Thule Air Base. A large part of the Fistclench facility, housing 150 personnel, lay beneath the ice and snow, so the work done on that camp had demonstrated that the idea of a military post beneath the ice cap was realizable. Nevertheless, the U.S. application for permission to build a new and larger camp under the ice underscored that the purpose of Camp Fistclench had not been to establish permanent military bases in the ice but to conduct preliminary investigations and technical tests in beneath-the-snow construction techniques. This specification that the installation was not permanent apparently reassured the Danish authorities, who pursued the matter no further.[28]

Be that as it may, the explanatory document from the Americans, dated February 20, 1959, did not make any mention whatsoever of a nuclear reactor, so the Danish authorities did not know that the application they had received related specifically to the very camp both Axel Serup and the Danish foreign ministry, back in November 1958, had asked the Americans to build in Alaska rather than in Greenland. Based on this, Danish permission to continue scientific activity was

FIGURE 2.3 The radar station DYE-2, located on the Greenland ice cap. DYE-2 was part of the Distant Early Warning (or DEW) line, which ran from Alaska across the northern reaches of Canada and over to Greenland. Its purpose was to give early warning of any potential airstrikes on the United States, and it was approved by the Danish authorities on March 20, 1958. During the negotiations about the DYE stations in Greenland (four in all), which took a number of years, Office Head Axel Serup had made a point of informing the Americans that Greenland was a very "sensitive area, politically speaking."

initially given without reservation. Later, however, on May 29, 1959, the United States sent yet another application requesting permission to build a subsurface camp in the ice sheet, and this new application spe-cifically stated that the facility's energy supply would come from "a semi-mobile (1500 kW) modular-type nuclear power plant"—which was about one-thirtieth the estimated size of the submarine reactor aboard the USS *Skate*.[29] This new American application was also deliv-ered, in person, by U.S. Embassy Secretary Ward Allen through the Danish Ministry of Foreign Affairs. Allen emphasized that this type of nuclear reactor had already been tested at the U.S. Army's Fort Belvoir facility, located near Washington, DC. The Danish government was welcome to see the information and data from Fort Belvoir, and the Americans were also willing to invite a Danish scientist—they pro-posed the chemist T. Kindt-Larsen, who at the time was working with the Babcock and Wilcox Company in Lynchburg, Virginia, not far from Fort Belvoir—to personally investigate the reactor in question. Finally, Allen emphasized, Danish scientists would be welcome to col-laborate with the American scientists working with such a reactor in Greenland.[30]

The American offer was very forthcoming, yet Hans Christensen, the administrative officer who prepared the foreign ministry's first internal memo on the request, still found it strange that during his visit Allen had not mentioned at all that "he had previously, unofficially, received a Danish refusal."[31] By this, Christensen was referring to the meeting between Axel Serup and Ward Allen in November of the pre-vious year, during which Serup had strongly recommended that the experiment with the nuclear reactor be conducted elsewhere, at which point Serup had understood from Allen's remarks that the Americans would be understanding of, or receptive to, the Danish position—the "thanks but no thanks" to having a U.S. nuclear reactor on Danish, and more specifically on Greenlandic, turf. In Christensen's interpretation, the Americans attributed "significant weight" to the construction of the camp under the ice, including the nuclear reactor.[32] Like all other written requests from the United States concerning scientific activities, this matter was forwarded, for comments and annotation, to the

Danish Ministry of Defense and the Ministry for Greenland. Because the plan involved a nuclear reactor, the Danish AEC was also asked to make a written statement. Neither the Ministry for Greenland nor the AEC had any major objections to the project, although the AEC did submit a statement expressing concern about certain aspects of the radioactive wastewater and potential health consequences.[33] Things were not quite so straightforward when it came to the Ministry of Defense.

NUCLEAR POWER IN GREENLAND

Ward Allen once again came calling at the Danish Ministry of Foreign Affairs on August 4, 1959. The Scandinavian Desk at the U.S. State Department had sent Allen an unofficial letter notifying him that three technical journals in the United States had run articles about the army's construction of its semitransportable nuclear reactor, which had also touched on the issue of the reactor's eventual location. Allen therefore wanted to know whether the Danish authorities would be in a position, any time soon, to respond to the American application to install the reactor in Greenland. Office head Torben Rønne was able to inform Allen that the matter was currently under advisement with the Defense Research Council, meaning that Allen could not count on receiving an immediate answer to his query and that consequently the installation could hardly be envisioned to take place in the current season but would have to await the summer of 1960. Rønne further said that "the Danes would most emphatically recommend that information about the reactor in question not appear in the American press."[34]

Then, a good two weeks later, after the urgently convened meeting held in Nils Svenningsen's office, the stage was set for new insecurity about the whole affair, bearing in mind Val Peterson's comments to Jens Otto Krag at the social event in Copenhagen. This was the backdrop against which the Danes decided to send the country's liaison officer, stationed at Thule Air Base, onto the ice sheet to view the site of the

FIGURE 2.4 Entry ramp leading down into the tunnel system of Camp Fistclench, photographed on July 11, 1960. Fistclench was the first military base the Americans established within the ice sheet. It was an experimental camp for testing out new techniques for "subsurface construction." The name "Fistclench," sometimes written "Fist Clench," undoubtedly alludes to the willpower it took to construct the camp and to live and work there.

camp. This officer reported back in a telegram dated August 25, 1959, stating that the facility's name was indeed "Camp Century" and that he had seen with his own eyes the first tunnels, which had been dug into the ice, but no sign of a nuclear reactor. Back in Copenhagen, the foreign ministry therefore concluded that "the American ambassador has exaggerated the information about the reactor's installation having commenced—perhaps in order to put pressure on the Danish government to speedily achieve the desired permission."[35]

Reassuring messages from Greenland notwithstanding, just a few days later various headlines in Danish newspapers included the words "nuclear power plant" and "Greenland."[36] They were not referring, however, to the American reactor but to tentative Danish plans to install a nuclear power plant near the already operational lead and zinc mine at Mestersvig, on Greenland's east coast. The news had been announced by two prominent figures: Committee Chairman Koch of the AEC and Viggo Brinch, the director of Nordisk Mineselskab (the Nordic Mining Company). The timing was highly opportune considering the matter of Camp Century, which was bound to reach the press sooner or later. With this announcement, "the concept of atoms" had been launched in the context of Greenland, and at this stage the atoms would be "Danish atoms." Even though the deposits of lead and zinc at Mestersvig had proved to be modest and were, in fact, almost depleted at this point, Nordisk Mineselskab, who ran the mining operations there, hoped that by exploiting the newly found deposits of molybdenum at nearby Malmbjerg, installing a nuclear reactor at the mine would be justifiable. Some years later, Arktisk Mineselskab (the Arctic Mining Company) became a reality, thanks to funding from the large American mining corporation AMAX. But the world market prices could by no means justify a nuclear-powered mining venture at Mestersvig and environs, so the plan was scrapped in the early 1960s.[37]

On September 7, 1959, the Danish foreign minister, Jens Otto Krag, briefed the Foreign Policy Committee on the American inquiry about a civilian nuclear reactor at Camp Century, adding that the government did not believe that responding to the U.S. request in the affirmative ought to cause any misgivings.[38] The following week, Nils Svenningsen was able to inform the American embassy that the Danish government took a positive view of the American plans.[39] Even though, at that time, foreign newspapers had already written various pieces about Camp Century, no information had yet been presented to the Danish public about the camp or the nuclear reactor. The Danes did not become aware of the situation until the journalist Finn Bergholt, a reporter for the large Copenhagen daily *Information*, got wind of the situation and contacted the Ministry of Foreign Affairs on November 13, 1959. Torben Rønne confirmed Bergholt's information, adding that "recently there was also talk of building a power reactor at Mestersvig, and that such reactors would be of great importance to the power supply in Greenland."[40] Rønne further stated that construction of the American reactor had not yet reached a stage that gave the Danes an opportunity to finalize their position on the matter. In his own internal memo on this inquiry, Rønne finished by noting that the journalist had not asked in any great detail "whether, from the Danish side, permission had been granted for the reactor in question, near Thule."[41] Strictly speaking, it had not.

3

THE CITY UNDER THE ICE

NORTH GREENLAND AS AN AMERICAN NUCLEAR BASE

It had become eminently clear to the Danish authorities during the summer of 1959 that the United States was extremely keen to establish Camp Century beneath the ice in northern Greenland, close to Thule Air Base. First, in November 1958, the United States had disregarded Danish concerns that their small country might find itself in big trouble were "the concept of atoms" to be mentioned in connection with Greenland. Not only would this create domestic policy problems in relation to the Danish defense appropriations and the stability of the government; ultimately, the Danish disagreements about "atoms" in Greenland might even weaken the national support for Danish membership of NATO. The following year, the Americans had begun building the camp without prior permission from the Danish authorities, which, under the 1951 Defense Agreement on Greenland between Denmark and the United States, was a prerequisite for American activity outside the agreed "defense areas." Beyond the substantial size of Camp Century, which the Danish authorities saw in itself as an indication that the facility must have some military purpose, it was probably the determination of the U.S. approach that made the political decision makers in Copenhagen particularly nervous about the project.

And the Danish authorities had even more reason to be nervous than they realized at the time. In 1995 through 1997, a research group based at what is now the Danish Institute for International Studies (DIIS) revealed that in 1959 parts of the U.S. Army were working on a new, grand plan that would involve Greenland and the rest of the joint kingdom even more deeply in America's nuclear deterrence policy—with Camp Century as a vital strategic element. The DIIS group's final report, a white paper entitled *Grønland under den kolde krig* (Greenland during the Cold War), is treated in depth in chapter 9 of this book. Suffice it to say here that the purpose of the group's work was to attempt to clarify some of the questions arising from the Danish debate in 1995, when it became publicly known that in 1957 the sitting prime minister, H. C. Hansen, had given the Americans permission to station nuclear weapons at Thule Air Base. In 1995, the United States also issued a statement confirming that nuclear weapons had been present at Thule Air Base from February 1958 for eight months (in the form of aircraft bombs) and once again from December 1959 until the summer of 1965 (short-range Nike Hercules missiles for use in the base's antiaircraft defense system). This fresh information provided important new insights into "the concept of atoms" in Greenland. Among other things, the historians found an American report previously classified as top secret but declassified in September 1996 as part of the effort to clarify events around that time; this report gave a detailed account of an American plan to use large swaths of northern Greenland as a nuclear base.[1]

This plan, code-named Project Iceworm, envisioned the installation of 600 nuclear missiles in tunnels beneath the ice sheet, covering a huge area of some 250,000 square kilometers (100,000 square miles), corresponding to 12 percent of Greenland's total land surface. Covered by ice and snow, the missiles would be largely invisible from the air, and the sheer scope of the tunnel network would also make the system more robust against attack. What is more, the American estimates found that the ice sheet alone, being extremely compact, would provide a certain degree of protection in itself. The completed system would have 2,100 launch positions, and missiles would be transported on subsurface railways in ice tunnels that enabled launching from any position. Operation and maintenance would be handled by no fewer than 11,000 personnel, who would be accommodated in quarters that lay inside the ice. Heat and power for the entire complex would come from a number of small nuclear reactors, like the one planned for installation at Camp Century.[2]

The "iceworm" in the project's name probably arose at Camp Fistclench, the U.S. military base set up in the summer of 1957 on the ice cap, some 350 km (220 miles) east of Thule Air Base, where the Americans first experimented on tunnel systems constructed in the ice. Camp Fistclench was built by the U.S. Army Polar Research and Development Center (part of the Corps of Engineers). During this work, "iceworm" became a popular nickname for the researchers, engineers, and military personnel who, much like actual worms, had to bore their way down into the frozen strata. (It should be noted that these iceworms knew nothing of the top-secret project of the same name.) The experience gained from Camp Fistclench—the world's first documented attempt to build a unified system of residential and storage tunnels in the ice sheet—showed that it would indeed be possible to establish military encampments that could exist for a certain length of time below the surface.[3]

Project Iceworm was the brainchild of the U.S. Army Engineer Studies Center, an army think tank that in the 1950s had been preoccupied with the consequences of the new weapons developed during this period, in particular the hydrogen bomb (H-bomb) and the intercontinental ballistic missile (ICBM). The center's analytical work focused on two interconnected problems: radioactive fallout from the powerful H-bombs and the precision of the missiles. The conclusion was that, depending on the prevailing winds, fallout from a potential H-bomb attack on the USSR could plausibly impact large parts of Europe, that is, America's allies. Also, since no solid facts about the precision of ICBM strikes existed at the time, using such weapons would quickly become difficult, if not impossible, without causing extensive and

unforeseeable devastation. As the army think tank concluded in 1957—
at a time when many in the U.S. military still saw "massive retaliation"
as the best atomic strategy—any nuclear response to Soviet aggression
would be equivalent to genocide, a situation that, obviously, would also
apply in the event of a nuclear attack on the United States.[4]

Even as the horrific consequences of a potential nuclear war were
beginning to dawn on the military and the public, two extensive missile programs were under way in the United States: the land-based
"Minuteman" run by the air force and the nuclear submarine–based
"Polaris" run by the navy. The Minuteman was a three-stage missile
propelled by solid fuel and with a range of up to approximately 10,000
km (6,200 miles), enough to reach Moscow from almost anywhere in
America. During the 1960s some 1,000 Minuteman missiles were
installed at U.S. airbases and reinforced launching silos sunk into the
ground across the Great Plains region.[5] The Polaris missile was also a
solid-fuel missile, and with a range of about 4,500 km (2,800 miles) and
launch capability from a submerged submarine, it was immensely flexible and almost impossible to neutralize.[6]

Unlike the air force and the navy, which had both seen funding
increases throughout the 1950s, the army's budget had been drastically
cut. Because of disagreements between the air force and the army, the
American secretary of defense, Charles E. Wilson, had pulled the army
out of the Jupiter missile program—Jupiter being the first U.S. medium-
range nuclear missile (MRBM)—in 1956 and subsequently sought to
limit the army's efforts to develop short-range defense missiles like
Nike Hercules. By the end of the 1950s, total appropriations for the U.S.
Armed Forces were allocating 22 percent to the army, 29 percent to the
navy, and 49 percent to the air force. In comparison, as recently as the
Korean War in the early 1950s, defense funding for the army and the air
force had been almost the inverse.[7]

In October and November 1957, the Soviet Union made it into space,
launching Sputnik 1, the first manmade satellite, closely followed by
Sputnik 2, containing the "space dog" Laika, the first living organism to
go beyond Earth's atmosphere. The Sputnik launches stoked American
fears that the United States was falling behind the USSR in the

development and production of missile technology, sometimes called "the missile gap." High-ranking military officials spoke strongly in favor of the United States now putting even more into developing ballistic nuclear missiles that could strike targets in the Soviet Union, and it was hard for President Eisenhower to withstand this pressure, although on several occasions he did state that in reality there was no "missile gap." His attempts to convince Congress that the U.S. nuclear missile capability was adequate were in vain, so he was unable to limit military spending—otherwise an integral part of his New Look strategy from 1953.[8]

When the U.S. Army Engineer Studies Center conceived the idea of Project Iceworm in the late 1950s, the army badly needed to demonstrate its relevance compared to the existing U.S. missile programs, not least the air force and its Minuteman missiles. Based on the widely held belief in a missile gap between the United States and the USSR, the army saw a potential political opening for a new missile project. While Project Iceworm did not involve any actual development work on missiles, in seeking out new missile-related opportunities for the army it ingeniously played on the weaknesses of the Minuteman program. In this context, Greenland's climate and location were crucial. Project Iceworm would need a shorter version of the Minuteman, one with only two rocket stages instead of three. This revamped missile, which, it must be noted, did not exist and would never be built, was fittingly christened "Iceman."[9]

Given its location in northern Greenland, the Iceman missile could make do with a shorter range than the Minuteman. It would also be able to reach targets in the Soviet Union faster than the Minuteman and strike with greater precision. What is more, the very construction and layout of the long, intricate tunnel system in the ice sheet would mean that even in the event of a surprise Soviet attack with nuclear warheads, the United States would be able to launch a rapid, effective counterattack using Iceman missiles launched from northern Greenland. And perhaps most importantly, unlike the Minuteman missiles, which would be launched from underground silos in America's heartland, the Iceman missiles would be located far from inhabited American territory and thus not constitute a potential risk should the Soviet Union attack U.S. missile sites.[10]

NAME AND LOCATION OF THE NEW CAMP

In 1959, the year the United States officially applied to Denmark for permission to establish Camp Century in the ice sheet, the concept of Project Iceworm was still not fully developed, although it must have been well underway. The application must be seen in the light of certain significant circumstances: First, the U.S. Army had previous positive experience building tunnels under the ice; second, there was a growing interest in making the United States the world leader in missile technology; and third, the army wanted to play a role in building the nation's missile-based defense capabilities. The people in contact with the Danish authorities presented the new camp as a scientific facility, leaving it up to the Danes to guess that activities there would also have a military aim—as Danish AEC chairman H. H. Koch did during the emergency meeting held in Copenhagen on August 20, 1959, and as Helge Larsen, the scientific adviser to the Danish liaison officer at Thule Air Base, had done in his report dated July 20, 1959.[11]

The American efforts were, in fact, well underway at this time, as described in the preceding chapter. The decision about Camp Century's physical location was made in May 1959, when a small, carefully selected team from the U.S. Army Polar Research and Development Center followed the marked-out trail that led from Camp Tuto, near the edge of the ice sheet, to Camp Fistclench, located a good 350 km (220 miles) further inland, on the ice cap. Transporting goods and personnel to this remote location was an arduous and expensive task. The mission of the small reconnaissance team, led by Colonel John Kerkering and Captain Thomas C. Evans, who had already been appointed as commanding officer of the coming Camp Century, was to identify the first location on this trail that met a series of requirements the army had stipulated for the new camp. The planners believed such a site might

FIGURE 3.1 In May 1959, the first American reconnaissance team, led by Colonel John Kerkering (center) and Captain Thomas C. Evans (left), pointed out the future location of Camp Century. The team was on the lookout for a flat area as close as possible to Thule Air Base yet unaffected by thaw during the summer months.

well lie about a hundred miles from the rim of the ice cap, hence the name "Century." But their assumptions were wrong. As it turned out, Kerkering and Evans had to move much further inland before finding an ideal location: 222 km (138 miles) from Camp Tuto, at an elevation of just over 2,000 meters (6,500 feet) above sea level.[12]

A film production by the U.S. Army released in 1961 as part of its series *The Big Picture*, which aired on the ABC television network, shows Kerkering and Evans in full polar gear and Ray-Ban sunglasses standing on the ice, establishing the position with sextant and chronometer. The narration track, a voiceover recorded later by Evans, calmly explains what the recon team was looking for:

We needed a flat surface, a level with less than one degree slope. This would minimize construction problems by enabling us to keep all of our tunnels on the same level. We finally picked this plateau, a smooth, white plane of ice for as far as you could see. This was the closest location to Thule, our supply base, which would not be affected by the summer thaw. That first day, we set our flags, marking the boundaries of the camp.[13]

CONSTRUCTION

Just one month later, the U.S. Army Corps of Engineers was ready to break ground, or, rather, ice, and the project management team was not prepared to let the brief Arctic summer slip away while waiting for the final go-ahead from Copenhagen. So in mid-June 1959—in other words, two months before the exchange between Danish foreign minister Jens Otto Krag and the American ambassador Val Peterson at the social event in Copenhagen—a caravan set off for the Camp Century site. Embarking on the laborious journey from Camp Tuto, near the ice rim close to the Thule Air Base, were personnel wagons carrying specially trained construction workers, accompanied by huge sledges loaded with construction materials, fuel, food, and other necessities. This type of ice caravan, called a "heavy swing," was drawn by huge tractors with extra-wide caterpillar tracks and immensely strong engines. The pace of a heavy swing is just a few miles per hour, so depending on the weather it would take three to six days of nonstop travel to reach a destination 222 km away. However, much of the personnel arrived at their destination in just a day or two, having been allowed to ride in the comparatively faster "polecats," personnel transports likewise equipped with caterpillar tracks but used specifically for transporting personnel and visitors. The first technicians on the scene immediately began to set up a primitive camp on the surface of the ice, consisting of prefabricated tent-like personnel quarters called "Jamesway huts." The huts' built-in electrical lighting and heating systems would enable the men who were to build

FIGURE 3.2 Camp Century had a total of 21 tunnels, stretching more than 1,800 meters (about 6,000 feet) in all. This figure indicates the function of each tunnel. For instance, Tunnel 2—labeled "Heat Sink"—was used to cool down the coolant (glycol) used in the nuclear reactor plant. After two years of operations, the heat sink had accumulated a reservoir of 76 million liters (20 million gallons) of water, which was completely pure and free of radioactivity. The small, jagged break drawn on the tunnel line just before Tunnel 2 shows that the heat sink was located at some distance from the camp. The same goes for the tunnel marked "Hot Waste Disposal," through which low-level radioactive wastewater was released directly into the ice sheet.

CAMP CENTURY

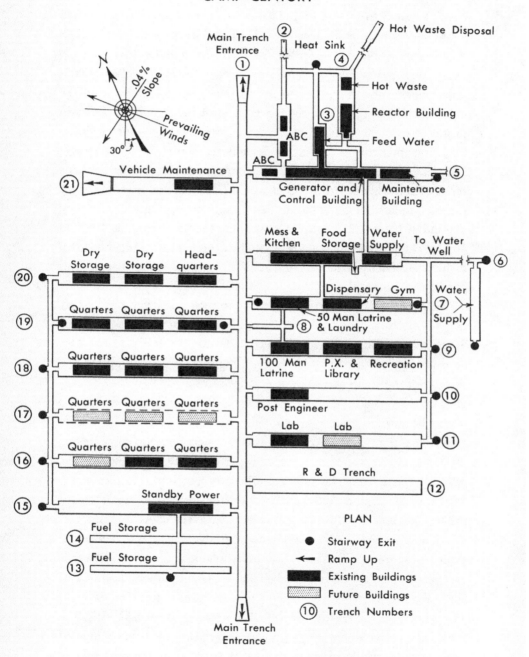

Main Trench Entrance ① — Heat Sink ②
Hot Waste Disposal ④

Hot Waste
Reactor Building ③
Feed Water

ABC

ABC

Vehicle Maintenance ㉑

Generator and Control Building — Maintenance Building ⑤

Mess & Kitchen — Food Storage — Water Supply — To Water Well ⑥

Dry Storage — Dry Storage — Head-quarters ⑳

Dispensary — Gym — Water Supply ⑦

Quarters Quarters Quarters ⑲

50 Man Latrine & Laundry ⑧

Quarters Quarters Quarters ⑱

100 Man Latrine — P.X. & Recreation Library ⑨

Quarters Quarters Quarters ⑰

Post Engineer ⑩

Quarters Quarters Quarters ⑯

Lab — Lab ⑪

Standby Power ⑮

R & D Trench ⑫

Fuel Storage ⑭

Fuel Storage ⑬

Main Trench Entrance

PLAN

● Stairway Exit
← Ramp Up
■ Existing Buildings
▦ Future Buildings
⑩ Trench Numbers

.04% Slope
N
Prevailing Winds
30°

Camp Century to survive on the ice for the few summer months when temperatures were at an acceptable level for human activity, although the mercury would still be far below freezing most of the time.[14]

As one heavy swing after another arrived with equipment and materials, the actual construction work on the camp got under way. The men began by digging into the ice. First came the trench for the main tunnel, predictably dubbed "Main Street," which was 335 meters (1,100 feet) long and 8 meters (26 feet) wide, making it large enough to receive fully loaded sledges from heavy-swing transports. The next step was a series of sixteen side tunnels that would house laboratories, barracks, showers, toilets, kitchen facilities, and a lounge, dining room, library, and movie theater. Last but not least, there were four tunnels destined for the camp's nuclear reactor, as well as the heat exchangers, steam turbine, electricity generator, and auxiliary diesel engines that were all part of the reactor plant.

The Americans excavated these many tunnels quickly and efficiently using a machine called a "Peter Plough" or "Peter Snow Miller." This Swiss invention uses rotating shovel blades to strip a one-to-two-foot layer of snow off the surface, blowing it high into the air and off to one side. By running this snowplow across the same area many times, stripping off a layer of hard-packed snow with each run, the plow dug the tunnel body and blew a plume of fine crystals up over the edge of an ever-deepening trench. Its capacity was an impressive 700 cubic meters (25,000 cubic feet) of compacted snow per hour. On each new run, the operator could make the plow cut a little deeper into the sides of the trench, resulting in a tunnel with visibly inward-slanting walls toward the top. Technically this was possible because the snow was progressively more compact as the depth grew. The advantage was that covering a narrowing trench was easier than covering one with completely vertical walls. Once a trench had reached 8 meters (a little more than 25 feet) below the surface, it was also about 8 m wide at the bottom but only 3 to 4 m at the top. The reactor tunnels, in contrast, had vertical walls. The trench was then covered over with wide, curved segments of corrugated metal sheeting while the plow moved on to excavate the next trench. Finally, some of the loose snow thrown up by the plow, sometimes referred to as "Peter snow," was blown over and across the corrugated metal roof. Within a few days the particles of snow would fuse into an ice roof that soon became so hard and stable that the sheeting could be removed and used as temporary roofing for the next tunnel.[15]

The side tunnels were accessed by way of Main Street and by ladders in the emergency exit tubes that went through the tunnel roofs. In the completed side tunnels, the construction crew assembled prefabricated houses with thickly insulated floors, walls, and ceilings. Each of these buildings, equipped with the necessary installations, had been assembled and checked in the United States before the long journey to Camp Century. This prevented the Arctic assembly crew from running into problems with lacking, faulty, or wrong components, which was a great advantage. An experienced construction team could complete a small barracks unit in just one day. Naturally, the larger structures with communal facilities took longer to erect. To make the process as practical, convenient, and efficient as possible, the engineers had opted for a modified version of the U.S. Army's standard T-5 barracks unit to accommodate personnel inside the tunnels, even though these structures were designed for outdoor use in wind, rain, and snow. The T-5 units were seriously overdimensioned for the purpose they would serve in Camp Century, but the project managers chose them as the best solution, lacking the time to develop an entirely new type of purpose-built prefab. A standard T-5 unit, being 6 meters wide, was too large for the narrow tunnels, so the units to be used in Camp Century were altered to be only 5 meters wide. This allowed inhabitants to pass between the houses in the personnel tunnels and also left enough room to accommodate various tubes, pipes, and cables between the units and the tunnel walls.[16]

All of the camp's subsurface structures were raised well above the tunnel floor to prevent the heat radiating from the structures (and the inhabitants) from affecting the floor surface. Powerful ventilation fans kept the air below and around the buildings ice-cold. Each tunnel was equipped with two ventilation systems: one that ventilated the living quarters, and one that blew the relatively warm air out of the tunnels. The American engineers wanted the houses to be comfortable and warm, but it was vital that the temperature in the tunnel spaces outside the buildings be kept as low as possible, preferably as low as −15°C (about 5°F), to prevent walls and floors from becoming soft and slushy or, in the worst case, melting. The ventilation system sucked in cold air and blew it through a number of channels drilled into the ice sheet, each about 30 cm in diameter and running down to a depth of 12 m below the tunnel floor. This cold air was transported through the tunnel, then blown out topside through purpose-built ventilation towers on the surface. This system worked, but it was not perfect. At certain times during the summer, tunnel temperatures rose higher than was desirable. This was just one of the factors that contributed to reducing the ventilation plant's lifetime compared to the ten-plus years the army engineers had projected.[17]

In 1959, the summer season ended in early September with the closing of Camp Century. Progress had been made, but much work remained. Thus far, energy in the form of heat and electricity had been supplied by oil-fueled diesel engines and electric generators. In September, most of the construction crew returned to the United States for the winter. Meanwhile, the U.S. Army Polar Research and Development Center, headquartered in Fort Belvoir, Virginia, spent the winter of 1959/1960 finalizing the plans needed to complete Camp Century, and in May 1960 the construction crew returned to the site. At the same time the remaining materials needed for the project were gradually transported by heavy swings that set out from Camp Tuto. By the latter half of September 1960, the construction of Camp Century was largely completed.[18] Only the nuclear reactor and the accompanying plant consisting of heat exchangers, steam turbine, and electricity generators remained to be installed.

WATER SUPPLY AND WASTE MANAGEMENT

Until the nuclear reactor was operating smoothly, electricity and heat at Camp Century had to be supplied by an auxiliary diesel engine linked to an electricity generator, exactly as had been done the previous year for the temporary Jamesway huts on the surface. The absolutely essential task of supplying water was resolved by the technical engineers at Camp Century, exploiting a concept conceived just a few years earlier by the Swiss-born geologist Henri Bader, who was head scientist at the

U.S. Army's Snow, Ice, and Permafrost Research Establishment (SIPRE). The gist of Bader's concept was to lead extremely hot vapor, produced in a diesel-powered steam generator, down through a hollow drill sunk into a hole at the end of Tunnel 6. This drill was suspended by a cable, and the hot steam from the drill tip melted more and more of the surrounding snow and ice, converting it into potable water, which the camp could use for all its needs. When heated continuously, the drill could melt its way through the ice to a depth of some 50 to 60 meters, at which point the surrounding layer of compacted ice was so dense as to be impenetrable to water. In this way, by introducing appropriate amounts of hot steam, it was easy to produce a natural well, a reservoir of ice-cold water that could comfortably meet the camp's requirements of some 30,000 liters (8,000 gallons) per day when fully manned. All the technicians had to do was adjust the steam supply up or down as needed. This turned out to be a simple, cheap, clean solution. In fact, the water supply operated impeccably throughout Camp Century's lifetime.[19]

Plumbing and sewage was a different story. All wastewater and sewage was pumped through tubes down into a hole, which had been melted in the underlying ice using Bader's method and was located about 50 meters from the barracks tunnels. The liquid waste was about 15 to 25°C when let out through the discharge tubes, so it penetrated a bit further down into the snow and ice, just like the water in the freshwater well in Tunnel 6. So far, so good. The camp's planners, however, had recommended that the liquid waste be dumped at a distance of at least 150 meters from the nearest habitation in order to avoid contamination and offensive odors. But the engineers, sorely pressed for time during the construction phase, found this to be impossible in practice, so the actual distance ended up being just one-third of what was recommended. To make matters worse, the sewage hole was not ventilated, causing an extremely unpleasant smell in certain parts of the camp, as witnessed in this passage from the final, official report on Camp Century: "The odor of sewage became almost unbearable in the nearest quarters by the following summer [1960] and traces of sewage odor were detectable throughout Trenches 18, 19, and 20. Subsequent venting of the sump reduced the odor to a more tolerable level but did not completely eliminate the problem."[20]

The sewage hole, or "sump," received substantial amounts of liquid and solid waste. The official report on Camp Century estimates that during the first two years of the camp's operation—from June 1960 to August 1962—12 million liters of waste were pumped into the sump, polluting the snow around the sump's central line to a distance of about 35 meters as of August 1962. The contamination continued to spread, and the daily influx of 17,000 liters of warm waste meant that the nearest tunnel (Trench 19) became so severely deformed that the camp's commanders were obliged to move the two most at-risk T-5 personnel units out of the tunnel.[21]

THE NUCLEAR REACTOR AND
THE APPROVAL PROCEDURE

Indisputably, the largest technical installation at Camp Century was the mobile nuclear reactor. As described in chapter 2, however, it was also the most controversial installation for the Danish Ministry of Foreign Affairs, which consistently handled "the concept of atoms" with extreme caution. The ministry's director, Nils Svenningsen, had written to the American Embassy in Copenhagen on September 14, 1959, and given permission, at least in principle, for the U.S. Army to build Camp Century. Nevertheless, at the same time he had drawn the Americans' attention to the fact that final permission to install a nuclear reactor in the camp would not be forthcoming until a team of Danish atomic experts had been given the opportunity to discuss "certain technical details" with their American counterparts.[22]

The Americans had no objections to this, and so from December 8 to 10, 1959, two Danish representatives attended a series of meetings in Washington, DC, with representatives of the U.S. Army Corps of Engineers, the body formally responsible for installing the reactor at Camp Century.[23] These Danish representatives were Christian L. Thomsen, head of the secretariat at the Danish Atomic Energy Commission (AEC), and Povl L. Ølgaard, from the AEC's own Danish nuclear research

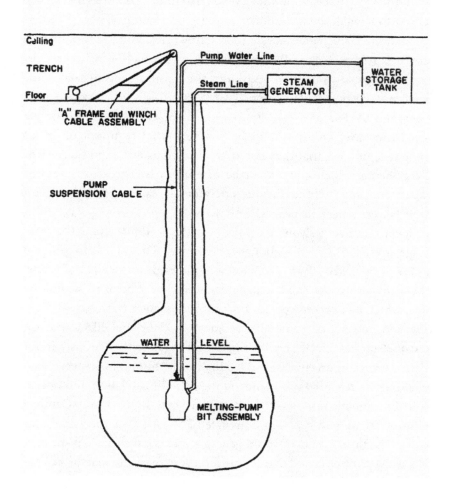

FIGURE 3.3 Conceptual sketch of Camp Century's water-supply system. Steam is led down into a hole in the ice sheet where it melts ice into water, which is then pumped up to the tunnel. The water was tested by the Sanitary Engineering Branch at the U.S. Army Corps of Engineers' R&D center at Fort Belvoir, Virginia. They found the quality excellent, so it was used without filtering, chlorination, or other treatment. In May 1962, they dug a new water well in the ice after the depth of the original well exceeded the water pump's maximum depth of 150 meters (500 feet).

facility at Risø. The meetings had been arranged as a result of the official Danish-American negotiations taking place soon after August 1959, when the U.S. ambassador Val Peterson had informed Foreign Minister Jens Otto Krag of the work under way at Camp Century.

First, the Danish guests were thoroughly briefed on the comprehensive U.S. Army Nuclear Power Program, which had been initiated in 1952 and aimed to develop and build small and medium-sized land-based nuclear power plants, constructed specifically for the U.S. Army, Navy, and Air Force to serve as energy sources at remote or inaccessible American bases around the globe.[24] An essential requirement for all these reactors was that they could be airlifted as a limited number of components, which could then be assembled by the army's reactor experts on site. Of the various operational reactors, the American experts were especially pleased with the SM-1, a pressurized-water reactor located at Fort Belvoir, Virginia, near the headquarters of the reactor group. The SM-1 was stationary (hence the "S") and able to generate 2 MW of electrical effect, which put it in the medium-sized ("M") class. The army also had a small experimental nuclear reactor in Idaho, the SL-1, which had become operational in August 1958. In this case, the L (for "low power") corresponded to 400 kW of thermal effect and 200 kW of electrical effect. The SM-1 had been made critical in 1957, and it mainly served as an educational facility for the military personnel who would act as reactor experts during the actual installation and operation of the mobile reactors. The reactor chosen to supply Camp Century with electricity and heat was designated PM-2A (P for "portable" and M for "medium"), and it would generate a maximum 10 MW of heat and 1.5 MW of electricity. This was a bit less than the reactor at Fort Belvoir but still significantly more than the army's SL-1. Calculations showed that this ought to be more than adequate to cover the camp's electricity and heating needs. Incidentally (the Danish experts were informed), the PM-2A was going to be built by the same company (ALCO Products of Schenectady, New York) that had built the SM-1 reactor—which, at that stage, had been operating to the experts' satisfaction for almost three years.[25]

Next, the Danes were briefed on the entire Camp Century project, after which, finally, the group could proceed to the pivotal issue of the meeting: a detailed look at all the individual components in the PM-2A reactor and at related aspects such as the built-in security features and the management of the radioactive waste that would be produced by the reactor while it was running. The American experts, notably including Captain Thomas C. Evans, who was in charge of building Camp Century, expected that the reactor components would arrive at the site between July 15 and August 16, 1960, and that assembly would begin at once. This piece of information alone already put considerable pressure on the Danish authorities, implicitly urging them to process the matter as speedily as possible. And the pressure rose a notch when the American reactor team showed the Danes a letter from the American Atomic Energy Commission stating that *if* the army had planned to install the PM-2A on American soil under conditions corresponding to those at Camp Century, the project would almost certainly have been approved and initiated, given the reactor's similarity to the tried-and-tested SM-1.[26]

Once the reactor had been installed and was up and running, the experts would, of course, meticulously monitor its radioactive emissions to the operators and immediate environment, making sure they did not exceed international norms. This was no different from Ølgaard's own place of work, the Risø Nuclear Research Laboratory. But what about the spent fuel rods? And what about other radioactive waste generated by the running reactor? As for the highly radioactive fuel rods, the Americans promised to take them back to the United States and also to take back all reactor components and radioactive fittings and fixtures from Camp Century when, at some point, the camp was shut down. However, when it came to the liquid, slightly radioactive waste—partly generated at the laboratory that would routinely test water from the reactor and partly arising from potential leaks in the pumps and the ion-exchange filters used to remove radioactive compounds from the water— the situation was rather different. Based on their experience with the SM-1, the American experts anticipated an annual production just short of 30,000 liters (7,500 gallons) of liquid radioactive waste, in other words, quite a significant amount in volume and in weight. This meant it would be extremely expensive and cumbersome to transport back to American soil, not least keeping in mind that it was only slightly radioactive. According to the experts, the maximum radioactive emissions would amount to 1.1 GBq (30 millicuries) each year, mainly stemming from fission products. Based on this, the Americans were requesting permission from the Danish authorities to lead this liquid waste away, into a hole in the ice located at a reasonable distance from the camp.[27]

As soon as Povl Ølgaard returned to Denmark, he and two of his colleagues—the physics professor Ole Kofoed-Hansen and the radioactivity expert Henry Gjørup—began a meticulous study of the PM-2A material Ølgaard had brought back from the United States, and they reviewed in detail the accompanying American documents about security procedures and waste handling. The work of this Danish expert group resulted in a letter, dated January 11, 1960, and addressed to the Danish AEC. Apart from expressing regret at the short time they had to complete their work, they declared "that we have found no technical or security-related objections to the project that would justify denying the application."[28] They additionally referred to the assurances from the American AEC that the PM-2A would have been approved had it been located on American soil. Then the Danish experts moved on to the issue of how to deal with the liquid radioactive waste, which the Americans were seeking permission to dump within the ice sheet:

> As regards the treatment of the liquid radioactive waste, we find it fully responsible that this be sent directly down into the ice sheet, provided it is deposited at a safe distance from the camp; and provided the annual amount of waste does not exceed 0.06 curie; and [provided] that the concentration of activity does not exceed 10^{-3} microcuries per cubic centimeter. Should it prove necessary to deposit larger amounts of activity within the ice, the waste must be cleansed with an ionic-exchange filter down to the permissible concentration for potable water (10^{-7} microcuries per cubic cm), after which it can be discharged down into the ice sheet. An account ought to be kept of the activity volumes deposited within the ice, and the Danish authorities ought to be informed of this once a year.[29]

The Danish AEC forwarded the experts' letter to the Danish Ministry of Foreign Affairs, which in turn sent a very precisely worded document—a *note verbale*, or "verbatim note"—dated February 10, 1962, to the American embassy in Copenhagen. This was the Danish response to the American application of May 29, 1959, for permission to install a nuclear reactor at Camp Century. The verbatim note granted the Americans such permission, on the following conditions:

1. that the Government of the United States of America assume full responsibility for any damage caused by the operation of the plant;
2. that the Danish authorities be kept currently informed of the amount and activity of all radioactive waste from the reactor;
3. that all technical changes which may affect the safety of the reactor be reported to the Danish authorities; and
4. that all radioactive parts be removed from Greenland by the United States authorities at the termination of the operational period of the reactor in so far as a request to this effect be made by the Danish authorities.[30]

This document was accompanied by a number of technical questions from the Danish experts at the Risø Nuclear Research Laboratory. They wished to clarify certain things in the existing reports about the PM-2A, and they requested a speedy reply from their American counterparts. The response was quick indeed: a letter dated February 29, 1960, sent from the Office of the Chief of Engineers and signed by William B. Taylor, head of the Nuclear Power Division of the Department of the Army. Taylor specified in his letter that the anticipated charge of liquid radioactive waste from the PM-2A would not exceed 1.85 GBq (50 millicuries) per year, slightly less than the Danish experts had concluded based on their visit at Fort Belvoir (which was an estimated 60 millicuries) but more than the initial American estimates of 30 millicuries. Taylor also emphasized that all radioactive waste that might exceed this limit would be removed from Greenland. The Americans would prepare an "environmental monitoring plan," which would be implemented beginning May 1960 and run until the reactor was decommissioned.[31]

After the Danish reactor experts had been able to scrutinize Taylor's clarifications for a few weeks, on April 20, 1960, they declared they were satisfied with his answer, provided the Danish authorities received "annual statements of the volume, specific activity, and total activity of liquid radioactive waste that is discharged into the ice sheet," as well as "immediate notification of any major accidents involving the reactor plant," in accordance with what the Americans had offered to make available.[32] The Danish AEC in turn notified the government that the American response was "satisfactory," adding that "the Commission, in processing this case, has generally assumed that once the reactor is operating, there will be appropriate access for the respective Danish authorities to inspect the reactor and the technical installations associated with it."[33]

It seemed that all the technical questions and issues had been dealt with. But what of the four conditions the Ministry of Foreign Affairs had set out in its verbatim note dated February 10, 1960? As subsequent events would show, these presented a prickly legal problem that would take more than two years to resolve. In their first reply to the verbatim note, the American authorities readily accepted conditions 2, 3, and 4. As for condition 1, however, the Americans made it clear that the U.S. government was prepared to pay all valid claims for compensation or damages raised in connection with the operation of the reactor, just as the United States offered to pay damages for harm or destruction that arose as a result of all other non-war-related military activities that fell under the 1951 Defense Agreement on Greenland signed by Denmark and the United States. This was possible because American legislation, specifically the Foreign Claims Act from 1942, permitted the authorities on a strictly administrative basis to cover all such valid claims for damages of up to 15,000 U.S. dollars. However, claims for amounts over and above this limit could only be dealt with if the U.S. secretary of defense presented them as a legal claim for payment, to be included in the financial appropriations bill and approved by the U.S. Congress.[34]

The verbatim note to the Americans caused the Danish authorities quite a bit of legal deliberation, and the matter was complicated further by ongoing work on an international convention that would govern liability and compensation obligations under the Organization for European Economic Cooperation (OEEC), a convention that was officially adopted (and ratified by Denmark) on July 29, 1960. Further confounding the legal interpretation work, there were existing agreements on liability and compensation within the NATO framework, as well as the question of whether the PM-2A reactor was a military or a scientific installation. On June 14, 1960, an employee at the Danish foreign ministry prepared a twelve-page memorandum on the problematic legal issues regarding the nuclear reactor at Camp Century and on the American comments on condition 1 in the Danish verbatim note. The memorandum concluded that "from the Danish side, one cannot acquiesce to the representations made in the American verbatim note but must maintain that the United States must bear full responsibility for the operation of the nuclear reactor." The memorandum also specified that any uncertainties pertaining to liability and compensation were to be decided "according to Danish law."[35] The Danes supported this conclusion at a subsequent meeting in the Ministry of Foreign Affairs, and it was communicated as follows to the American embassy in Copenhagen in another verbatim note, dated July 29, 1960:

> As understood by the Danish Government, Condition 1 as stipulated in the Ministry's Note of February 10, 1960, will involve that Danish law courts will be competent, in conformity with Danish law and international conventions to which Denmark is a party, to hear and adjudicate cases raised to ascertain what damage has been caused by any nuclear accident arising out of the installation and operation of the reactor in question and ascertain who should be entitled to receive compensation for any such damage, while the Government of the United States would undertake to pay in full any such compensation. The Danish Government hopes that the Government of the United States will accept Condition 1 as explained above.[36]

At a meeting in the Danish foreign ministry on September 12, 1960, a representative of the Pentagon, Mr. Sophocles A. Hero, presented a new draft wording of condition 1 that aimed to unite the views of both countries. According to the draft, the United States was "prepared to pay in full all valid claims arising out of the operation of the plant."[37] After a few words were inserted to the effect that Danish law and international conventions were to be applied in the event of disagreements between the parties, both sides adopted the new wording. Nevertheless, the issue gave rise to further complications when the draft forwarded by the

American embassy on September 23, 1960, was found to contain a modified passage stating that "the Government of the United States will take appropriate action and if necessary seek appropriations to pay in full all valid claims arising out of the operation of the plant."[38] The Danish Ministry of Justice was unable to approve the modified wording, since it "does not place upon the American state a duty to pay compensation."[39] The parties were therefore obliged to conduct a new round of unofficial discussions before finally agreeing, in November 1960, on a mutually satisfactory wording of condition 1, including a specification of how to interpret the expressions "pay in full" and "if necessary seek appropriations for such claims."[40] Agreement notwithstanding, the compromise was further postponed by a proposal from the American government, communicated to the Danes on April 7, 1961, suggesting that questions of liability relating to the operation of the Camp Century reactor could be decided under the regulatory framework of NATO. Once again the Danish Ministry of Justice was unwilling to consider the American proposal, and the Danish government maintained that the United States would have to assume unlimited liability for running the PM-2A reactor.[41]

After this, apparently nothing further happened regarding the matter during 1961 or in the first half of 1962. One reason for this might be that around this time the Danish government was working on national legislation concerning nuclear installations, including the scope of the owner's liability. On May 16, 1962, the Danish parliament adopted the Nuclear Installations Act, which became effective on July 1 of that year. It stated, in section 13, that "should a nuclear accident occur in an installation in this kingdom, or in another convention state, the owner of the installation is under obligation to compensate the damage thereby caused."[42] Shortly after this, on September 24, 1962, Denmark and the United States agreed on the final wording of condition 1 regarding the nuclear reactor at Camp Century:

> The United States Government recognizes its responsibility to pay in full all valid claims arising out of the operation of the plant and will take appropriate action and, if necessary, seek appropriations for such claims, any difference of opinions to be resolved in the normal manner,

taking into consideration pertinent Danish legislation and international conventions.[43]

Thus, a protracted diplomatic affair came to an amicable conclusion. The Danes had staunchly insisted that the Americans must take full responsibility and assume full liability for operating Camp Century's nuclear reactor and covering any claims for damages that might arise. What is more, during the negotiation process the Danes had maintained the view that the legal basis for the agreement and its conditions was to be Danish law and international conventions rather than American law. In a historical light it is ironic, but also a testimony to the parties' mutual trust, that during the negotiation process the PM-2A reactor had physically been installed at Camp Century as the Americans wished and had in fact been up and running for a year and a half. Let us now take a closer look at the technical details of how this came about.

THE AMERICAN NUCLEAR REACTOR IN GREENLAND

The reactor at Camp Century was installed during the summer of 1960, coinciding with the final stages of the camp's construction. The construction teams were gradually replaced by army officers, soldiers, and various types of technical personnel arriving to man the camp permanently. The reactor components were transported from the United States by aircraft, ship, and truck, arriving at Camp Tuto by way of Thule Air Base and making the last leg of their long journey, from Camp Tuto to

FIGURE 3.4 The May 1962 issue of *National Geographic* contained a feature article about nuclear power in polar regions. Naturally, the article mentioned Camp Century, and it also gave an illustrative overview of the camp's layout. This illustration, done by Robert Magis, depicted Camp Century as a miniature city with an unmistakably futuristic feel. The article was written by George F. Dufek, head of the first Operation Deepfreeze expedition to the South Pole in 1957–1958 for the International Geophysical Year, who described Camp Century as "a fantastic city hidden in the Greenland icecap."

Workers test one of 15 hatches through which men could escape in emergency.

KODACHROME BY W. ROBERT MOORE © N.G.S.

Ramp permits vehicles to descend into trench

Coolers, jutting above the ice, exhaust waste heat from the nuclear power plant

Cutaway View of
Camp Century
and Its Nuclear Power Plant Under Greenland's Icecap

Red flags mark snow-covered trenches

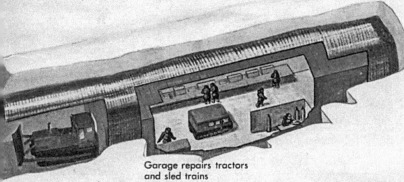

Garage repairs tractors and sled trains

Corrugated-metal arches shelter the trenches

Plywood prefabs can accommodate 20 men each

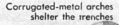

Camp headquarters Century's nerve cen

Radio shack houses camp's telephone center and wireless system

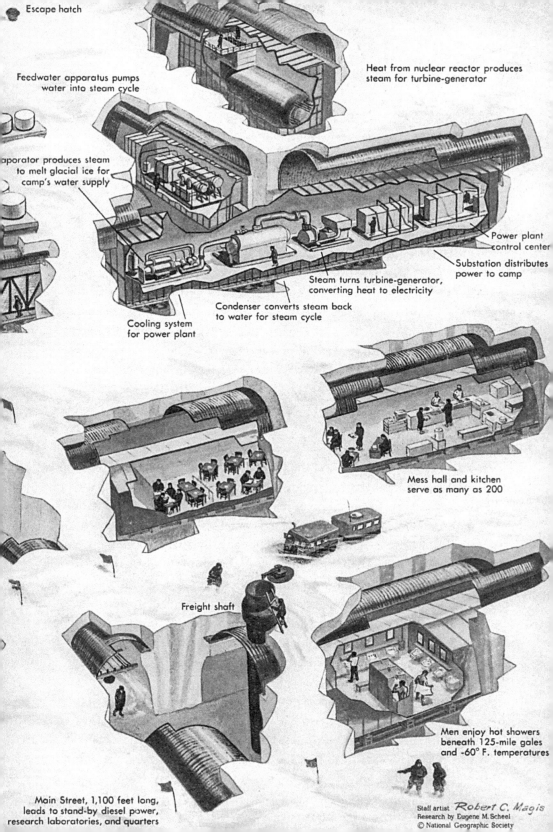

Escape hatch

Feedwater apparatus pumps water into steam cycle

Heat from nuclear reactor produces steam for turbine-generator

aporator produces steam to melt glacial ice for camp's water supply

Power plant control center

Substation distributes power to camp

Steam turns turbine-generator, converting heat to electricity

Condenser converts steam back to water for steam cycle

Cooling system for power plant

Mess hall and kitchen serve as many as 200

Freight shaft

Men enjoy hot showers beneath 125-mile gales and -60° F. temperatures

Main Street, 1,100 feet long, leads to stand-by diesel power, research laboratories, and quarters

Staff artist *Robert C. Magis*
Research by Eugene M. Scheel
© National Geographic Society

Camp Century, on heavy-swing transports. The first components arrived on July 17, 1960, and the last components on July 28,[44] so the time schedule shown to the Danish representatives Christian Thomsen and Povl Ølgaard at their meeting with the Americans in Washington, DC, in December 1959 was followed quite precisely.

After arriving at the ice-cap site, the components, none weighing over 13 metric tons, were maneuvered into the special trenches equipped to receive them. The tunnels for the reactor and related plant elements like the feed-water pump, steam generator, and electricity generator were numbered 3, 4, and 5.[45] The trenches dug here were significantly wider than the others and were also designed with vertical walls. The trench width of 12 m (rather than the standard 8 m, with inward-sloping walls), meant that the roof construction of the reactor-plant tunnels came to consist of semicylindrical corrugated metal elements known among army engineers as "wonder arches" for their incredible versatility. But this had not been in the original plan. The U.S. Army Polar Research and Development Center, the body formally responsible for the entire construction project, had wanted the reactor tunnels to be the standard 8-meter design. Meanwhile, the responsibility for building the PM-2A reactor and the tunnels that would house it had been allocated to another army engineering organization, the Nuclear Power Division. They, in turn, had brought in a subcontractor, ALCO Products, to handle the actual design and construction of the nuclear reactor.[46] So when ALCO Products notified the army that it was impossible to develop such a small PM-2A unit in the brief time available, the planners accepted a deviation from the original tunnel width, permitting excavation of 12-meter-wide trenches for the reactor plant. Nevertheless, despite extra ventilation capacity and the more spacious tunnels, all meant to ensure that the snow above the roof could be kept sufficiently cold, the roof construction in the reactor tunnels would soon prove to be one of the weak spots in the design of Camp Century.[47]

After the reactor components had been dragged and maneuvered into the tunnels, it was up to a team of 36 reactor technicians, led by Captain James W. Barnett, to assemble the PM-2A plant and make it run reliably. Needless to say, the reactor itself—and the huge effort needed to install and run it in such an isolated location—was enormously expensive. Camp Century's total construction budget was 7.92 million U.S. dollars, in 1960 prices. Of this amount no less than 5.7 million USD was allocated to the reactor plant. The justification for the expenditure was based on an assessment that the alternative—two or three large diesel engines that would have to run 24/7—would be even more expensive. Calculations showed that each year these diesel engines would use almost 4,000 metric tons (1 million gallons) of oil to supply the camp with electricity and heating, all of which, obviously, would have to be transported from the United States. By comparison, the PM-2A was projected to handle the same task using just 20 kilograms (44 pounds) of uranium 235, encased in 32 fuel rods within the reactor core.[48]

These numbers were easy to understand, but what is more, the subsurface installation of a nuclear reactor within the Greenland ice sheet was an enormous and difficult engineering endeavor that, in itself, was an astonishing achievement. Almost all the journalists invited to visit Camp Century in 1960 were fascinated by the camp's reactor. Among them was the reporter and writer Walter Wager, one of the first journalists to do a feature article on Camp Century for an American weekly, which appeared in 1960.[49] The following year Wager published a book about the facility based on his visits there: *Camp Century: The City Under the Ice*.[50] His description of the events on the day the reactor first went critical gives a vivid impression of the atmosphere in the reactor plant's control room. But between the lines, it also tells us what sort of images Wager—and the U.S. Army—wished to communicate to the American public of the die-hard American iceworms who lived and worked under the ice. Wager had stayed at Camp Century in the spring of 1960 while the PM-2A was being assembled, and he probably returned that fall around the time it was to be commissioned. According to Wager, all the camp's officers gathered in the reactor's control room on the morning of November 12, 1960. In his book, Wager's distinctive reporting style conveys the intensity in the room as Captain Barnett gave the order for the technicians to begin inserting control rods and fuel rods into the reactor core, one by one, right

up to the final insertion of "rod No. 37. . . . There was almost no talking as all eyes were focused on the instrument dials on the complex
control console," Wager writes. And apart from a single officer who
forgot about safety protocol and lit up a cigarette, there was no sign of
nerves. Captain Barnett and his team had the situation completely
under control:

> And then it happened. At 6:52 A.M. on the morning of November 12,
> 1960, the conventional power plant was cut off and the atomic power
> complex began to feed electricity. To the troops and scientists in the 28
> buildings . . . there was only a brief flickering matched by the fluores-
> cent lights overhead. Few of them fully appreciated that they were
> neighbors to a modern miracle, a remarkable scientific achievement in
> which all Americans can take pride. Busy with their daily concerns in
> the tunnel town, they did not pause to reflect that this newly proven
> combination of subsurface living and nuclear power might open the
> entire Arctic and Antarctic.[51]

In fact, at this point in time the reactor had already been operating on a
test basis for a good month. In his own report on constructing Camp
Century's nuclear reactor, James Barnett mentions the difficulty of
defining a precise date for when the reactor was fully operational or
formally commissioned for service. The reason is that the equipment
and components were continuously being tested throughout the assembly and mounting phase. On October 1, 1960, the military engineers
began inserting the fuel rods into the core, and on the morning of
October 2, the reactor was set to go critical from the control room.
After a mere five minutes, however, the technician hurriedly shut down
the reactor again because of a leak in the steam generator. The problem
was fixed within a few days, but other problems arose. That is why it
was not until the morning of November 12, 1960, as Wager describes,
that the reactor actually became operational, meaning that from that
time onward it produced superheated water under high pressure. The
superheated water was converted into hot steam in a secondary circuit,
causing a steam turbine to rotate, which in turn made a generator produce the electricity needed to keep Camp Century running.[52]

Overall, the reactor's first period in operation was beset by unfore-seen problems, which must have caused no small concern in the camp. Within a few days it became clear to the reactor team that radiation levels were "unacceptably high" in the vicinity of the reactor.[53] Immedi-ately after the results of the first "sketchy" radiation tests were commu-nicated to Thule Air Base, there was a ten-day radio blackout, during which the camp was completely cut off from the rest of the world. For-tunately the problem was limited to the reactor tunnel, with radiation levels in the adjacent tunnels remaining acceptable. Further investiga-tions in late November 1960 showed that the radiation had been caused by a leak in the reactor's upper casing. A decision was made to shut down the reactor altogether and await the arrival of a large shipment of lead, which would serve as extra protection on the upper reactor com-ponents. The first shipment arrived quickly, on December 10, 1960, but although it improved the situation it was still not enough. The next shipment of lead arrived in early January 1961, along with experts from ALCO, and after thorough testing the reactor finally resumed operation on February 9, 1961. Measurements showed that the radiation level near the upper part of the reactor was in the range of 1.5 to 2 mSv/hour (150 to 200 mrem/hour), which was acceptable, although higher than the 1 mSv/hour (100 mrem/hour) originally planned. Following another 400 hours of operational testing, on March 8, 1961, responsibil-ity for operating the reactor was handed over to the U.S. Army's reactor crew in the camp.[54]

It had been a busy winter at Camp Century and probably a more dramatic one than meets the historian's eye. The authorities in Wash-ington, DC, and Copenhagen had followed events as closely as was possible at such a great distance. On December 16, 1960, Christian Thomsen, from the Danish AEC, made a telephone call to Poul Steen-berger at the Danish foreign ministry to report something he had learned (from a very reliable source): during operational testing of the reactor, the upper portions had turned out to be inadequately protected. The reactor had been stopped, and it could hardly be expected to resume operations before spring.[55] Then, ten days later, Thomsen was able to provide additional information: the radiation intensity had been "very great," prompting the foreign ministry to ask the Danish embassy in Washington to contact the American authorities.[56] In the response from the Americans, received on January 11, 1961, Lieutenant Colonel E. L. Faust of the U.S. Army's Nuclear Power Division explained that "high radiation levels were detected in an area near the reactor that was designed for limited access while the plant is in operation." The radiation level measured while the reactor was running at low power had been "extrapolated to a full power value of about 40 r/hr [400 mSv/hr]."[57] However, as Faust assured the Danes:

> This problem has resulted from a design deficiency but has not resulted in undue exposure to personnel and has never resulted in a hazardous condition. The criteria for limited access to this area did present an extremely complex shielding design problem and consequently the plant test program was developed to thoroughly demonstrate the adequacy of the plant shielding. Radiation in other portions of the plant is well within safe levels.[58]

As far as we can discern, after this response the Danish authorities took no further action regarding the matter. They must have found Faust's description of the new shielding measures using lead and other materials reassuring. We have come across no further information to contradict Faust's statements that the incident never resulted in a dangerous situation for the inhabitants of Camp Century. Nevertheless, measurements conducted from October to December 1960 and presented in ALCO's final report on the installation of the PM-2A plant show much higher figures than those Faust reported to the Danish authorities. One table with measurements of gamma-radiation levels made on October 19, 1960, show a maximum radiation dose of "1150 r/hour," and another table shows a maximum radiation dose as high as "28,500 r/hour."[59] These numbers are indeed extrapolations of individual measurements made while the reactor was running at low capacity, meaning they in no way reflect the actual radiation level at Camp Century. Still, the fact remains that they are vastly higher than the extrapolated maximum radiation-dose figures Faust presented to the Danes.

It is also part of the story that around this particular time, in January 1961, the U.S. Army's reactor engineers must have been acutely aware of problems with the army's experimental reactors. There had been a serious incident at the SL-1 reactor in Idaho. This was, admittedly, a different type of reactor than Camp Century's, but like the PM-2A it was still a new, experimental design. An explosion and subsequent meltdown had occurred in the SL-1 on January 3, 1961, killing its three operators. The ensuing investigation concluded that the root cause of the incident was faulty removal of a control rod from the reactor core. The accident did not directly affect the U.S. Army's Nuclear Power Program, but it did lead to a greater focus on security procedures in reactor operations, which had apparently also taken effect by the time the PM-2A reactor at Camp Century was being commissioned.[60]

One cannot help but wonder: What was it like to live in Camp Century in the winter of 1960/1961, when the denizens of the city under the ice had to get used to living next door to a functioning nuclear reactor? How did the camp's nearly 100 men, effectively voluntary captives under the ice, feel about their own situation and about living in such close quarters throughout the long Arctic winter? Obviously, there is no single or simple answer to this question. Each man—to our knowledge only one woman, a Danish medical doctor, ever visited the camp— had his own personal experience of living and working in Camp Century, and very few of their accounts were ever shared with others, much less made available to the general public. There is, however, one tunnel-town inhabitant—likewise a Dane—whom we are able to follow very closely indeed, sharing his personal observations about living in one of the most unusual military facilities ever to exist. We will do this in chapter 5. First, however, we offer a selection of rarely seen images from the camp and then discuss, in chapter 4, what news was actually disseminated to the public from Greenland in general and from Camp Century in particular.

THE MAKING OF CAMP CENTURY

A Photographic Tour

FIGURE P.1 A lineup of "polecats"—small, agile caterpillar-track vehicles mainly used for personnel transport—preparing to leave Camp Tuto, near the rim of the ice sheet, with fresh troops for Camp Century, located 222 kilometers (138 miles) to the northeast. Undated; around 1960.

FIGURE P.2 A "heavy swing"—a slow, ground-based cargo transport—bringing building materials and equipment from Camp Tuto to the construction site in the summer of 1959.

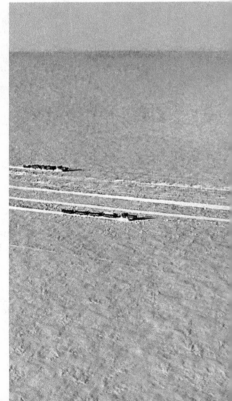

FIGURE P.3 A feature article in the May 1962 issue of *National Geographic* included this panoramic aerial photo of a heavy-swing train on its way from Camp Tuto to Camp Century.

FIGURE P.4 Technicians setting up an installation in the temporary surface camp at the Camp Century site, enabling fairly regular communications with the base at Camp Tuto. June 15, 1959.

FIGURE P.5 Soldier pushing a snow-filled wheelbarrow up to the mouth of the snow melter, which supplied the temporary surface camp with fresh water. June 22, 1959.

FIGURE P.6 A "Peter Plough"—
a high-volume snow mover—
excavating a trench that would
become a permanent tunnel in
Camp Century. July 8, 1959.

FIGURE P.7 Crane lifting iron bars down into a tunnel, for use in testing to determine how much the snow and ice are compressed over time. Note the temporary camp on the surface. July 9, 1959.

FIGURE P.8 Preparing an excavated trench for roofing over with corrugated metal arches. The excavation technique used here makes the tunnel narrower toward the top. July 18, 1959.

FIGURE P.10 Snow mover blowing snow across the sheet-metal roof. After several days, the snow freezes into shape, becoming so hard that the sheeting can be removed, leaving a roof consisting only of snow. July 20, 1959.

FIGURE P.9 Corrugated metal roof laid over one of the narrow tunnels, in which construction crews would soon be assembling prefabricated T-5 barracks for the men. July 19, 1959.

FIGURE P.12 Pile driver in action at Camp Century, driving foundation timber into the ice sheet in Tunnel 3. The building in this tunnel housed the reactor's feedwater. August 17, 1959.

FIGURE P.11 Emergency escape tube being maneuvered into place through the roof of a tunnel at Camp Century. These tubes, with escape hatches at the top, also served as ventilation ducts. July 27, 1959.

FIGURE P.13 A Peter Plough excavating Tunnel 4, the future home of the nuclear reactor. Note the vertical sides and the layers removed. August 20, 1959.

FIGURE P.14 Readers of the May 1962 issue of *National Geographic* were able to look into "Main Street," the central tunnel at Camp Century. This main thoroughfare, 330 meters (1,100 feet) in length, accessed all other tunnels in the subsurface complex.

FIGURE P.15 *National Geographic*'s May 1962 issue also showed readers the prefabricated barracks units in one of the Camp Century tunnels, which housed personnel sleeping and living quarters. The buildings were raised well above the ice floor to prevent melting.

FIGURE P.16 Using "wonder arches" to roof over one of the wide trenches
that would house the PM-2A nuclear reactor plant. June 20, 1960.

FIGURE P.17 Roofing over one of the Camp Century trenches, while personnel from the U.S. Army's photo unit prepare to document the work. August 2, 1960.

FIGURE P.18 Aerial view of the "parking lot" in front of the Camp Century tunnel complex, where numerous vehicles and sledges with heavy equipment await unloading and installation. At the top, the entry ramp to Main Street and the reactor tunnel. Just beyond the ramp, a sledge with the large steam condenser that would soon be hauled down and maneuvered into place in Tunnel 5. July 1960.

FIGURE P.19 After unpacking the large heat exchanger from its protective covering, the reactor crew prepares to haul it into the tunnel next to the reactor. July 17, 1960.

FIGURE P.20 Here the steam condenser, another component of the reactor plant, waits on a sledge coupled to a tractor on caterpillar tracks. Photographed in July 1960.

FIGURE P.21 The steam condenser being hauled down into Tunnel 5, which it shared with the heat exchanger and the electricity generator. Photographed in July 1960.

FIGURE P.22 Plant components in place in the tunnel. First, the heat exchanger; in the middle, the electricity generator; and at the far end, the steam condenser. July 18, 1960.

FIGURE P.23 Crane in the reactor tunnel, maneuvering and positioning the collector tank, where radioactive wastewater was held before being discharged into the ice sheet. Although there is no precise date, this event certainly took place in the summer of 1960.

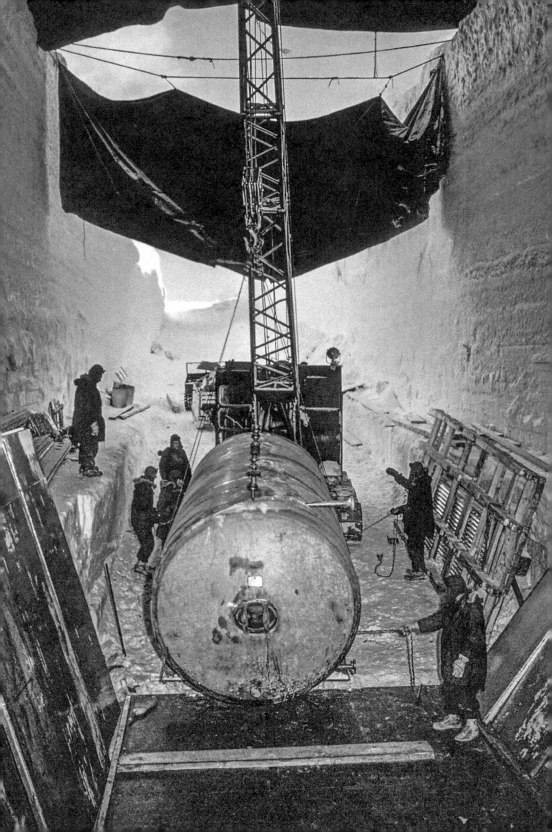

FIGURE P.24 The PM-2A reactor in place inside Camp Century. The lid of the reactor, still unstarted, is open, revealing the reactor core with room for fuel rods and control rods. Photographed in the summer of 1960.

FIGURE P.25 Technician wearing rubber gloves—but no other safety equipment— lifting a fuel rod out of its transport container. The fuel rod would soon be placed in the reactor core. Photographed in the summer of 1960.

FIGURE P.26 Several hundred yards away from the camp was a wastewater well in the ice sheet, where slightly radioactive water from the reactor and heat exchanger was deposited about once every two weeks. June 2, 1961.

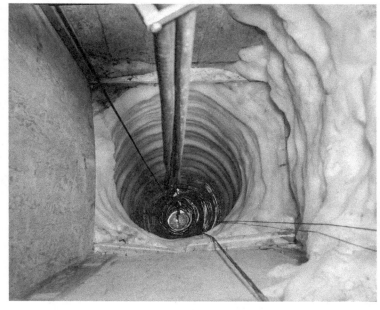

FIGURE P.27 A look down into the water well that supplied Camp Century with pure, fresh water as needed. The well was located in an annex to Tunnel 6. August 17, 1960.

FIGURE P.29 This relatively primitive T-5 unit housed the headquarters of Camp Century's commanding officer, Captain Thomas C. Evans, seen here outside the unit, next to the U.S. ambassador to Denmark, Val Peterson (at left). August 8, 1960.

FIGURE P.28 To our knowledge, no actual opening ceremony was held at Camp Century. On this occasion, however, the nearly finished camp is being inspected by a group including (at front, right to left) the Danish ambassador to Washington, DC, Count Keld Gustav Knuth-Winterfeldt; U.S. Army Colonel John Kerkering; and U.S. Army Brigadier General Robert Hackett. August 13, 1960.

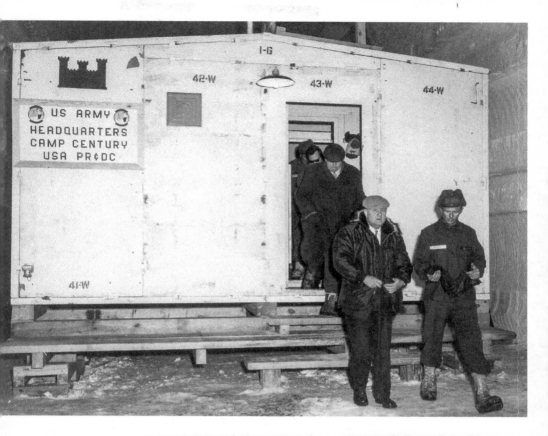

FIGURE P.30 The lower part of the reactor area's emergency exit, leading to the escape hatch on the surface. If an accident occurred, people in the reactor area could climb to safety using a ladder fastened to the wall of the tube.

FIGURE P.31 Main Street being cleared of snowdrifts blown in through the tunnel mouths—a frequently recurring problem. The top of the black vehicle, just barely visible behind the piled-up snow, belongs to the D-8 Caterpillar used for this task. July 20, 1961.

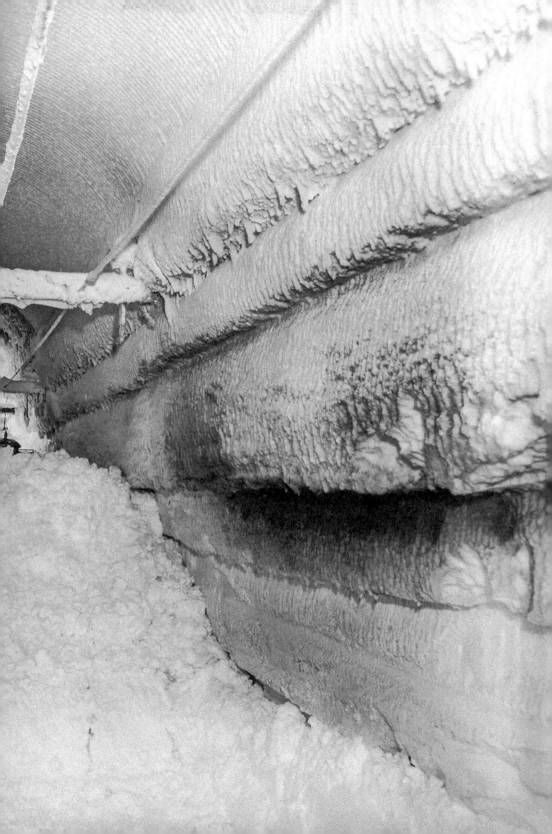

FIGURE P.32 A group of men at Camp Century feed loose snow into a snow blower that forces it out of the tunnel. This method was used to deal with snow that had drifted in and with snow and ice scraped off tunnel walls and ceilings. August 18, 1961.

4

NEWS FROM GREENLAND

THE 1952 PRESS AGREEMENT

When the American weekly the *Sunday Star* revealed on August 23, 1959, that the building of Camp Century was under way, the hunt was on for news about the U.S. Army camp dug into the Greenland ice sheet. American news organizations were willing to expend considerable sums to send their best reporters on the long journey to Camp Century so they could report from the exotic, miniature "city" in one of the most inhospitable and inaccessible regions on Earth. The army, which was responsible for constructing and operating the facility, was only too pleased to assist reporters seeking to reach northern Greenland. The army was under pressure at home after the national decision to opt for a missile-based defense strategy, so top army commanders were keen to show everyone—not least the American taxpayers—that the army was actively and innovatively contributing to the nation's defense through their numerous initiatives in Greenland, which included Camp Century.[1]

The army therefore saw no problem in allowing visiting reporters to deal with scientific, engineering, and military perspectives at the camp. On the contrary, this would only help demonstrate how the army was relying on state-of-the-art research and the best available engineering techniques in its endeavors to defend the North American continent by building bases in Greenland. The only problem was that the Danish authorities took a very different view. In Denmark, the actual purpose of Camp Century, including the question of why the army was interested in investing so heavily in the endeavor, had the potential to become a political hot potato in Copenhagen. Given the sensitive nature of "the concept of atoms" in Greenland, the Danish government had no interest whatsoever in the press covering the camp, especially if they mentioned its importance to U.S. military strategy. Interestingly, contrary to what one might think, in this case the Danish authorities actually had an opportunity to limit or, some would say, censor the articles written by visiting reporters.[2]

As a byproduct of the 1951 Defense Agreement on Greenland, the spring of 1952 saw the signing of a press agreement between Denmark and the United States. It stipulated that all written work about U.S. military installations and activities in Greenland that was intended to appear in print in the United States, Denmark, or elsewhere had to be presented to the Danish embassy in Washington, DC, before publication. The embassy would then have the text reviewed by the Danish Ministry of Foreign Affairs, which would first gather feedback from the Defense Ministry and the Ministry for Greenland. Only then would the embassy be able to notify the author of the changes Denmark officially recommended before the piece was published. What is more, the Ministry of Foreign Affairs had demanded—and the United States had accepted—that all press material arriving in this context in Copenhagen would be made fully and freely accessible, at no cost, to the Danish press.[3]

The 1952 Press Agreement, which had been made to give Danish media easy access to news from Greenland, was soon challenged by the American press community. At a meeting held in Copenhagen on March 7, 1953, between the American embassy and the Ministry of Foreign Affairs, the topic was raised by a group of American reporters who, shortly before the meeting, had visited Thule Air Base and were dissatisfied with the regulations applicable to non-Danish journalists traveling in Greenland. In their interpretation, the 1952 Press Agreement permitted the

Danish authorities to "censor" articles, to unnecessarily protract the approval procedure (for up to six or seven weeks), and to violate author copyrights by making texts and images available to Danish newspapers for free. During the meeting, the Danish civil servants argued "that news relating to the defense areas ought not to come overwhelmingly from American sources to the Danish public. It is very important that the Danish public does not get the impression that the Americans have more or less taken over portions of Greenland, also because this occasions anti-American sentiments."[4]

At the meeting, Ward Allen from the American embassy asked whether the Danes were prepared to give up the press agreement if more Danish journalists were permitted access to the defense areas. The Danes answered yes, in principle, but financially such visits would still pose a tremendous problem, given that traveling between Denmark and Greenland was extremely expensive. While American journalists could often travel for free on military aircraft, Danish journalists had no such opportunities, except on very rare occasions. Quite simply, the Danish news media could not afford to send their own journalists to Greenland to cover events in this newly formalized country in the joint kingdom. That made it hard to comply with the Danish authorities' wish to supplement the wealth of news about Greenland coming from American sources with Danish-sourced content. The articles from American journalists were, and would remain, an important source of information and news from Greenland not only for the Danish authorities but also for the country's citizens and media. The meeting concluded with the ministry's representatives agreeing to acknowledge, in part, the American criticisms and to discuss how to improve the prevailing practice thus far, focusing in particular on shorter processing times for the Danish ministries reviewing the American draft articles. With this accommodation, the 1952 Press Agreement remained in force.[5]

Despite mutual confirmation of the agreement at the March 7 meeting, new problems quickly arose. Over the following months the Danish foreign ministry ascertained that several American newspapers had run articles about Greenland in which reporters had written about U.S.

scientific testing on the ice cap, far outside the agreed defense areas and without first consulting the Danish authorities by allowing them to review the articles' contents. Therefore, in the autumn of 1953, the Ministry of Foreign Affairs instructed Henrik Kauffmann, the Danish ambassador in Washington, to make two points unequivocally clear to his contacts at the U.S. State Department: (1) that the existing agreement between Denmark and the United States concerning official press releases from the American side was still in force as originally agreed and (2) that journalistic material based on visits to Greenland was to be delivered to the Danish embassy in Washington, which would immediately send such material to the Danish Ministry of Foreign Affairs, which would then ensure that "material of interest to the Danish public [would be] publicized simultaneously in Denmark and the United States."[6]

This exchange laid the issue of press coverage to rest for a couple of years. It then returned with a vengeance. In April 1956, Ambassador Kauffmann had to inform Director Nils Svenningsen at the Danish foreign ministry that "American press activity relating to the defense areas in Greenland have, unfortunately, come into the spotlight." A group of American journalists had approached the House of Representatives with fresh grievances about "Danish censorship," and a number of them had now requested information about the scope of American reporting material made available to the Danish press and whether such material had, in effect, been used with or without explicitly stating the source.[7]

Ambassador Kauffmann's letter to the Danish foreign ministry would set off a long exchange of diplomatic memoranda, back and forth across the Atlantic, aiming to find new wording that was acceptable to both parties. The arguments on both sides were largely the same as in 1953. On one side stood Denmark, which did not want important news from Greenland to reach the Danish public from American sources. On the other side stood the United States, which wanted to safeguard the interests of American journalists, including the freedom of the press and the reporters' ability to meet deadlines. The matter seems to have remained at an impasse for some time. Not until autumn 1960 do we find the parties agreeing on the wording of certain terms all non-Danish journalists would be obliged to sign before being permitted to enter Greenlandic territory, as follows: "Approval by the Danish government for your entry into Greenland is contingent upon your agreement to submit all copy, photographs, films, etc., prior to publication for review by the Danish authorities and whatever further use the Danish government may desire."[8] In other words, an unconditional victory for the Danish view. At least, so it might seem.

AMERICAN ATTEMPTS TO "SELL" GREENLAND

The 1952 Press Agreement was important to Denmark and to the United States, given that the authorities in both countries were interested in having whatever influence they could on the information being published about Greenland. To a great extent, the Cold War was a struggle for approval in popular opinion and the public debate. It was "total cold war," as President Eisenhower said in 1958—a war to win not only the arms race but also, and equally, the ideological battle going on in much of the media landscape.[9] Both the United States and the Soviet Union initiated large-scale campaigns to disseminate international propaganda, attempting to bolster their influence as superpowers in their respective spheres, which included many countries around the globe. Incidentally, their campaigns were very precisely coordinated to link into various financial support and collaboration programs—today called "soft power."[10]

The word "propaganda" covers a variety of different communication activities specifically aimed to propagate or spread a certain worldview in order to encourage people to think, believe, feel, or do a certain thing. In military parlance, "the battle for hearts and minds" is a frequently used expression, and military propaganda is highly reminiscent of psychological warfare. Although propaganda often gives a distorted or even untruthful version of reality, this is not always the case. Good, effective propaganda—like all other good, effective communication—links factual information with a strong and convincing message. In this context, news of American defense activities in Greenland could be both reliable and informative while still supporting the message that the United States was the champion of the free world. The line between spreading propaganda and disseminating information was—and is—a difficult one to draw.

Between 1951 and 1964 the U.S. Army produced a television series called *The Big Picture*, which was organized as propaganda for the army while at the same time showing program content that richly illustrated the multitude of different army activities. The series was offered free of cost to all American television networks and so was aired extensively.[11] The message was unmistakable: the U.S. Army was prepared to defend the United States and American interests no matter where it had to go or what it had to do. What is more, U.S. soldiers had what it took to make sure America would win the Cold War,[12] as this quotation from the introductory sequence to *The Big Picture* shows: "From Korea to Germany. From Alaska to Puerto Rico. All over the world the United States Army is on the alert to defend our country, you the American people, against aggression."[13]

Greenland was an area of special interest to the U.S. Army and therefore also a topic of special interest to *The Big Picture*. The series dedicated a full eight programs to Greenland, including the 1961 episode on Camp Century mentioned in the previous chapter. The first *Big Picture* broadcast on Greenland was about the construction of Thule Air Base in 1951. These programs were an attempt by the U.S. Army to "sell" Greenland to the public, promoting it as an example of the army being a vigilant presence wherever a threat arose against the United States or American values,[14] even in the hostile environment of northern Greenland, a vital defense fortress in the Cold War. "Here," the program about Thule Air Base explained, "where temperatures have dropped to fifty below zero and where winds rise to 150-miles-an-hour gale force, where the bright sun is abruptly succeeded by dense fog and blinding snow, American ingenuity and daring has built a new outpost in this country's defense, a giant air base on top of the world."[15]

Propaganda was not just an important tool for the U.S. Army. It was an integral part of the nation's Cold War strategy. Around 1947 and 1948, President Harry S. Truman developed what he called the strategy of "containment," the object of which was to give the United States an opportunity to influence other countries—governments and populations—around the globe, enhancing the American sphere of influence while diminishing the influence of the Soviet Union. In other words, the aim was to contain the spread of communism. Information campaigns and other types of soft power were seen as important instruments of political, economic, and ideological containment, since often it was not possible or viable to exert power directly in the countries in question. In 1953, President Dwight D. Eisenhower set up the U.S. Information Service, with the explicit aim of understanding, informing, communicating with, and influencing the public outside the United States.[16]

One example of successful propaganda staged by the United States was the "atoms for peace" initiative, which President Eisenhower launched in a speech he gave at the United Nations on December 8, 1953, promoting the idea of a new, peaceful view of atomic energy. After A-bombs were dropped on Japan at the end of World War II, the world had witnessed the steady development of new and increasingly terrifying nuclear weapons, not least the hydrogen bomb, or H-bomb, which the United States had tested in 1952 and the Soviet Union had tested the following year. Since those first strikes, the words "atoms" and "nuclear" had been perceived as dangerous, almost apocalyptic. Eisenhower emphasized in his 1953 speech that there were also peaceful civilian applications for atomic energy and that these could benefit the whole world, regardless of political convictions. He proposed that all nuclear powers, at that time meaning the United States, USSR, and United Kingdom, ought to hand over their uranium and other fissile materials to an international "Atomic Energy Agency," which could put it to good use. Simultaneously, the nuclear powers would begin preliminary negotiations on nuclear deescalation.[17]

Eisenhower's speech may have been an earnest attempt to direct developments in the realm of nuclear power toward more peaceful purposes. At the same time, however, it was one element in America's effort to discredit the Soviet Union in the strategic game of high-level world politics, the ploy being to present some apparently realistic cooperation and disarmament measures that the United States already knew the USSR would refuse. The "atoms for peace" speech was also the opening move in an intense information gambit called Operation Candor, in which the U.S. government tried to affect the perception everyday Americans had of nuclear weapons, thereby increasing acceptance among the populace of the nuclear deterrence policy the nation had been pursuing.[18] Efforts also included a major information campaign featuring pamphlets, articles, films, and exhibitions all meant to spread the message that the United States was intent on moving toward exploiting the peaceful options atomic energy had to offer.[19] The American-made message about the peaceful uses of nuclear energy was also promoted in Copenhagen, among other things by Danish and non-Danish displays and other materials appearing at the electricity and nuclear exhibition held in October 1957 at Forum, a large Copenhagen exhibition venue.[20]

As part of the "atoms for peace" initiative, the Walt Disney Company produced a film in 1957 accompanied by a book bearing the same title: *Our Friend the Atom*. (Two of the quirky coincidences in our story show that just four years earlier, the Danish foreign ministry had called the atom bomb "our friend," as noted in chapter 1, and three years later Søren Gregersen, the Danish scout who lived in Camp Century, was photographed for a newspaper article for *Politiken* holding a Danish translation of this very book, as shown in chapter 5.) The film was narrated by the German physicist Heinz Haber, who had served as a reconnaissance pilot and scientist in Nazi Germany during World War II. After the war, Haber (and more than 1,600 other German scientists) had been brought to the United States, and he later became associated with Disney in the capacity of scientific consultant. In the production about the "friendly" atoms, Haber compares the atom to the genie in the bottle, widely known from the adventures of Aladdin as recounted in *The Arabian Nights*. The moral of the film is unmistakable. Just like the genie, the atom is capable of helping or harming humanity, and it is up to us how we avail ourselves of the newfound power that has fallen into our hands. The atomic genie in the film fulfills the three greatest wishes of humankind: energy, food, and peace.[21]

CAMP CENTURY IN THE DANISH MEDIA

The American propaganda or information campaigns about the U.S. Army's efforts in Greenland and about the peaceful, even friendly atom were significant for the press coverage of Camp Century and for the way the authorities responded to it. Throughout the summer and autumn of 1959, when the Camp Century project was initially mentioned—first by the international press and then in the Danish media—attention was already massively focused on American activities in Greenland and on the potentially peaceful applications of nuclear energy. The publicizing of Camp Century and its little nuclear reactor created an obvious connection between the two topics. Indeed, part of the idea driving the "atoms for peace" campaign was to put atomic energy to work in developing countries and in areas where it was difficult to set up and run large-scale energy-supply systems. Some thought that small-scale nuclear plants might even help supply energy to Greenland's many secluded towns and settlements.

At any rate, this was the journalistic angle chosen by the vast majority of Danish newspapers when covering the story of Camp Century from late summer 1959 onward, exemplified by these few selected headlines:

- "Greenland May House Our First Atomic Plant," in *Politiken*, August 28, 1959
- "American Nuclear Power Plant in Greenland," in *Information*, November 14 and 15, 1959
- "Miniature Atomic Plant. Americans Plan to Build Small Test Plant at Thule Air Base in Greenland," in *Aktuelt*, November 15, 1959
- "Yes to Atomic Power Plant in Thule," in *Berlingske Aftenavis*, February 3, 1960

FIGURE 4.1 Acting with the utmost flexibility and caution, Denmark hosted exhibitions from both the United States and the USSR on "peaceful atoms." Niels Bohr (center) and the Danish finance minister Viggo Kampmann (far right) flank Ambassador Kliment Lyovychkin at the opening of the Soviet exhibition on the scientific and technical uses of atomic energy on November 28, 1959, in Copenhagen City Hall. Meanwhile, the Danish defense minister Poul Hansen was visiting his American counterpart to explain why the Danes had not allowed the submarine USS *Skate* to visit Copenhagen earlier that year.

- "Greenlandic A-power Plant to Be Commissioned This Year," in *Aktuelt*, March 11, 1960
- "Atomic Plant Beneath the Ice Sheet," in *Land og Folk*, March 23, 1960
- "Wish to Bring Atomic Power to Greenland's Plants" in *Information*, February 10, 1961

Obviously, many Danish reporters chose to emphasize the nuclear power plant as the most striking news item when covering the Arctic subsurface facility. A couple also emphasized their hopes for the future energy supply of Greenland, inspired by the news of a "Greenlandic atomic power plant." The idea was that in the future, nuclear reactors like the one at Camp Century could be installed to resolve the energy-supply problems of remote settlements where it was very expensive to set up and run other types of power plants. Even Denmark's communist-minded broadsheet *Land og Folk* ran the same story and made none of its usual allegations against the Danish government for playing fast and loose with world peace by silently letting the U.S. military do whatever it pleased in Greenland.

The Greenlandic media also wrote about Camp Century. *AG (The Greenland Post)*, the largest and most widely circulated newspaper in Greenland, ran a long feature article in April 1960 under the headline "The Atomic City on the Ice Cap Will Be Built During the Summer." The article's anonymous author reviewed the official presentation from the U.S. Army of how Camp Century had been laid out, of the progress being made in installing the nuclear reactor that would supply the tunnel town with electricity from the autumn of 1960, and of how there were already plans for the following summer to build a railway tunnel inside the ice sheet that would run the more than 200 km from Camp Tuto to Camp Century. Presumably that would not pose any major problem, the author reasoned, seeing that "in one day, twelve excavating machines can dig a full eight kilometers of tunnel." But despite great faith in American technology, the reporter still did "not dare believe that some years from now, people will be able to take the Thule

Express and ride under the ice sheet to Narssarssuak, then change to a train headed for Julianehåb."[22]

Only one Danish newspaper took a different angle: the large Copenhagen daily *Politiken*. In May 1960, their man in the field, the journalist Paul Hammerich (later a well-known writer and public figure) had spent several days in Camp Tuto, near the ice cap's rim. His stay had included the opportunity to meet with Colonel John Kerkering, the commander-in-chief of the U.S. Army Polar Research and Development Center, and Kerkering briefed Hammerich about the ongoing construction work. This enabled Hammerich to state in his article, very precisely, that "the first portable atomic-power plant outside the United States will be sailed and airlifted to Thule, transported 200 km eastwards, and dug deep down into the snow to become, on the 1st of October, the central-heating plant for the 125 Americans who constitute the citizenry of Greenland's first underground community: Camp Century, the city of our century." However, Kerkering was apparently more outspoken than might have been expected, animated perhaps by a "bottle of Scotch . . . cooled with a lump of ice which you know was formed long before Columbus discovered America." The two men shared just such a bottle after a rough day "in the wretched ice-fog, which makes you feel like a fish swimming around in coffee-cream." As Hammerich concluded after his visit,

> For a visitor to Camp Tuto, the summer headquarters of Colonel Kerkering, located just a few kilometers from Thule at the edge of the ice sheet, it is obvious—although not stated in so many words—that the [American] wishes point in four directions.
>
> 1. Exercises in defense against an all-out Arctic war. This summer, the first major military maneuver on the ice sheet will be initiated.
>
> 2. Investigation of the ice cap, which, by virtue of its sheet of ice reaching up to three kilometers in thickness, can safely be seen as Nature's best safeguard against hydrogen-bomb detonations and the radioactive emissions in their wake.
>
> 3. Huge cavities beneath the block of ice, which in the case of a protracted war could contain stores of provisions for every need,

guaranteed deep-frozen. Nothing rots and nothing rusts in the eternal, arid cold.

4. The American defense authorities run the [U.S.] space program, the leaders of which take a keen interest in northern Greenland, partly as a launching location and practical uplink site for satellites, partly as a training location for spaceship passengers. The moral is: If you can stand a winter in the ice sheet, you're ready for the Moon, or for Mars.[23]

Hammerich was by no means trying to conceal the military objectives of the Camp Century project. He did emphasize, however, that the American experiments—such as airstrips and roads built on the ice sheet and "subsurface tunnels for fast electric trains"—were of "general public interest to Greenland and Denmark."[24] If Hammerich presented all the information he had learned from Kerkering, the colonel had refrained from touching upon the question of nuclear weapons beneath the surface of the ice sheet, the key component in the top-secret Project Iceworm plan, which may well have been kept secret even from Kerkering.

At any rate, Hammerich's article was remarkably straightforward on the issue of Camp Century and U.S. strategic interests in northern Greenland, and it is hard to believe that before appearing in print it passed through the Danish Ministry of Foreign Affairs for review. Indeed, we have found no hint of any such review process in the archives we have been able to access for the Danish ministries for Greenland and for foreign affairs. The few native Danish journalists who ventured to visit Thule Air Base and the Far North were probably exempted from the 1952 Press Agreement, which, as noted, applied chiefly to non-Danish journalists and gave the Danish authorities a certain ability to "contain" press statements about Camp Century.

WALTER CRONKITE IN CAMP CENTURY

Visits by American and other non-Danish journalists are a particularly interesting aspect of Camp Century's history. All were obliged to sign the special terms agreed upon by Danish and American authorities in the autumn of 1960. As a result, all journalistic products—articles, photographs, and television recordings—had to be sent to Copenhagen for review and commenting and also made freely available to the Danish media before publication in the United States or elsewhere. The camp's most noteworthy visitor was probably Walter Cronkite, ace reporter at the television network CBS, who arrived in the summer of 1960 with a camera crew in tow. The massive exposure the camp received through his coverage is hardly surprising, since his visit resulted in a television broadcast, "The City Under Ice," which aired as part of the popular Cronkite news series *Twentieth Century* on January 22, 1961.[25]

The program was seen by millions of Americans, who got a good overall impression of the many difficulties the U.S. Army Corps of Engineers had overcome to make Camp Century a reality. Cronkite's relaxed conversation with the head of the camp at the time, Captain Thomas Evans, could only reinforce the confidence of the American people in the army's achievement at having conquered "one of the last frontiers on Earth" by stationing an entire unit *inside* the ice sheet. The program demonstrated that life at Camp Century—"the city under ice"—was quite comfortable and safe, even though during the winter months the temperature "falls to 70 below zero [-57°C] and the wind howls with a speed of 130 miles [210 km] per hour." Meanwhile, Cronkite asked no questions at all about why so much money was being spent on the project, nor did Evans volunteer any information on that point. His remarks stayed on a general level and dealt with the camp's three official purposes. According to Evans, these were to test new ideas for survival on and within the permanent ice sheet, to test a mobile atomic reactor, and to establish a permanent base scientists could use when studying the properties and dynamics of the region's snow and ice. Cronkite explained to his American viewers that Greenland was a Danish island "on top of the world" and that Denmark, "a fellow NATO member," had been so kind as to give the Americans permission to set up an important radar station and a large air base at Thule—in addition, of course, to Camp Century, located on the ice cap. Summarizing his report, he underscored the scientific and technological aspects of

Camp Century without saying a word about any military applications. The focus of his coverage was the battle to subdue Nature, not the Soviet Union. "Men will stay behind here, in their city under the ice, to continue Man's battle against Nature. He has brought his greatest scientific achievement, power from the atom, to the very top of the world, but can he live here? Can he stop the crushing force of the ageless ice?"[26]

We do not know whether Cronkite's television program was reviewed by the Danish authorities, as stipulated in the 1952 Press Agreement. Perhaps it was out of the question, or perhaps it was not deemed necessary at all. Cronkite was renowned for his diplomatic finesse in handling potentially volatile topics. His program was a story of the heroic military personnel and scientists who defied the ice-cold Arctic in their search for new knowledge and new technologies, helped in this quest by Camp Century and its nuclear reactor. Cronkite's contribution merged seamlessly into the bigger story of the American involvement in Greenland and of the many peaceful uses for atomic energy that the U.S. Army and authorities had tried to "sell" to the United States and the wider world over the preceding years.

DANISH ATTEMPTS TO "CONTAIN" CAMP CENTURY

As a news story, Camp Century traveled beyond the American and Danish media. In the archives of the Danish Ministry of Foreign Affairs we have also found articles from Peru (probably the second article published about the facility, after the story initially broke in the *Sunday Star* on August 23, 1959), West Germany, Italy, and the United Kingdom.[27] The task of keeping up with news stories about Camp Century cannot have been easy for the Danish authorities, who surely had ongoing discussions about what issues they ought to officially make public, and how. Even so, we have found no traces of such discussions of principle, although we have found several examples of the foreign ministry trying to stop the proliferation of information considered dangerous to the keystones of Danish security policy—including the recurring declarations that Denmark did not want nuclear weapons on Danish soil in the current situation.

A good example of Danish intervention in the camp's international press coverage is found in the work of the American journalist Walter Wager, whom we met in chapter 3. Wager visited the camp in the early spring of 1960, and his six-page illustrated article "Life Inside a Glacier" appeared in the *Saturday Evening Post* on September 10 of that year.[28] Naturally, his readers were never informed that the Danish authorities had recommended that Wager change three things: "the remarks on p. 1 about the placement of rockets; on p. 13 about Greenland being owned by Denmark; and on p. 14, where the Greenlanders are referred to as eskimos."[29] The last two corrections were suggested in order to alter wording in Wager's draft that would be offensive in Greenland, whereas the first aimed to have a specific paragraph deleted. The pivotal passage, which followed immediately after an initial, factual description of the new camp, could not leave the reader in any doubt that in addition to the scientific purposes of Camp Century, the installation also served decidedly military purposes. It was equally clear that these military purposes could threaten the credibility of Danish security policy if they became publicly known in Denmark, as can be discerned from the original wording of Wager's draft:

In the future, similar Arctic tunnel-clusters may house rocket batteries to knock down enemy bombers and ICBMs heading over the north Pole towards the United States; they may also house planes and paratroopers of crack airborne teams assigned to wreck launching pads and H-bomb depots in aggressor territory, or American long range missiles ready for instant retaliation. Invisible to both aerial and radar reconnaissance but constantly cocked like an ever-ready Sunday punch, they could seriously discourage any power-crazed foreign regime considering another Pearl Harbor. Some optimists feel their existence may even prevent World War III.[30]

In the archives of the Danish Ministry for Greenland we have found Wager's draft article, complete with underlining and deletions, as well as a single exclamation point after the first sentence. We do not know precisely how the Ministry of Foreign Affairs communicated the Danish authorities' proposed changes to Wager, but we can see that he chose to amend his manuscript in keeping with the comments. The above-quoted, fairly detailed paragraph has been replaced with a much briefer remark that "in the future, lessons learned at Camp Century could be applied to other regions of the Arctic if the need ever arose to build additional early-warning or air-defense facilities at locations where extensive operation is now impossible."[31]

Wager was obviously not the only journalist who received proposals from the Danes for significant changes to written material. Another example is the Italian journalist Luigi Romersa, who worked for the Italian magazine *Il Tempo Illustrato*. Romersa was in Greenland in the autumn of 1961, and his manuscript is dated November of that year. It was notably the introduction to Romersa's piece that found disfavor with the civil servants in the Ministry for Greenland when they received his manuscript from the foreign ministry as part of the review procedure.[32] The Italian began his article by writing that immediately after his arrival, a fierce storm had confined him to "the military base Camp Tuto, which the Americans have built in the proximity of Thule. Several of these U.S. military bases are scattered over the 1,726,240 square km of Greenland, but the most important of all is the so-called Camp Century, a gigantic anti-atomic fortress, dug deeply like a catacomb below the ice, near the Pole."[33] Naturally, both the Ministry for Greenland and the Ministry of Foreign Affairs were displeased at the prospect of such a description of U.S. bases in Greenland reaching the public, particularly if linked to Camp Century, which both Danish and American authorities preferred to call a "scientific" facility. The description could potentially have been exploited by the enemies in the East and by Danish groups opposing NATO. The Ministry for Greenland therefore proposed that the Ministry of Foreign Affairs seek to have important passages in the article altered:

The manuscript does, however, contain certain information which, in this Ministry's view, most appropriately ought to be corrected. We are alluding to the 1st section, 2nd sentence, which could potentially be construed in such a way as to make the reader think that military bases have been set up, spread evenly across all of Greenland. The sentence further suggests that in Camp Century there is a very sizable installation of major military importance, particularly intended for anti-atomic contingency. Overall, the article expresses that Camp Century is to be described as a significant military fortification.[34]

The letter ends by pointing out that Camp Century, "according to the information provided to the Ministry for Greenland . . . has, first and foremost, a scientific purpose, such that the designation 'a gigantic anti-atomic fortress' is, at any rate, misleading."[35]

In the cases of Wager and Romersa, the Danish comments gave rise to significant corrections in the printed articles and were thus a step in toning down reportage on the military purposes of Camp Century. This can only be interpreted to mean that the Danish authorities consciously wished to limit or "contain" any mention of the expansive U.S. military base strategy in northern Greenland. Much like the American government, which attempted to contain communism, among other means by attempting to influence the information reaching regular citizens across the world, Denmark actively tried to influence the press coverage of Camp Century.

Although in several instances the Danish authorities did, in fact, successfully promote a representation of Camp Century as a purely scientific project in many international media—an angle that, incidentally, was frequently employed by the U.S. Army—containing the outflow of news and reporting from the camp proved to be an insurmountable task.

While there are several examples of the Danish authorities successfully containing information about Camp Century's military significance, there are many examples of the opposite. One is courtesy of an American journalist who wrote under the witty pseudonym "Ivan

Colt"—linking a typical Russian moniker with the legendary American arms manufacturer—and supplied a considerable number of articles and stories to men's and boys' magazines such as *Men*, *American Rifleman*, *Male*, and *Real Men*. In an article appearing in October 1960, Colt included a vivid description of missile-launching bases beneath the surface of the ice sheet that would be "able to plaster every major Soviet city, H-bomb depot and missile plant."[36]

Another American journalist, Herbert O. Johansen, who wrote for *Popular Science* magazine, published an article in their February 1960 issue that likewise took no pains to veil Camp Century's military and strategic implications. Still, the most intriguing thing about Johansen's piece is not its description of what Camp Century meant to the United States in military terms, since other American articles had also dealt with this topic. Rather, it is the fact that the article also appeared in Denmark, unabridged and in Danish, in the July 1960 issue of *Reader's Digest*. The circulation of the Danish-language version of the family digest, called *Det Bedste* (literally, "the best"), was translated directly from the American original. In its heyday in the 1950s, *Det Bedste* had a phenomenal circulation (by Danish standards) of 300,000 copies. Johansen's article offered the many Danish subscribers a very strong hint at the otherwise top-secret Project Iceworm: "The working areas will be dominated by scientific laboratories, but should the need come for a similar military installation—perhaps an under-ice launching site for intercontinental ballistic missiles or interceptors—we have the blueprints, the techniques, the machines."[37] His message could hardly have been clearer: behind the scientific image of Camp Century lay a sweeping plan for potentially incorporating the Greenland ice sheet into the nuclear missile–defense strategy of the United States. And given that a popular-science journalist such as Johansen was aware of the existence of Project Iceworm, although probably not its name, it is hard to imagine that many others were not also discussing the topic around that time. Nevertheless, the plans Johansen mentioned never became the object of any major debate in the media or among Danish civil servants and politicians. It was an aspect of Camp Century that was, and would remain, a public secret.

WAS THIS CENSORSHIP?

In the early 1960s, more and more Danish newspapers were able to send journalists to Greenland. Paul Hammerich of *Politiken*, mentioned earlier in this chapter, is a good example. Around the same time, the Danish authorities were obliged to acknowledge that they had not entirely succeeded in containing the press coverage of Camp Century's military aspect and also that their inability to do so had only had minor consequences for the political debate about Denmark's position on nuclear weapons on Danish soil and the enforcement of the country's position in Greenland. These circumstances no doubt influenced the decision taken by the Danish Ministry of Foreign Affairs in December 1963 to terminate the 1952 Press Agreement.[38] The détente between the two

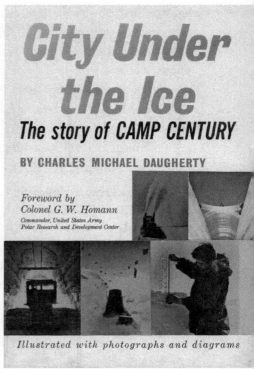

superpowers after the Cuban Missile Crisis in 1962 probably also played a role, since Denmark no longer had to exhibit the same diplomatic caution as before in its dealings with the Soviet Union.[39]

From then on, journalists and writers visiting American bases and other military installations in Greenland did not have to make their manuscripts and other work available to the Danish authorities. Nor did they have to fear several weeks in limbo, awaiting courteous suggestions for corrections from Denmark before publication.

Beyond this, alleged actions taken by the American authorities to make things difficult for reporters wishing to visit more or less secret locations in Greenland is another issue altogether, one we will not deal with here. At any rate, without the 1952 Press Agreement, reporters given access to Greenland could write whatever they wanted and publish it at any pace, as agreed with their publishers or editors in chief.

FIGURE 4.2 Covers of the three American popular-science books about Camp Century that were published in 1962, 1963, and 1964, while the camp was still operating. Wager's and Daugherty's books, both intended for the general public, were written in a journalistic style. Hamilton's book, appearing as part of a series called The Wonders of Science Library, was "written in simple language [and] will appeal to the reader who desires a clear view on the developments in science."

FIGURE 4.3 The February 1960 issue of *Popular Science* had a spectacular cover illustration of Camp Century.

The question remains whether the Danish authorities really did censor foreign reporters and writers who visited Camp Century between 1960 and 1963, a claim that was certainly purported by a number of American journalists in that period. The *Oxford Dictionaries* define censorship as "the suppression or prohibition of any parts of books, films, news, etc. that are considered obscene, politically unacceptable, or a threat to security."[40] In light of this definition one can fairly say that the 1952 Press Agreement between Denmark and the United States, in force from 1952 to 1963, granted Danish authorities the right, before publication, to review in detail and comment on articles written by non-Danish journalists following a visit to Camp Century, although they did not have the right to suppress or prohibit the material or its publication. Furthermore, the press agreement did not stipulate the extent to which the journalists were obliged to comply with the changes proposed by the Danish authorities. It was impossible to go that far without also violating the freedom of the press. This leads us to conclude that a very mild form of censorship did occur, which can best be understood as a partially successful Danish attempt to contain the news flowing out of Greenland, in keeping with the joint kingdom's national security and its best interests.[41]

5

SCOUTING IN THE HIGH ARCTIC

A STROKE OF LUCK: "AN ORANGE HAS FALLEN INTO MY TURBAN"

This is a horrible, desolate place. At least that's the general opinion and the daily topic of conversation among the Americans here. In a way I do understand their point of view. They are made to work on just one single task during the three months at a time they spend here. In the U.S., they could go out at night. Here, they are confined to playing cards, reading or talking in their quarters, playing billiards, going to the movie theater, which mainly shows old, lousy movies, or sitting in the library, which is not very well stocked. Even so, I feel like an orange has fallen into my turban.[1]

These are the opening lines of the first newspaper article about Camp Century written by the nineteen-year-old Danish Boy Scout Søren Gregersen, which appeared in *Politiken* on November 27, 1960. The article was preceded by a sequence of events that played out just right for the young, hopeful Gregersen—"Søren Scout from Korsør," as the article's photo caption called him—making him the lucky Aladdin who, borrowing a phrase from a well-known Danish production of *Arabian Nights*, catches "an orange in his turban."

FIGURE 5.1 The seven finalists in the American Boy Scout competition and members of the selection committee, seen here at the final meeting in Washington, DC, in August 1960. Kent L. Goering (seated, second from right) was announced as the national winner, seated here between Committee Chairman Harry M. Adinsell (seated, center) and Major General Stephen R. Hanmer, deputy chief of engineers, who is pointing out the location of Camp Century on a map of Greenland. The bald gentleman (standing, back row) is Dr. Paul A. Siple, scientific advisor to the director of army research.

The previous year, the U.S. Army Corps of Engineers had invited the Boy Scouts of America to select an accomplished member who would be offered five months' work as a "junior scientific aide" in a military camp built under the surface of the Greenland ice sheet—Camp Century. The news was announced in major American newspapers, including the *New York Times*, on June 26, 1960,[2] specifying that candidates for the job had to be high-school graduates aged 17 to 19½ and physically qualified to spend a length of time in the Arctic. An initial field of 120 candidates was quickly narrowed down to seven. The seven finalists were invited to New York City in August 1960 for another round of testing and interviews before a special selection committee, which finally awarded the job to an eighteen-year-old Eagle Scout from Neodesha, Kansas, by the name of Kent L. Goering.[3] *Scouting*, the magazine of the Boy Scouts of America, listed all of Kent's excellent qualifications and also historically contextualized his upcoming adventure as part of a proud tradition:

> As you read this Kent L. Goering, Explorer and Eagle Scout, may be taking a hot shower down inside a Greenland glacier. . . . For the third time the Boy Scouts of America is honored by having a member as a junior scientific aide on a government polar expedition. Our deep freeze Explorer is following the example—if not the direction—of Dr. Paul Siple who, as a Scout, went to Antarctica with Admiral Richard E. Byrd in 1928, and Richard L. Chappell who went there with the International Geophysical Year expedition in 1958. Both of them served on the committee that selected Kent.[4]

This coincided with a similar invitation from the United States that would enable a Danish Boy Scout to visit Camp Century. After just a few weeks of consultations among the leaders of various Danish Scouting organizations, in September 1960 the selected Dane was announced: eighteen-year-old Søren Gregersen from the coastal town of Korsør. "Atomic theory, Greenland, and American terminology are vying for attention in the mind of a young recruit as he sweats his way around the military drill grounds near Slagelse," *Politiken* wrote.[5] After graduating with honors from the venerable upper-secondary school Sorø Academy, "where he had worked as a good friend and comrade in the school's Scout troop," Søren had begun his conscripted military service in the Danish army. This meant his application had to be reviewed by the Ministry of Defense for prior approval.[6] In it, Søren wrote that he wanted to examine Camp Century's nuclear reactor in every detail and that his ambition was to study "atomic science."[7]

ADVENTURE UNDER THE ICE

Kent Goering and Søren Gregersen both lived and worked at Camp Century from October 1960 to March 1961. Their story is that of an odd adventure. Who would have thought that two Boy Scouts would travel to the northernmost reaches of Greenland, spending five months there submerged in the ice cap in the company of American military personnel and researchers, in a camp where power and heating were supplied by a mobile nuclear reactor? But the story has many facets and can be told in two very different ways.

The first version is a fascinating account of everyday life in a tunnel town under the snow and ice, as seen through the eyes of two young men—in other words, a story told at the micro level, putting a human perspective on the topics treated at a more general historical level in the other chapters of this book. Most particularly we see the physical surroundings, the people, and the events in the unusual camp through the firsthand narratives of the Danish scout Søren Gregersen—who, at nineteen, was well aware of the Cold War between the two nuclear superpowers, although he would hardly have realized that his physical presence in Camp Century put him in one of the hottest spots on Earth in that ice-cold conflict. We will now embark on the first version of the story, saving the second for the last part of this chapter.

The Arctic adventure of the two Boy Scouts began when Søren and Kent first met, shortly after Søren landed in Washington, DC, on October 13, 1960. Here they were received not only by Paul Siple but also by the acting chief of engineers, Major General S. R. Hanmer, along with prominent representatives from the Boy Scouts of America and employees from the Danish embassy in Washington. This was indeed a distinguished reception. That evening they dined with Captain William F. Cahill, who had been appointed to serve as commanding officer at Camp Century from January 1, 1960. Cahill briefed them on what they would soon be seeing and feeling for themselves, enclosed in Greenland's perpetual ice cap. Over the next two days they met numerous important figures and photographers in Washington and at Fort Belvoir, a nearby U.S. Army base in Virginia. They were tailed around the clock by photographers from the army's press corps, resulting in a wealth of photographs that appeared in a wide variety of American and Danish newspapers over the following days and weeks. The young men also had time to enjoy some of the landmarks in the American capital, including the White House, Capitol Hill, Lincoln Memorial,

FIGURE 5.2 The serving officer of welfare at the Danish army's barracks near Slagelse had reportedly purchased "a couple of thick volumes about atomic theory and nuclear physics" for Søren Gregersen before his trip to Greenland. For a feature article portraying the young recruit, the journalist asked whether he was, in fact, studying these tomes: "'I try to. But I can't, because every time I sit down, I fall asleep,' answers Søren Gregersen, whose whole person seems every bit as sincere and honest as this response." The image and accompanying article appeared in *Politiken* on September 11, 1960.

FIGURE 5.3 On October 14, 1960, two days before their journey to Camp Century began, Kent Goering and Søren Gregersen were in Washington, DC. Here they met a number of prominent figures, including Dr. Paul A. Siple, who stated on this occasion: "It is vital to the Nation's future that young people's interest in science be stimulated through real field work of this kind."

Washington Monument, and Arlington National Cemetery. Before leaving on the next leg of their journey to Thule Air Base in Greenland, they took on assignments for various newspapers and magazines to report on their experiences in the ice camp. Among other things, Søren Gregersen agreed to write several pieces for *Politiken* and for the Danish Scouting magazine during his stay, of which more later.[8]

To fulfill his obligations, Søren kept a diary, in which he made entries almost daily, short and long, chronicling his experiences.[9] Our attempts in the following to describe the remarkable but also curiously mundane everyday life at Camp Century are built in large part on accounts from this unpublished diary. Søren Gregersen's information is sometimes supplemented by contributions from Kent Goering, who to our knowledge did not keep a diary, and by the author Walter Wager, who had the opportunity in 1960 to spend a few weeks in Greenland in the extraordinary U.S. facility.[10] We would, however, ask readers to bear in mind that the two youths had a very special status in the camp. Neither of them had any academic degree or special knowledge of the sort needed to bring Camp Century's overall purpose to fruition or to make the camp's installations run more smoothly. Even though Søren and Kent were assigned to help a variety of changing work crews during their stay, their importance to the camp lay not in their value as labor but elsewhere.

DAILY LIFE AT CAMP CENTURY

Kent Goering and Søren Gregersen arrived at Camp Century on Saturday, October 22, 1960, after a long, arduous journey, first by airplane from McGuire Air Force Base in New Jersey to Thule Air Base, then by truck to Camp Tuto, where they spent a few days before traversing the last 222 km across the ice sheet to Camp Century in a "polecat" personnel vehicle. Fortunately, the day following their arrival was a Sunday, so they could sleep as long as they liked and relax. But on Monday morning, duty called. It was time for them to begin earning their keep as "junior scientific aides." They also had to get used to the routines that structured daily life in the winter of 1960/1961 for the camp's seventy or so inhabitants, about half of whom had a degree in science or technology.[11]

Although Camp Century was a military research station, the facility was not governed by rigid military discipline. Most of the people in the camp had been specially assigned because of their educational background, often a bachelor's degree in science or engineering, and they expected their stay to be a unique learning experience.[12] A regular workday for those who had not been on evening or night shift tending the camp's power, heating, and other vital installations ran something like this:[13]

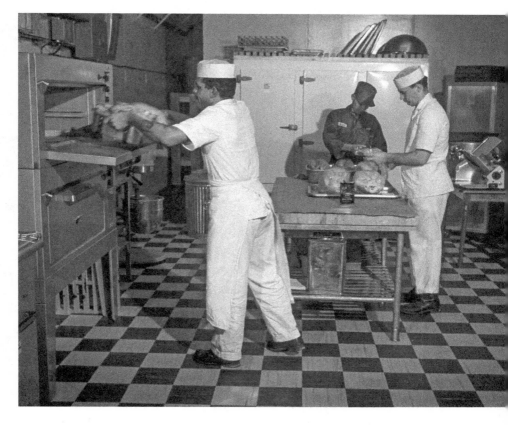

FIGURE 5.4 The two Boy Scouts, and everyone else in the camp, enjoyed the good food prepared daily in the mess kitchen and served up in generous helpings. With deep-freeze capacity for provisions virtually unlimited, shelf life was not a problem at Camp Century.

Wake-up time in the personnel barracks was 0600 hours. After quickly donning underwear, shirt, trousers, and shoes, the men would hurry through the barracks tunnels, down Main Street, and into the communal bathrooms, also called "the 100-man latrine." There were so many sinks, showers with hot and cold water, outlets for shavers, and toilets that no one had to stand in line for long to complete their morning routine. Freshly showered and shaved, the men would make double-quick time back to their quarters to dress for whatever work awaited them that day. For those going outdoors, up onto the surface of the ice sheet, this meant multiple layers of woolen clothing, a fur-lined parka coat, and special boots—which, according to Søren, were so thickly insulated that "it is virtually impossible to feel cold in these boots."[14] In contrast, those working inside would generally just dress in normal clothing. The heating system maintained regular room temperatures indoors, at the warmer end of the normal range: the citizens of the "ice city" liked their quarters hot.

Dressed to meet the exigencies of a new day in the ice sheet, it was time for the morning meal in the camp's mess hall, which could seat 150. The tables were arranged so small groups could eat together, creating a more homey atmosphere than the long mess tables typically seen on U.S. military bases. Meals were served buffet style, each man fixing himself a tray with dishes and utensils, then taking his fill of the heaps of eggs and sausages, cornflakes, bread, milk, and coffee.

After breakfast, the actual workday began around 0700. There were many different jobs to do in and around Camp Century. Some were extremely specialized and could only be handled by people with expert training and education. One such task was manning the nuclear reactor, steam turbine, and generator in Tunnels 3, 4, and 5. These elements made up the plant generating the electricity that kept the camp's lighting and heating systems running. Here, an advanced academic degree in engineering or physics was effectively a precondition. Likewise in the "dispensary," the camp's medical clinic, which obviously had qualified staff, and in most of the research laboratories, where the work was done by military or civilian scientists specializing in such fields as geology, glaciology, and seismology. Besides the academic positions there were a number of jobs for skilled craftsmen and even some for electricians, plumbers, carpenters, and snow-maintenance personnel. The last group was responsible for keeping Main Street free of snowdrifts and buildup and for scraping ice off the walls, an important task because the moisture in the tunnels would quickly condense and freeze into ice, and the gradual shifts in the ice sheet slowly but surely deformed the tunnel cavities.

Around 0930 it was time for a half-hour coffee break, then back to work until 1145 and the second meal of the day. Huge amounts of food were served up and eaten. Those who had worked outdoors were especially

FIGURE 5.5 After arriving at Camp Century the two Boy Scouts—Kent from Kansas and Søren from Korsør—spent the first few days touring the entire facility. They are seen here, with a person from the U.S. Army, in front of transport crates containing parts for the PM-2A nuclear reactor, built by ALCO Products, Inc., of New York.

hungry, since working in the cold takes its toll in extra calories. As Walter Wager reported after his visit in the spring of 1960, Camp Century was probably the only military camp where each man was offered two big steaks—and wolfed them down. Once lunch was over, almost everyone would smoke a cigar or cigarette and drink a mug of steaming-hot coffee while chatting with lunchmates at the table.[15]

At 1230 hours it was back to work for the rest of the afternoon. The workday ended at 1745, giving the men time to wash and change into fresh, comfortable clothes before the third meal of the day, which was served at 1830. Usually it would be meat with mashed potatoes and gravy, plus side dishes of peas, fried tomatoes, and salads, followed by

FIGURE 5.6 One piece of hardware the Boy Scouts really looked forward to seeing was the PM-2A reactor. Here a reactor technician shows Kent and Søren, still in their scout uniforms, how the control panel works. The two young men briefly worked in and around the reactor plant, and Søren was also involved in measuring radioactivity in the vicinity of Camp Century.

cheese, bread, cakes, and dessert. The beverages, served in large pitchers, were water, milk, and fruit juice. The air on the Greenland ice cap is extremely dry, so everyone at Camp Century was explicitly instructed to drink lots of liquids to avoid dehydration.

After the evening meal, the men had about three hours of free time for hobbies, card games, letter writing, reading, or a movie. Camp Century had a well-equipped workshop and a library with fiction and non-fiction, as well as a "movie theater" that usually showed at least one film

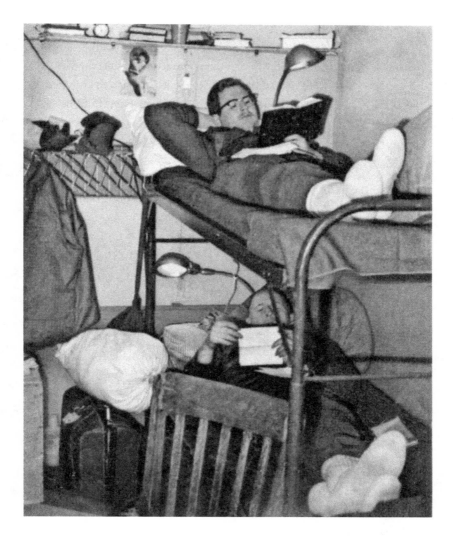

FIGURE 5.7 During their stay at Camp Century, Søren and Kent shared a bunk room like the one seen here. The reclining occupants are not the two scouts but U.S. Army personnel.

every evening. The repertoire ranged from Shakespeare's plays, to documentaries, to pure entertainment, catering to virtually every taste, apparently even the poorest. Kent Goering was well satisfied with the leisure facilities and even found Camp Century a perfect locale for one specific group of people:

This is Greenland, a vast ocean of ice and snow three times the size of Texas. . . . Camp Century is our city under the ice, and it was built here with the consent of the Danish Government. It is a city of not much more than a hundred residents, scientists, engineers, and soldiers, occupying an area about eight blocks long, three blocks wide. . . . Mail reaches us via heavy swings every third week, weather permitting. We have a well-stocked library, and a theatre with first run movies. Although the atmosphere is always sharp with a cold tingle, it is almost 100% dust-free. We do have to admit that Camp Century is a veritable paradise for hay fever victims.[16]

The men would start getting ready for bed around 2200 hours. Unless it was a Saturday evening, a new, demanding workday was scheduled to begin the next morning at 0600. There was no bedtime curfew, though, and sometimes a group would stay up longer in one of the communal living rooms. Normally almost everyone would be asleep before midnight, and silence would reign in the small, subsurface city, even if snowstorms raged topside and temperatures dropped to new lows in the months-long Arctic night.

EXCERPTS FROM SØREN GREGERSEN'S DIARY

When Søren and Kent were awakened on the first workday after their arrival, they were instructed to put on their Boy Scout uniforms. After breakfast they would be taking a guided tour of the camp, led by the commanding officer, Captain Andre G. Broumas, and accompanied by one of the U.S. Army's own photographers. Numerous pictures were taken on the tour, many of which later appeared in the United States, Denmark, and elsewhere. Afterward, the young men were allowed to change into clothes better suited to their glacial surroundings. At last they could begin "the peaceful but exciting work in Camp Century," as an optimistic Søren wrote in his diary. By this point he was fed up with going everywhere with a photographer in tow.[17]

FIGURE 5.8 The Boy Scouts pausing at a shield wall in the reactor tunnel. Much of the shield wall consisted of oil drums. While working around the nuclear reactor, Søren learned a few things about the Danish security requirements for the reactor, which he shared with the readers of *Politiken* in his third travel report, dated February 19, 1961: "Concerning the disposal of radioactive waste, Captain Arnold told me later that day that permission has been given by the Danish government to pour up to 50 millicuries of liquid waste out into the ice per year. All solid waste must be sent to the United States to be buried in the ground."

Over the following days and weeks, Kent and Søren were tasked with assisting one crew, then another, then another. First they helped engineers and scientists from the U.S. Army Chemical Corps, who were wrapping up some experiments apparently meant to show whether the residents of Camp Century could be protected against attacks with chemical or biological weapons, using the materials at hand. We base this deduction on Søren's diary entry for that day: "Capt. Bronson shows us gas masks that have been tested in the cold, and we see a collective gas filter that filters the air for a whole house." The Chemical Corps was also testing some smoke generators for use in case of enemies approaching the base at close range. The equipment was meant to lay out a white smokescreen on the surface that would make the camp's entry ramps, marking flags, containers, and special-purpose huts invisible on the white expanse of ice. The following day, which was Tuesday, October 25, the two scouts were allowed to take apart the camp's gas filter, weigh it, and reassemble it. "Bored stiff" was Søren's unimpressed comment on this task. The afternoon was not much better. They waited for Captain Bronson to appear for over an hour, and when he did he handed them a couple of pamphlets on "bacterial warfare" and sent them to their quarters. As Søren succinctly concluded: "Quite an unfruitful day."

The next day, Wednesday, they once again "went to the Chemical Corps, but they had already had enough of us," as Søren put it. Captain Bronson immediately sent them on "to Sig-Met [the meteorological team of the Signal Corps], where for the first couple of hours they showed us and told us a bit about the instruments in their 'wanigan' [living quarters mounted on a large transport sled] and out on their tower," which logically was placed on the surface at some distance from the tunnels. After this thorough briefing, "we moved on to playing chess, talking, reading. . . . We went home at four thirty. In the evening in the library, I started working on my first article for 'Politiken' and wrote on a typewriter, for the first time ever." Søren's initial attempts at typing were somewhat fumbling, but during the stay he became quite an accomplished typist.

FIGURE 5.9 "Søren Scout" passing through a visibly shrinking transit tunnel in Camp Century between Main Street and one of the side tunnels. The picture documents that less than a year after the camp was built, the movements in the ice sheet were causing serious problems.

Thursday was very much the same:

All day [we were] with Sig-Met, where we read, played chess, and talked. They still haven't taught us much about their instruments. However, we did get to call up Tuto's weather station over the radio. Every hour, the fellow working at that moment sends in his observations to Tuto, Station 1. At the same time, Tuto gets observations from Tuto West and from Tuto East. On with "Politiken" and typing.

This is the style of the entire diary, although the daily entries vary in length, from a mere three to four lines up to ten to fifteen lines. Naturally, we will not follow the two scouts day by day but concentrate on days when their experiences shed light on topics or events treated elsewhere in this book. Let us therefore fast-forward a couple of weeks to Monday, November 7, 1960, quoting Søren Gregersen's entire entry for that day:

Up for breakfast, but we didn't start work until 0845. Until coffee we were indoors, i.e. inside the tunnels. After that, until noon, we were topside. Topside, it's pretty much time to wrap things up. It's getting too dark. We worked in the mess tunnel, where our job was to put little pegs in the walls as the basis for measuring the width of the tunnels at various heights, at various times, since they know very well that the tunnel sides are coming in, the floors coming up, and the ceiling coming down. Also, we hung a wire with a plumb weight from a nail in the ceiling so that Burch can read, on a vertical measuring stick every week, how much the roof of the tunnel has come down. It's becoming a problem, that mess tunnel. Then in the evening, in the library, I wrote an article for "Spejdernes Magasin" [the Danish Scouting magazine].

Interestingly, here Søren Gregersen's diary touches on a problem—the gradual collapse of the tunnels—which was identified very early on as the greatest unsolved problem at Camp Century. As mentioned in the previous chapter, the American journalist Herbert O. Johansen wrote an article about the camp that was translated and appeared in *Det Bedste*, the Danish version of *Reader's Digest*, in July 1960. This piece stated that there was one problem the army's engineers had not yet found a way to solve, namely, the difficulties with the physical shifts occurring in the tunnel systems because of movements in the ice sheet.[18] The problem had already been recognized some years before, during the first tunnel experiments at Camp Tuto. Based on the assessments, the army could expect to use Camp Century for ten years at most before having to start from scratch somewhere else.[19]

Sundays at Camp Century were special, since they normally meant no work and an opportunity to sleep late. The men could also go to a religious service in a designated worship space if they so wished; there was no compulsory attendance. On Sunday, November 13, 1960, Søren confessed in his diary that he did not get up until eleven thirty. He also noted that after lunch he was "with the photographer inside the steam tank in the reactor plant. We were able to do this today because the reactor is now non-operational, between two 6-hour test runs supplying the camp; most places the radiation was under 5 mr."[20]

This tells us that Søren was present in the camp when the nuclear reactor went critical and began supplying the camp with energy—an event that, according to Walter Wager, took place on November 12 of that year at 0652 hours, as described in chapter 3. Meanwhile, it also tells us that this event, which Wager regarded as sensational and saw as the absolute climax of his visit to the camp, was something Søren Gregersen hardly noticed. To him it was nothing special, perhaps because during his previous tour of the reactor section he had become convinced that making a reactor go critical was a routine operation. On the other hand, it was by no means routine that the reactor had to be shut down almost immediately, which was necessary because the radiation intensity above the reactor was rapidly nearing the maximum level permitted, so security procedures prescribed a shutdown until the problem was resolved. The reactor crew had to order—and await—a fresh shipment of lead sheets with which to enclose the reactor, to reduce radiation to an acceptable level.[21]

So much for the scouts' stint in the reactor section. There was nothing more for them to do there, so they had to move on. They asked to be allowed to assist Burch, an enlisted soldier and a good acquaintance of theirs in the camp, in measuring the various tunnels "inside" and marking their positions "topside," where piled-up snow quickly hid the original marking flags, but obviously the camp's management did not think this was a good idea. The following Wednesday, November 16, the Boy Scouts were "transferred to the thermo-drilling project, which is housed in tunnel 12. Capt. Broumas wouldn't let us continue [to work] with Burch, even though I pointed out to him that Burch needed us, whereas Herb Ueda has enough people for the things that have to be done at the moment in the thermo-drilling project."[22]

Captain Broumas did not want the two young men to serve as cheap labor for a single group. He saw it as his duty to make sure they became familiar with all of the various jobs and tasks in Camp Century. The upshot was that Søren and Kent were tasked with helping a person by the name of Brady "in stretching out a cable along the wall in tunnel 12. It was a big, heavy cable, which in the cold had become quite stiff and unwieldy. The rest of the day we took part in the work to move the 'drilling tower' down to the 'winch,' the small, heavy base building of the tower. Meanwhile, this tower is still lying down."

Over the next ten days, the two scouts spent the better part of their working hours in the company of Herb Ueda and his team. They had just begun preparing for what, in the long term, would turn out to be Camp Century's greatest scientific achievement: drilling to the very bottom of the ice sheet and extracting an unbroken core of ice 1,390 meters (4,560 feet) long. This sample from Greenland's permanent ice cap helped Danish and American glaciologists attain a new and deeper understanding of Earth's climate over the past hundred thousand years, as will be described in detail in chapter 7.[23] Still, the youths were not overwhelmed by their workload, having lots of time to read, play chess, and watch movies, in addition to writing some of the articles they had promised to send to various newspapers and magazines in their homelands far away.

On Saturday, November 26, Søren wrote: "We tidied up the tunnel (12) and watched Herb and the others get ready to begin the drilling (or rather, the melting). After dinner I took 'Polaroid' photographs for 'Politiken,' and they began to drill the first 15 feet down during the afternoon . . . Bob et al. drilling all evening."

FIGURE 5.10 Camp Century's library, where Søren and Kent spent many hours and which they also managed for several months. The selection was not large, and Søren found good reads to be few and far between. As he told the readers of *Politiken* on Sunday, January 15, 1961: "For me the evenings, outside movie time, are spent in the library, where the few good books include a Danish–English dictionary and an encyclopedia."

This sounds promising, but in practice the drilling operation did not run nearly as smoothly as the scientists had hoped and expected. The following Monday, Søren was able to relax and have a good read—the Danish polar explorer Peter Freuchen's book *Ice Floes and Flaming Water*—because that day the drill was undergoing repairs, as it would for the next many days. The problem was that the original drill had an unfortunate tendency to melt the piece of ice core inside it. This was counterproductive, to say the least, given that the whole point of the exercise was to bring up the lengths of ice core frozen and intact. On Sunday, December 7, the problem remained unsolved, and the following day the entire ice-core project team left the camp on a heavy swing headed for Camp Tuto. For them, the season was over. They were going back to the United States to celebrate Christmas and enjoy the winter holidays, to return early the following spring. One of the few team members who remained behind was the American head of the project, Lyle Hansen, who had decided to spend the long winter searching for a solution that would make the recalcitrant ice-core drill operate as intended.

The two Boy Scouts took no part in this effort, for now they had been reassigned to the reactor team, which was working hard to get the reactor operational. But these efforts were beset with problems too. As Søren wrote on December 6:

My goodness, what an awful start to our stay in the reactor section! A "pole-cat" came in at 12 o'clock; three others came in around 1 o'clock. Two "pole-cats" of the six that set out from Camp Tuto had been abandoned along the way, one about 70 [miles] and one about 100 miles from Tuto. We didn't think we would be working in the afternoon, since the mail had arrived, but at 2 o'clock Mr. Embleton made an angry telephone call to us and asked us to saw up some sawdust. Sgt. Honeycutt helped us. This sawdust is intended for use in "shielding" tests.

It was a strenuous task, and the scouts also had to saw the next day until after their coffee break. Afterward they were rewarded by seeing the reactor in operation, albeit very briefly:

We . . . watched the control man make the reactor go critical and make it work, very little and without transferring this work to the secondary water system ("zero power"). At around 1 o'clock, after 55 minutes of work, he pressed the "scram" button, causing the reactor to immediately stop its work. Then our task was to fill plastic bags with measured amounts of water and sawdust, [which contains] a lot of hydrogen ions that are meant to absorb neutrons, which are the big problem in the protection here, around this reactor.

The young men had not been involved in executing the eventual solution to the radiation problem, as the extra sheets of lead had not yet arrived. They only contributed to a temporary emergency solution that could limit the radiation enough for standalone testing of the reactor. After the operator had shut it down, they returned to their quarters around four thirty. Søren Gregersen was tired but not completely worn out: "I was really not in the mood for writing, but I did succeed in writing [the piece for] 'Sorø Amtstidende'. . . . Editor Corneliussen has asked me for an article for the New Year's issue of 'Sorø Amtstidende.'"

Around this time the two Boy Scouts were also given another task: managing the camp's little library. It was thought this activity might bring them into contact with many interesting people, and they were certainly well qualified to do the job. Indeed, Søren's diary entry for Friday, December 9, reflects a certain self-confidence: "We began to create order in the library. The previous librarian did not take any interest in it at all." This task did not exempt them from other duties, however, nor was it their intention that it should.

On Monday, December 12, they were once again assigned to the reactor team. A large shipment of goods, including the lead sheets, had just arrived, and the two young men were able-bodied helpers in the practical work of shifting, stacking, and stowing the materials:

We [were] put to work, helping to transport the goods from the swing into the main tunnel. After lunch we spent a little while in the control room. We were told that the reactor has 37 elements, 5 of which are control rods with boron and uranium. For the rest of the afternoon we carried or dragged boards and beams into the ABC tunnel, and the lead was brought into the main [reactor] tunnel.

This information enables us to say, with certainty, that at least some of the lead required to insulate the reactor had arrived at Camp Century a couple of weeks into December 1960. Apparently, however, it was not enough, given that the reactor did not begin regular operations until February or March 1961. In the interim the camp had to be supplied with heat and electricity from the diesel generators installed during the setup phase, which were meant to serve as an auxiliary power system once the reactor was up and running. At one stage the camp's management was worried that its store of conventional fuel might run out. This was also an issue that involved the two scouts when, on December 16, Kent was asked "to find out how much oil the camp has left; and I, how much water is formed by the steam produced. Perhaps savings can be made here."

The oil was primarily meant for use in the diesel generators that were the camp's backup system when the nuclear reactor was offline. In an interview from 2002, Herb Ueda explained that sometimes problems would suddenly arise in the reactor, which would cause the lights throughout the tunnel system to go out. You might think the white snow would transmit some faint glow or shimmer, but as Herb Ueda explained: "The power would go out and believe me, when you are down in that camp, and the power goes out, it is pitch black. You can't see the hand in front of your face. . . . [But] they had a very elaborate back-up system. I think they had four 500 kilowatt generators. Huge. And in the end, the backup generators operated longer than the nuclear reactor."[24]

Then came December 24 and 25. The Christmas holidays inspired the Yuletide spirit, with lots of good food, beer, and whiskey. Even so, Søren, who was the only Dane at Camp Century, confided in his diary that during his days off, his thoughts were often with family and friends back home. Fortunately the mail bag arrived on December 27, an eagerly awaited event for all the ice-town's inhabitants, but according to Søren's entry for that day there was more than a little drama involved in the delivery:

"Mail drop"—I got a big envelope from home containing a flat Christmas-season calendar;. . . my first article, as a newspaper cutting from "Politiken" ([the editor] Paul Hammerich has changed it, not for the better in my opinion) and Christmas notes and letters. This letter was found far away from Camp Century in the snow. Twelve sacks were dropped [from the mail plane], and they have been searching since 2 o'clock, 4 or 5 hours, for loose letters from three of the mail sacks, which tore open.

Mail deliveries were evidently irregular and unreliable, and, as the diary entry hints, the camp's personnel had to spend hours outside in the brutal Arctic winter locating and picking up what in the end was just a fraction of the letters from the torn sacks, which the icy wind had scattered far and wide.

The new year immediately brought the scouts an important task, described in Søren Gregersen's diary entry for Monday, January 2, 1961:

> I woke a couple of minutes too late to have breakfast. Kent had received instructions from Capt. Cahill, so he instructed me about these instructions until the coffee break. After that, until two thirty we examined the laboratory building and compared its installations with the original

FIGURE 5.11 A view of Camp Century's "movie theater," which showed a film almost every evening. The projector reels were so small they had to be changed several times during a regular full-length movie. Not everyone was equally enthusiastic about the available selection, although as Søren Gregersen wrote in the article that appeared in *Politiken* on January 15, 1961: "I have now determined that the films I can see for free in the movie theater are actually not as bad as my first impression led me to believe."

plan ("blue print"). And the rest of the afternoon Kent very nicely drew corrections onto this plan. We posted a notice in the mess hall: "The Library will not be open tonight. Go to the movie!" We went, and we saw "The Bridges of Toko-Ri" [an American film from 1954 about the Korean War]. Good movie!

Over the next two to three weeks Kent and Søren systematically went over all the buildings in Camp Century. Each structure was measured, its installations checked, and the results matched up against the original blueprints. All differences were meticulously incorporated onto a revised plan of the facility. The object of this exercise—in addition to giving the young men a meaningful activity—must surely have been to enable the maintenance crews to do their work faster and cheaper, since without reliable reference drawings they might expend a lot of time and effort on a problem without finding the root cause, or fixing it.

On Wednesday, February 1, just a few days after completing their comprehensive survey and registration job, Kent and Søren boarded a heavy swing bound west and arrived, after a long and arduous journey of several days and nights, at Camp Tuto, near the ice-cap rim. They stayed there for a couple of weeks, and Søren took the opportunity to visit several tunnels (including one in the ice and one in the permafrost layer) and various other scientific sites in the vicinity. He also went as a passenger by truck to Thule Air Base to do some shopping and to speak to some of his fellow Danes working at the base. On Monday, February 20, around midnight, the Boy Scouts embarked on the journey back to Camp Century, arriving back at their ice-bound burrow town on February 23 after three days, the normal transit time from Camp Tuto to Camp Century for the slow-moving heavy swings.

Judging from the entries in Søren Gregersen's diary, the remainder of the scouts' stay in the camp seems to have been fairly uneventful, bordering on tedious. The camp, having lost its novelty, was no longer intriguing, and the officers in charge seem to have been hard pressed to keep finding interesting tasks for their two "junior scientific aides." Kent and Søren spent most of their time writing articles for newspapers and other publications in their respective countries and converting part of one tunnel into an ice-skating rink—thoroughly inconveniencing the men of the Chemical Corps, who were obliged to cross the incredibly slippery area multiple times each day, en route from their living quarters to the laboratory. At this point both young men were becoming sick and tired of camp life, which shines through in Søren's frank disclosures in his diary entry dated March 10, 1961:

> We don't care much for the Chemical Corps, and all the talk about sex here in the camp annoys us. More and more things and more and more people annoy us. A lot of the personnel are "short timers" [a term coined during the Vietnam War for personnel with only a short time left on their tour of duty and so unwilling to do demanding tasks] with yellow [count-down] ribbons hanging from their breast pockets and such.

At long last came the moment they had been anticipating for several weeks. On March 22, 1961, they left Camp Century in a polecat, completing the trip to Camp Tuto in just over twenty-four hours. They once again spent a few days in this larger, more-well-equipped camp before being driven to Thule Air Base, where they boarded an aircraft bound for the United States. On Wednesday, April 5, they touched down at McGuire Air Force Base, where they had begun their journey six months earlier. After landing they went directly to a waiting car that drove them to New York City, where they were installed in the Hotel Commodore, right next to Grand Central Station. In practical terms, this marked the conclusion of their stay at Camp Century, but the two Boy Scouts still had various obligations to fulfill before their adventure was over.

The very next day Kent and Søren were the center of attention at a press conference held by the Boy Scouts of America at the organization's Park Avenue headquarters. The two appeared before a throng of press, radio, and television reporters who asked for details about their five-month stay in the "city under the ice." Camp Century was still good media material. The next morning, Søren and Kent awoke to flattering headlines and in-depth articles in American newspapers from across the country. The following three quotations will suffice to exemplify the reporting.

Belvoir Castle, the base newspaper of the U.S. Army's center for engineering R&D at Fort Belvoir, Virginia—which headed up the entire Camp Century project—stated in its headline that the scouts had assisted the army with an important scientific assignment in Greenland. Kent Goering, still full of energy after the long trip, concluded that "the winter in Greenland was no hardship, even though temperatures often dropped to minus 70 degrees."[25]

The headline in the *New York Times* simply stated: "2 Scouts Return from Arctic Trip." The article emphasized that the two young men had been through ninety-seven days of darkness, with temperatures around –57°C (–70°F)—and more than 280 km (175 miles) from the nearest girls. Kent Goering was once again quoted, this time for observing that "the principal lectures he had learned were not scientific but social: 'how to live with others and myself, in isolation, at close quarters, every minute of every day for months.'" Søren Gregersen, on the other hand, had stressed that "he had learned much about scientific research from the engineers at the camp, as well as better English."[26]

New York World-Telegram & Sun reflected the perception in its headline that the two Boy Scouts liked Greenland, despite the subzero temperatures. The reporter listed all the activities the young men had taken part in with "great enthusiasm" during their stay at Camp Century. The article concluded with a passage on how it was not Camp Century but the land itself that had made the biggest impression on them: "It was the eternal Greenland that awed them, not the modern trappings. 'I can see the weird romance of a country that has lured explorers,' said Kent. 'It is a land of desolate beauty.'"[27]

THE OTHER VERSION OF THE STORY

At the time, no journalists expressly queried a situation that, rationally speaking, was fairly bizarre: the United States, a nuclear superpower, builds a military facility dug into the ice sheet, then invites two Boy Scouts to work there as "junior scientific aides." An obvious question for a critical journalist would have been: Why? This question was never asked in any of the newspaper articles we know of, leaving us the opportunity to ask it—and attempt to offer an answer. This is the very question that opens our second version of the story of Søren Gregersen, Kent Goering, and their adventures in Camp Century.

The answer is that the two Boy Scouts were part of the U.S. Army's endeavors to "sell" their activities in Greenland, primarily to the American public but also to Danes and numerous other groups and countries in the global sphere of American influence around the world. Thus, the story of Kent and Søren was not merely one of how two young men dealt with working and living in a secluded subsurface camp in a frigid, high-altitude wasteland of ice and snow and of what they thought about the experience. It was also a story of how the U.S. Army was prepared to defend "the free world" at this outermost bastion in the extreme north; of how the army's ingenious, hard-working engineers were able to overcome all difficulties, even in one of the most hostile environments on the planet; and of how the two scouts were also able to contribute to these efforts and to learn about the nuclear technology that helped make it all possible. Søren and Kent personified the cooperation in Greenland between Denmark and the United States—a cooperation that, led by the United States as the world's leading nuclear superpower, was able to guarantee the safety of Danes and Americans alike. Having Kent and Søren as prominent figures in the coverage of Camp Century put a human and hence more congenial face on the graver security aspects of America's presence in Greenland.

The second version of the story also has an implied aspect that goes beyond the U.S. Army's significance for American security policy and for the wider NATO collaboration. There is a moral narrative, too, about the human preconditions for successfully defending the United States, Denmark, and the Western world at large. Time and again, the army's propaganda films, when dealing with the efforts in Greenland, underscored that the army's men were brave, tenacious, honest, and God-fearing.[28] In this context, the two Boy Scouts also played a key role as representatives of Scouting as such. Founded by the British war hero Lord Robert Baden-Powell in 1907, the Scout Movement's purpose was to support young people's physical, social, and moral development by means of a structured patrol system, outdoor life, and varying degrees of edifying religious ministry. Ever since the movement swept across the United States in 1910, the U.S. military has given it significant moral and financial support. But the U.S. military also gained much in return, particularly during the two world wars in the twentieth century, but also during the Cold War. Especially during the first fifteen years of the Cold War, the American Scout Movement underwent huge growth, going from a membership of just under 4 million in 1950 to some 7.5 million in the early 1960s.[29] At this point, Scouting in the United States was increasingly being seen as part of civilian society's contingency planning in the event of a crisis—with the motto "Be Prepared" taking on a new shade of meaning—and the young Scouts' guidance and training shifted more toward American patriotism and liberal, democratic values. The two Boy Scouts at Camp Century showed the world that mentally and physically young people were willing and able to take part in fighting the enemy, too, wherever and whenever the need might arise.

This is most clearly expressed in one of the programs in the army's television series *The Big Picture*, described in chapter 4. The episode, from 1961, was entitled "The U.S. Army and the Boy Scouts." Like the rest of the series, it took no pains to hide that part of its underlying purpose was to tell the public about some of the many beneficial things the army, and in this case also the Scout Movement, was doing for the United States. As the narrator explained, the Boy Scouts of America was "one of the few institutions to balance the rather softening effects of our modern way of life," giving American boys and adolescents an opportunity "to develop the initiative, the resourcefulness, the character, the quick thinking, and the leadership they really need in the somewhat jittery, insecure world in which we live."[30]

Kent Goering and Søren Gregersen are only included in the program's brief introduction. The rest is dedicated to relating how the U.S. Army had always supported the Boy Scouts of America, which, in turn, had helped to support the army's endeavors. The main character was the geographer and head of the U.S. Army's Office for Polar Affairs, Paul Siple, who was a prominent figure at the time. Shortly before the program was broadcast, Siple had chaired the committee that, in August 1960, selected Kent Goering for the mission as America's junior scientific aide in Camp Century. Siple too had been a Boy Scout, and like Kent he had achieved the rank of Eagle Scout, the highest in American Scouting. More than three decades earlier, Siple had won a similar competition, earning a trip with U.S. admiral Richard E. Byrd's expedition to Antarctica in 1928, likewise as a junior scientific aide.[31] In the program, Siple speaks of how the experience was decisive for his later career as a scientist and member of the armed forces.

Being a Boy Scout is a good thing if you want to do something for your country. That is the program's underlying message, which (as the host explains in closing) can easily be confirmed by asking Kent and Søren, the two Boy Scouts who spent five months together in the camp within the Greenland ice sheet. The host then rises from his chair and slowly walks toward the wall, stopping next to a large portrait of U.S. president John F. Kennedy. As the camera zooms in on the portrait, patriotic music plays as the following quotation from President Kennedy rolls down the screen:

> Training and associations of boy scout life are invaluable to the individual development of young men and to the quality of community life. More than 20 million persons have taken an active part in the scouting movement since its foundation. It has been a most valuable influence in our national life, and I know that future energies of the boy scout movement will add even more to the vigor and strength of our nation.[32]

Numerous channels and networks across the United States showed *The Big Picture* programs, also as reruns, and the program mentioning the two scouts in Camp Century may well have been seen by millions of Americans throughout the 1960s. And the television programs did not stand alone. The articles and other written contributions by Søren

Gregersen and Kent Goering played a role in promoting the army and the Scout Movement. As Søren's diary indicates, an important part of their stay was spending many hours writing to readers back home about their experiences in Camp Century.

In the winter of 1960/1961, every Danish newspaper worth mentioning ran at least one article about "Søren Scout" living in the ice sheet. Most published several. The large Danish daily *Politiken* had something of an advantage, though, having been the first to make Søren Gregersen an offer he couldn't refuse, when its editor Paul Hammerich contacted him almost immediately after the proverbial orange had landed in the young man's turban. Søren sent Paul Hammerich eight articles from Camp Century, but to Søren's chagrin, Hammerich exercised his editorial right to alter and abridge the contributions, and only four articles reached the readers of *Politiken*. Still, there is no doubt that they were much read and often quoted, for the newspaper did a professional job on the layout, including many striking illustrations and photographs and running the articles as a sort of series under a consistent headline: "The Scout in the Ice Cap."[33]

The articles by the two Boy Scouts helped reinforce the narrative about Camp Century that the authorities, both American and Danish, wished to promote: the story of the camp as an unconventional, exciting scientific facility, with negligible focus on its implications for U.S. military strategy. The accounts from the two young men contained not the slightest hint of Camp Century having anything to do with plans for a gigantic American nuclear missile base under the surface of the ice sheet—which is by no means surprising, since they had no inkling of the plan. The camp's small nuclear reactor was primarily cast as a step in the potential peaceful utilization of atomic power in Greenland, which is precisely how it was represented in the vast majority of articles penned by Danish journalists.

Thus, both versions of the story about the Boy Scouts at Camp Century underscored how the United States was building upon a crucial, rock-solid foundation not only of moral values but also of technological and scientific knowledge.

6

U.S. MILITARY R&D ON
THE NORTHERN FRONTIER

RESEARCH AS MILITARY GROUNDWORK
AND CONTROL

According to the 1951 Defense Agreement, the United States had almost unlimited authority within a number of precisely specified "defense areas" in the western part of Greenland, most notably centered around Thule Air Base, Kangerlussuaq (Søndre Strømfjord, or "Stromfjord"), and Narsarsuaq. When the Americans wanted to carry out research or testing outside these defense areas, the picture was very different. The relevant projects—typically more than thirty each year—first had to be described in terms diplomats could understand, then cleared with the U.S. State Department, and finally submitted for approval to the Danish authorities by way of the U.S. embassy in Copenhagen. A reasonable attempt to summarize the extensive American research and testing activities is found in the Pentagon's own explanation: that its aim was to provide the three branches of the American military with the knowledge of geophysical conditions in the polar regions needed to give them "an ability to predict and even to control the environment in which [they are] required to operate."[1]

At the end of World War II it was already clear to influential figures associated with the upper echelons of the U.S. defense community that research was an absolutely crucial precondition for the nation's military operations in the air, on land, and at sea. One such figure was the geographer Paul Siple, who also played a prominent role in the preceding chapter on the Boy Scouts in Camp Century. In 1947, he wrote a memorandum to high-ranking officers in the U.S. Armed Forces that held a clear warning: "We must realize that in reality the Arctic Ocean is a Mediterranean Sea in the middle of the populated land masses of the northern hemisphere. We must make certain that this sea cannot be crossed by an enemy who considers it less difficult than we do. Technically the research and development to cope with the Arctic will not be insurmountable if we put our minds to it."[2] Siple, who had strong connections to the U.S. Army, also believed that although at the time the Soviet Union had a sizeable lead in Arctic research and warfare, a decade of vigorous efforts would enable the United States to surpass its opponent in both fields. Siple's call to action and similar assessments soon energized American geophysical research, and a good deal of the polar research most relevant to the military took place in Greenland. It is quite telling that in the American military parlance of the time Greenland was sometimes referred to as "the world's largest island and stationary aircraft carrier."[3] During the Cold War, substantial amounts of R&D funding were allocated to geophysical research, the motivation being that the American defense planners of the 1940s and 1950s saw a number of unsolved geophysical problems as the greatest threat to new (and future) weapons systems. They were concerned not only with the reliability and efficiency of bomber aircraft, land-based missiles, and submarines armed with nuclear warheads but also with the combat capabilities of soldiers operating in polar conditions.[4]

One such problem was a lack of knowledge about gravitational-field variations in the Arctic—knowledge that would enable remote-controlled missiles to hit their targets precisely enough to be effective. Another crucial field of study was the phenomena around the magnetic north pole, particularly how the magnetic field reacted to solar-flare events. Understanding these better would make it possible to keep vital communication channels open between Thule Air Base and various military command centers in the United States. Yet another promising aspect lay in the huge advantage the U.S. military would have in Greenland if they became able to control the weather and operate in any conditions. These few examples hint at the enormous scope of potential work awaiting geophysical scientists in Greenland. They also indicate why the budgeting authorities were highly receptive to messages like the one delivered in 1947 by Charles Piggot, the chairman of a geophysics panel under the Pentagon, who declared that "all progress in the geophysical sciences sooner or later will contribute to the strengthening of the nation's strategic and tactical potential." And to make sure even his dimmest readers would get the message loud and clear, Piggot added that "in many cases the development of weapons and countermeasures are predicated on advances in certain phases of geophysics."[5]

Although the Danish foreign ministry would hardly have been aware of the statements and reports from Siple or Piggot, the Danish diplomatic community was undoubtedly aware that most of the tests and experiments the Americans wished to conduct outside the defense areas were primarily military in nature. This knowledge was best kept out of the public sphere, however, as it had the potential to provoke debates in the Danish political landscape about the aim of a massive American presence in Greenland, a situation that any incumbent Danish government, whatever its composition, would rather avoid.

Fortunately for the parties in power during this period, the frequent negotiations between the United States and Denmark on the framework and substance of America's experimental activities were conducted within a very small, very official circle—at least until 1962. The participants in these negotiations were civil servants from the Danish Ministry of Foreign Affairs, officials from the Danish embassy in Washington, and representatives of the American embassy in Copenhagen.[6] The setup made it relatively easy for the Danish government to control the flow of information about the American requests, and little news of the negotiations ever really became common knowledge. The Danish authorities did have a practice of sending military liaison officers to the various defense areas, as well as a "scientific advisor" who, tasked with staying abreast of the ongoing American research projects, would report to the Danish liaison officer at Thule Air Base. Still, as early as the mid-1950s the American experimental activities were already so numerous and so far-flung that in practice it was impossible to keep track of everything that was going on.[7]

Given this situation, and given the considerable pressure America exerted on Denmark to have its applications approved and get the permits required to proceed, the Danish Ministry of Foreign Affairs almost consistently chose to place its trust in the United States. This meant giving the go-ahead for all American project proposals unless for some reason a specific project looked like it might create serious problems for Danish foreign policy—as was indeed the case when the Americans first raised the idea of building a nuclear-powered camp in the Greenland ice cap. The small circle of applicants and decision makers combined with the absence of independent bodies to monitor the process meant that it held little risk for those involved.

Between 1951 and 1959, until the building of Camp Century began, most of the American science projects were based either at Camp Tuto, which was located near the rim of the ice cap, 23 km (14 miles) from Thule Air Base, or at Camp Fistclench, located all of 350 km (220 miles) inland on the ice cap, almost due east of Camp Tuto. The better part of this research was headed by the U.S. Army Snow, Ice, and Permafrost Research Establishment (SIPRE), which in 1961 merged with a similar army body under a new joint name: the Cold Regions Research and Engineering Laboratory (CRREL).

Among many other things, the American research projects conducted in Greenland during the 1950s investigated the properties of upper-layer ice and its suitability as a transport surface for heavy vehicles; new methods of identifying dangerous glacier crevasses; ways to predict and counteract episodes of the weather phenomenon known as "whiteout"; the construction of camps on or in the ice sheet; and the vulnerability of such camps to attacks with conventional, chemical, and bacteriological weapons. The research was conducted by scientists from military and civilian organizations and ran the gamut from the most basic studies to concrete military applications. In practice, projects often mixed elements from both ends of the scale. From the late 1950s onward, the U.S. Air Force took over more and more research

Research projects in and around Camp Century

Project 6	Trafficability
Project 13a	Constructions and snow
Project 14	Water supply
Project 23a	Whiteout studies
Project 23b	Snow fences
Project 25a	Deep vertical drilling using electrically heated drill bit
Project 25b	Examination of drill cores
Project 33	Foundation laying
Project 40	Model testing with beams of snow
Project 42	Movements of the ice
Project 44	Cooling well for the reactor

As listed by the Danish scientific adviser, who visited the facility in the summer of 1961. The first three projects were being conducted by the U.S. Army Chemical Corps, the rest by CRREL.

Source: Report by Vagn Buchwald, dated August 25, 1961; UM 105.F.8, Archive for the Ministry of Foreign Affairs, Danish National Archives.

projects in northern Greenland, mainly because the justification for Thule Air Base came to be primarily linked to the Ballistic Missile Early Warning System (BMEWS), constructed in 1958–1960. The colossal BMEWS radar network had stations in Alaska, the United Kingdom, and Greenland (near Thule) and was designed to protect the North American continent against nuclear-armed missiles crossing the Arctic, launched as surprise attacks from the Soviet Union.[8]

There is no space here to recount all the research projects conducted on the ice sheet in and around Camp Century during its existence. We therefore dedicate the remainder of this chapter to describing, in some depth, three very different projects that involved both civilian and military scientists but nonetheless mainly had a military aim. Although all three projects had been initiated before Camp Century was built, they all relied on Camp Century as an important inland research station on the ice sheet. In the next chapter, we will also take a detailed look at another major research project that posterity has recognized as perhaps the most important scientific legacy of Camp Century: the drilling of an ice core to the very bottom of the ice sheet, aimed at obtaining new knowledge about Earth's climate in prehistoric times.

WHITEOUT: WHEN NATURE ERASES ALL THE LINES

There is no Danish term for the meteorological phenomenon the Americans call "white out," which is a sort of wiping-out of all contours, resulting when the influx of light from the sky has the same value as the light reflecting off the snow [so that no shadows are cast]. All contours disappear; it is not possible to see the horizon. . . . Having no view of the horizon causes dizziness, and one loses the sense of what is up and down. If one bends down to pick an object up off the snow, one will often end up on one's back. . . . Losing one's sense of equilibrium also afflicts pilots, who therefore find it difficult to keep their planes on course and maintain full control of the aircraft. More than one pilot has flown his plane down vertically, directly into the snow, believing he was actually ascending.[9]

This description is from the Danish geographer Børge Fristrup's book about the Greenland ice cap, published in 1963. Whiteout is not a new phenomenon, of course, but one well known to the peoples of the Arctic. Nonindigenous participants in the famous Arctic expeditions of the late 1800s and early decades of the 1900s also became acquainted with whiteouts, learning the hard way to bring all activities to a halt and simply wait it out. The U.S. military's new interest in this natural phenomenon, beginning early in the Cold War, was based on more than merely wishing to understand whiteouts. They also wanted to learn how to control and counteract them. The massive time and effort being allocated to scientific geophysical research and polar engineering made military decision makers optimistic about achieving their goals.[10] At the same time, the U.S. military was developing a variety of technologies to modify weather in temperate climates, making it all the more logical for them to try them out in Greenland, too.[11]

As early as 1954, whiteout studies were one of the pivotal fields of endeavor in the American research catalog for Greenland. In the summer of 1954, the U.S. Army's polar research unit, SIPRE, sent a caterpillar-track expedition more than 290 km (180 miles) inland, across the ice sheet, to set up a small radar station simply referred to as Site 2 (near the location of the later Camp Fistclench). The expedition experienced several whiteouts while traveling inland, enabling the mission's scientists to measure thousands of fog and mist droplets to determine the physical properties of the events. Their studies showed five different types of whiteout. In subsequent years, follow-up studies examined details of the frequency and duration of fog formations and of prevailing temperatures and wind conditions during the occurrence of the different whiteout events.[12]

In the late 1950s, scientists had embarked on a program of specific experiments, albeit on a very modest scale, aimed to counteract whiteouts with a variety of chemicals. The most frequently used method consisted of bombarding whiteout fog with mortar grenades filled with tiny crystals of silver iodide. This technique, called "cloud seeding," builds on a theory that the silver iodide crystals will act as condensation cores for the microscopic particles in the whiteout fog. Researchers also tried spreading dry ice (carbon dioxide in solid form) from balloons to reduce whiteout. None of the experiments showed convincing results.[13] The need for further research was clear.

A new and more comprehensive round of testing began in the summer of 1963, this time at a testing ground laid out roughly 800 meters (900 yards) upwind of Camp Century, to the southeast. A wanigan (sled-mounted living quarters) served as a headquarters and field laboratory during the experiments, which took place in August and September, northwestern Greenland's main whiteout period. The most important equipment consisted of (1) helium-filled balloons that could lift the instruments taking temperature and particle-density measurements to various heights in a whiteout fog; (2) CRICKET rockets, designed for launch into a curving trajectory with a maximum height of 1.2 km (4,000 feet) and a maximum range of 5 km (3 miles); (3) tried-and-tested cloud-seeding substances such as dry ice or the organic compound phloroglucinol in powder form, lifted as the CRICKET's payload and released at a predefined point along the rocket's trajectory; (4) parachutes to give the rockets a soft landing after each use, enabling

FIGURE 6.1 Preparing to send up cloud-seeding material (dry ice) near Camp Century in 1963. The launching platform, built on a one-ton sled, is seen here with an operator (holding a CRICKET rocket) and a number of dry-ice containers. Experiments aiming to mitigate "whiteout" episodes were part of a comprehensive U.S. Army campaign to investigate weather-modification techniques, including experiments in rainmaking, fog dissipation, and cloud formation.

reuse; and (5) equipment to register visibility in the area before and after the seeding operation.[14]

This equipment was used in 1963 to perform 135 launches between August 8 and September 4, a period with more than 60 hours of recorded whiteout. Only a handful of rockets crashed, the rest being partially or completely reusable. In most cases the seeding agent was dry ice, but quite a few experiments were based on phloroglucinol, which was easier to store and therefore quicker and easier to use.[15]

The American scientists concluded, based on their many experiments, that the CRICKET rocket and auxiliary equipment worked well, and that "it can . . . penetrate fog or clouds to heights of about 4000 ft, and it is less expensive to buy and operate" than any other system tested. Unfortunately, this did not mean that whiteout-related problems had been resolved. On the contrary, the final lines of the report are almost painfully frank:

> It was concluded that better tracking and observing techniques are needed to determine if the seeding is effective. Monitoring a test from the ground in a dense low fog is very difficult for two reasons: (1) It is very easy for the observing personnel to get lost in the fog when they attempt to track a seeded section. (2) Air movement, even in so-called calm, is variable and one cannot be certain which way the seeded area is drifting.[16]

All in all, this was a discouraging conclusion for the U.S. Army. After a decade of intensive and expensive research, the scientists, not to mention their military leaders, were obliged to recognize that as in so many other respects, the Greenland ice sheet was a formidable opponent when it came to whiteouts. During the Arctic summer, the ice cap gave rise to numerous whiteout episodes, a phenomenon that had proved impossible to combat effectively with technological means. The American dream of subduing the natural world in Greenland remained a dream, at least for the time being. The Canadian historian of science Janet Martin-Nielsen, who has studied the topic in depth, has described the result of the research project as follows:

In the end, the only lasting approach to polar whiteouts was the earliest and simplest: to halt (or greatly reduce) ground operations and divert air operations for the duration of the whiteout. From the point of view of military strategy, waiting for polar whiteouts to pass was clearly imperfect—and yet this approach provided the only sustained solution to the phenomenon. It was ultimately rooted in practicality and functionality; it did not involve an effort to overcome and control nature, but rather consenting (and even submitting) to nature's course.[17]

Martin-Nielsen describes the United States' attempts to battle whiteouts as "the other cold war." While the "first cold war" had the United States pitched against the Soviet Union in an arms race with nuclear weapons, as well as open military confrontations with conventional weapons in so-called proxy wars, the "second cold war" was a battle against Nature. The U.S. military attempted to win over Greenland's special climate conditions by means of research and technology, but in vain. Martin-Nielsen's phrase "the other cold war" shows that the Cold War was something more and something other than merely a nuclear arms conflict between two superpowers. The Greenland ice cap was an important and intractable player, one often forgotten or overlooked in historical analyses of the conflicts of the Cold War. Beginning in the 1960s, the Americans gradually relinquished their one-sided aspiration to control and manipulate the harsh Greenlandic environment as they saw fit. This resulted in what Martin-Nielsen describes as a "détente with nature" and "strategic cooperation with that space."[18]

RAILROADS UNDER ICE

If this winter's experiments [at Camp Century] yield the desired results, the Americans are prepared to begin next summer on continuing the project of installing a railroad, which running within an ice tunnel of about 200 kilometers is intended to connect the ice-city with the research base [Camp Tuto] established at the edge of the ice cap. . . . If there really proves to be a reality underlying the American plans—and so far we have no reason to disbelieve them—it opens up very interesting perspectives. However, we do not dare believe that some years from now, people will be able to take the Thule Express and ride under the ice sheet to Narssarssuak, then change to a train headed for Julianehåb.[19]

Through this tongue-in-cheek description, which appeared in *AG* (*The Greenland Post*) in April 1960, the Greenlanders were able to read for the first time that railroad tests were taking place at Camp Century, the "city under the ice," whose very existence had only recently become publicly known in Greenland and Denmark. Just a few years earlier, no one in their right mind would have imagined that Greenland might ever have railroads, much less regular train service. Then, after the construction of Camp Century was revealed, it seemed like nothing was impossible. Apparently the Americans could do anything, and they seemed to have unlimited resources, so why not a Greenlandic railroad, too? Anyone who knew anything about polar conditions was acutely aware that transporting personnel and materials from Camp Tuto to Camp Century along the surface was slow, risky, and expensive. If it really could be done on a railroad inside the ice sheet, the advantages would be enormous, and in the longer term similar rail-tunnel projects might even benefit the whole island.

When discussing why the U.S. Army was prepared to spend massive amounts of money on investigating whether a facility like Camp Century could operate over a prolonged period of time, and whether railroads embedded in the ice sheet were more than just science fiction, an important underlying motivation was Project Iceworm, described in chapter 3. The viability of this brainchild of the U.S. Army's think tank—a gargantuan atomic-deterrence network, installed under the ice cap in northern Greenland—was inextricably linked to the outcomes of a variety of efforts investigating the properties of the ice and the opportunities it offered. As early as 1955, the Americans had made their first attempts at rail-based installations inside the ice, although on a very small scale and with a very specific practical purpose. The test was conducted close to Camp Tuto, where the U.S. Army engineers made a tunnel in the ice sheet by digging and drilling almost horizontally into the vertical ice wall that made up the rim of the ice cap at that particular location. The aim of the exercise was partly to study how long such a tunnel might last and partly to provide good storage spaces for frozen food and other materials, including diesel fuel for the engines that kept the camp running. By the end of 1955, the crew had succeeded in digging an ice tunnel 152 meters (166 yards) long with a cross-section of 7 by 2 meters (a good 7 by 2 yards). Over the following years the tunnel was extended several hundred meters and expanded internally with the excavation of several large storage rooms. Initially the crew used compressed-air jackhammers to excavate, removing the ice debris on sledges. Later on, heavier excavation equipment was used, and the crew began removing the larger volumes of ice on tip wagons that ran on rails.[20] The setup was described by Børge Fristrup, mentioned earlier in this chapter, whose position as scientific advisor to the Danish liaison officer at Thule Air Base kept him abreast of American experiments and testing at Camp Tuto in 1955.

Evidently the setup worked smoothly, as Fristrup wrote nothing negative about it. A few years later, preparatory tests also went on at Camp Fistclench, but the real proof-of-concept testing took place at Camp Century under the auspices of an extremely diverse project group called "Trafficability," alluding to the ability of the terrain or surface to allow certain types of vehicle to cross. The group covered all manner of projects that had to do with transport upon or inside the ice sheet. The tunnel railroad was one of these projects, headed by the U.S. Army Polar Research and Development Center, which in 1960–1961 had dug out a horseshoe-shaped, covered tunnel several hundred yards from the main facility's tunnel network. The Danish scientific advisor at the time, a civil engineer named Vagn Buchwald, visited the camp in August 1961 and wrote a report to Denmark's liaison officer at Thule Air Base right after his visit:

The ring tunnel has various curve radii, and the plan is to cover the floor with different types of snow, planks, and mats, after which the

FIGURE 6.2 This little rail system, installed near Camp Tuto, proved extremely efficient for transporting loose material out of the ice-sheet tunnel during its excavation in 1955.

floors will be tested for durability of use with heavy-duty vehicles, particularly 5-ton trucks. Like the other Century tunnels, this tunnel has been excavated with a Peter Snow Miller, which has proved to be incredibly useful up here. It carves its way into the snow, leaving behind a trench that is 2.7 m wide and 1.2 m deep, and in ideal conditions it can handle up to 900 m³ per hour, corresponding to an average of 4.5 m [of trench dug] per minute.[21]

Buchwald's report also noted that the Americans had drawn some conclusions on the basis of the preceding year's initial testing, which, although preliminary, were quite positive: (a) that rail traffic seemed to be possible on the evenly ascending and fissure-free portions of the ice sheet; (b) that floors covered with aluminum mats were durable under wear and tear, though quite costly; (c) that untreated virgin snow could not carry heavy loads but that snow that has passed through a Peter Snow Miller and recrystallized had outstanding properties; and (d) that after one year of use, the plank floor in the main tunnel was remarkably well preserved.

The U.S. Army's scientists and engineers were clearly interested in shedding light on the possibilities of rail- and wheel-based transport inside ice tunnels. From the outset it had been a military goal to build the installations embedded in the ice sheet, which would serve to camouflage and protect equipment and personnel. The preliminary conclusions were uplifting, but given the lack of detailed knowledge about the tunnels' long-term viability in view of the natural movements in the ice, constructing major tunnel systems in the ice cap was still an uncertain proposition. One problem about building down in the ice is that its various layers do not move at the same speed, which rapidly leads to tunnel deformation. The studies near Camp Tuto (before Camp Century was set up) had led to the preliminary conclusion that subsurface tunnel systems in the ice *could* be built but that they would have a limited lifetime—a conclusion that later proved to be premature, in part because of the pressure the scientists were under to achieve applicable results.[22]

The conclusion on the railroad tests at Camp Century was also cast in an overly optimistic light, at least in the official eight-page press release featuring six large photographs and issued by the U.S. Army's press office in the summer of 1963. Its fanfare-worthy heading, "TOP OF THE WORLD RAILROAD," is followed by a somewhat convoluted explanation about the long series of tests conducted by the U.S. Army engineers and scientists at Camp Century. The text emphasizes that the studies were based on the expectation that at some point the army would be building "a sub-surface railroad track network in a polar ice mass." The test railroad at Camp Century, built in August 1962, was of

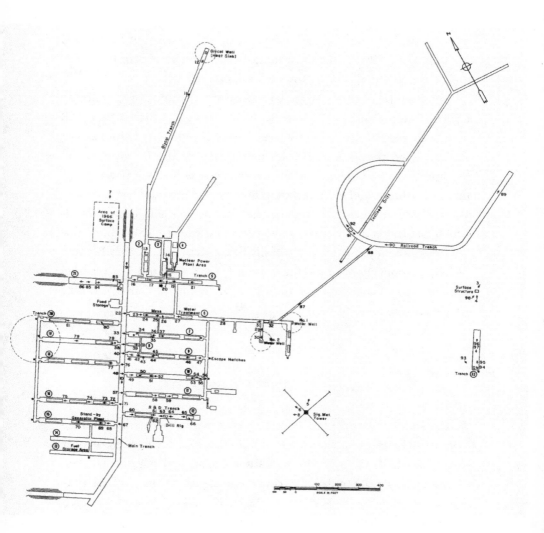

FIGURE 6.3 Plan of Camp Century, which in addition to the camp, shows the position of the railroad tunnel (top right), "the Glycol Heat Sink" (top left), and the "Sig. Met. Tower" (bottom right).

the same type and standard specification as many stretches of railroad in the Midwestern United States—an area noted for accommodating the bulk of the army's underground missile silos, which were being constructed at the same time. The army had therefore hired consultants from the Spur and Riding Constructors Company, Inc., of Detroit to evaluate the test results. Perhaps it is hardly surprising that the company's president, Paul J. Suarka, heaped on the praise, not least in his final analysis: "This is the most fantastic railroad system in the world and . . . its potential . . . is beyond consideration."[23]

The army thereby attempted to represent the results of the railway tests at Camp Century as an unparalleled success, which it may well have been, seen in isolation. However, before any visions of hundreds or perhaps even thousands of miles of railroad in the ice sheet could become a reality, potential investors—be they public or private, military or civilian—had to be certain that the tunnels would last for many years. However, long-term integrity had not been tested in the project, which had lasted a mere one to two years and had studied a short tunnel, where small problems could easily be corrected before they became serious complications. Like the results from the Camp Tuto tunnel tests, the conclusions on the railway experiments at Camp Century were by no means definitive.

BUILDING INSIDE THE ICE SHEET

Geologists specializing in ice have long known that the ice cap covering Greenland behaves like a viscous liquid. This means that any holes or cavities made in the ice will gradually collapse, first deforming, then shrinking in size, then disappearing completely. The speed of the process depends on the temperature in the cavity and on the cavity's depth and location, chiefly its distance to the ice cap's rim. The huge number of research projects conducted by the U.S. military on the ice sheet had many different purposes, but a particularly important theme for the army was how to build installations under the surface of the ice sheet using ice as a construction material. The grand idea behind Project Iceworm was founded on the feasibility of establishing major subsurface tunnel systems in the Greenland ice sheet. The army's most important camps near or on the ice sheet were Camp Tuto, Camp Fistclench, and Camp Century. Among other purposes, these facilities served as a sort

FIGURE 6.4 The horseshoe-shaped tunnel near Camp Century, built in 1961–1963, was used for experiments with subsurface truck and rail transport inside the ice sheet. The aim was to test the ice's load-bearing capacity and deformation when systematically subjected to substantial pressures.

of preliminary study to test the applicability of the basic concept. It is a fair claim that in many ways Camp Century itself was one large research project, the primary goal of which was to demonstrate a sufficiently long lifetime for tunnels similar to those envisioned for Project Iceworm, if and when it came to fruition. Obviously, however, this does not mean we believe any individual scientists at Camp Century would have known anything about Project Iceworm, given that the project was classified top secret.

Between 1954 and 1959 an extensive series of tests was carried out at Camp Tuto and Camp Fistclench, where certain walls in a number of excavated cavities and tunnels were marked with a squared-off net of colored string, making it easy to observe and measure deformation as a function of time and temperature. These experiments clearly demonstrated that the deformation occurring in the Camp Tuto system, on the rim of the ice sheet, was more pronounced than in the Camp Fistclench system further inland, just as expected. It turned out that the temperature of the ice was a critical parameter: the higher the temperature, the greater the deformation over a given time span. Researchers found that the temperature definitely had to be kept below freezing, at −6°C at the least (corresponding to 21°F). Otherwise a cavity would rapidly implode.[24]

How long could an ice cavity last without needing major repairs? That was the critical question for the U.S. Army in 1957. It needed a quick answer, so the scientists and engineers at Camp Tuto were urged to speed up their investigations as much as possible. The idea they conceived was to load so much snow onto the roofs of the cavities being studied that it would correspond to many years of snowfall. The hope was that the extraordinarily heavy load would enable them to examine in one single season the equivalent of five years' worth of deformation under normal load. On the face of it the conclusions of this experiment were positive: it really was possible to build ice caves and tunnels below the surface for military purposes. The lifetime of the cavities was estimated at ten years, provided the temperature was kept sufficiently low.[25] In 1957, one of the army scientists concluded his report on an optimistic note: "The author can visualize . . . that an entire airbase could be built under the ice with the exception of runways."[26]

There can be little doubt that these preliminary research findings played a crucial role in the decision to develop Project Iceworm and initiate the planning and construction of Camp Century, which, when completed, gave the U.S. Army a unique opportunity to study ice deformation in a complex tunnel system with internally connected tunnels of varying width, depth, and ventilation efficiency. Tunnel deformation quickly proved to be a major issue, perhaps even the greatest practical problem the camp had to deal with. In the previous chapter, we described the Danish Boy Scout Søren Gregersen's experiences during his stay at Camp Century in the winter of 1960/1961, shortly after the facility was completed. He remarked in his diary on the well-known problem "that the tunnel sides are coming in, the floors coming up, and the ceiling

FIGURE 6.5 Network of colored strings on the wall of a tunnel in Camp Tuto. The experiment began with rectilinear squares, but after ten months the effects of ice-sheet deformation were clear.

coming down." Gregersen and Kent Goering, his fellow Boy Scout from America, helped measure the deformation in various tunnels to see "how much the roof of the tunnel has come down." They found that it was already "becoming a problem, that mess tunnel."[27]

Bearing in mind that at this point the mess tunnel was just a few months old, Goering and Gregersen's observations did not bode well. Many of the other tunnels were faring little better. Measurements of the distance between floor and ceiling in the main tunnel (designated 1, or Main Street) and in Tunnels 6–21 showed reductions of up to 1.2 m

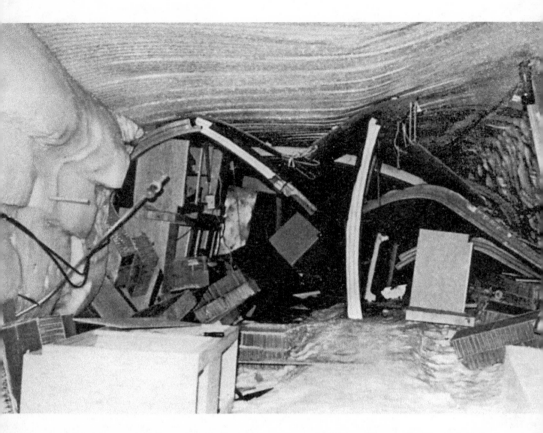

FIGURE 6.6 In the summer of 1969, three years after Camp Century had been definitively closed, a U.S. Army photographer took this picture of a compressed personnel tunnel in the erstwhile "city under the ice," celebrated as a technological marvel just a few years before.

(4 feet) in just a single year, from the summer of 1962 to the summer of 1963. Since the original height of Main Street was 8.5 m (28 feet), this was a significant reduction. The most pronounced deformation took place in the tunnels where temperatures were highest—the mess tunnel and the tunnels with personnel quarters, where the heat given off by electric radiators, light bulbs, various electrical apparatuses, and numerous human bodies was so great that the ventilation systems could not keep up. While the temperature in Main Street fluctuated between −40°C and −10°C (−40°F and 14°F) in the summertime, during the same period

the temperature range in Tunnel 20, which housed personnel barracks, varied between –15°C and –5°C (5°F and 23°F).[28]

The situation was even worse in Tunnels 2–5, which housed the reactor, the heat exchanger, the turbine, and the generator. This was not only because of the significant heat emissions but equally because these tunnels, as described earlier, were much wider than the others. The roof was therefore under significantly more load, leading to even greater compression and sagging. The deformation problems quickly reached a point where it was necessary to "shave" or scrape considerable amounts of snow off the walls and ceilings of the most severely affected tunnels at regular intervals. The Danish geologist Valdemar Poulsen, who also served as the scientific adviser to Denmark's liaison officer at Thule Air Base, reported after his visit to the camp in August 1963 that "by this time the risk of the roof above the reactor caving in had become so serious that Major Meeken decided to stop it. This was done on July 9, 1963."[29] The arduous task of removing the reactor from Camp Century began at once and was completed the following year, in a process we cover in detail in chapter 8.

The final report about Camp Century, submitted by Elmer F. Clark—commanding officer of the U.S. Army Engineer Arctic Task Force and the Greenland Research and Development Program from 1955 through 1957—concluded that it would be necessary to scrape and remove approximately 15,000 cubic meters (530,000 cubic feet) of snow and ice from the tunnel system each year to maintain its original dimensions, adding:

Even for a camp no larger than Century, the snow trimming effort is burdensome, and particularly so if done with hand tools alone. Efficient mechanical equipment systems capable of trimming the trenches and transporting the snow out of the camp could be developed. However, the cost would be high (estimated 0.4 million dollars), and this expensive development effort would not be justified unless a number of subsurface installations such as Century were planned.[30]

Based on the experience gained from Camp Century, in 1962–1963 a select group of high-ranking military officers close to Robert McNamara, the serving U.S. secretary of defense, decided to shelve Project Iceworm. The Danish historian Nikolaj Petersen concludes that one reason Iceworm was abandoned was that Camp Century had demonstrated that subsurface tunnel systems in the Greenland ice sheet were far more difficult and expensive to build and maintain than anticipated.[31] Maintenance in particular—the constant shaving and scraping of tunnel walls and then transporting the heaps of ice to the surface—was costly in terms of manpower and money. And as Clark had stated, without many miles of tunnels to keep up in "a number of subsurface installations such as Century," the heavy investments in more efficient maintenance technology would not be justified.

Ultimately the U.S. Army was obliged to draw the same conclusion about tunnels below the ice as it had about whiteouts above the ice: Greenland's ice cap was a virtually unbeatable opponent. The best strategy was to prepare to coexist with it, rather than attempt to subjugate and control it.

7

THE COLD WAR AND
CLIMATE RESEARCH

THE MILITARY ORIGINS OF
CLIMATE RESEARCH

In chapter 6 we described three examples of research projects in and around Camp Century that were clearly relevant from a military perspective. On the face of it, the project to which we now turn our attention seems quite different. Could anyone imagine a more peaceable, archetypal scientific project than drilling through the Greenland ice sheet, top to bottom, in order to meticulously study every inch of the extracted ice core? The answer, perhaps somewhat surprisingly, is "yes." While it is true that many modern observers would consider ice-core drilling a textbook example of pure science, as a pursuit primarily aimed at gaining new insights into climate variations of ages past, this has not always been the case.

From the early 1920s to the mid-1940s, the Arctic went through a brief warm spell, relatively speaking.[1] The average temperature rose, and warmer ocean currents began circulating in the North Atlantic, the Norwegian Sea, the Barents Sea, and the waters around Greenland. Warmer water brought cod and other new species to the region, and Greenland's cod catch swelled.[2] The warming trend also sparked new speculations about an escalating "greenhouse effect" caused by carbon dioxide emissions from human activity. In the mid–twentieth century, however, very few researchers concurred with the British climatologist Guy Callendar in thinking that the two phenomena might be linked.[3]

Despite widespread skepticism about the idea of manmade climate change, many scientists were interested in understanding climatic changes and their impact on all sorts of human endeavors in the Arctic. In the late 1940s, a Swedish-born meteorology professor at the University of Chicago, Carl-Gustav Rossby, noted that Russian steel-hulled ships were navigating certain parts of the Arctic Ocean and that Scandinavian fishing vessels had resumed their activities around Spitsbergen—which they had given up centuries before, in the late 1500s. Rossby concluded, "These things can only be the result of a long period change in the climate of the high latitudes."[4] Rossby's message reached his fellow meteorologist Howard B. Hutchinson, who worked for the U.S. Navy and was a member of an influential body under the Pentagon called the Research and Development Board. Hutchinson in turn underscored the importance of climate change research to military operations: "If officers in the Navy become cognizant of these long period changes that are going on in the polar regions [we would have a] much better understanding of long range climatic changes and could possibly use them to our advantage in national defense."[5] As noted, few scientists espoused Callendar's idea that climate changes in the Far North could be a result of human activity. The phenomenon nevertheless caused concern among high-ranking officers in the U.S. Armed Forces in the early years of the Cold War. In certain military circles that were thinking strategically about the growing military threat in the North, across the Arctic Ocean, the ability to predict climate changes in the Arctic was seen as almost on a par with the ability to forecast the weather reliably. The U.S. Air Force knew Arctic missions could be extremely dangerous because making trustworthy weather reports was impossible, while the U.S. Navy obviously had a crucial interest in knowing the extent of the sea ice along the coasts of Greenland and in having some idea of how it was expected to develop in the years and decades ahead. The U.S. Army was no less interested in knowing whether conditions on the permanent ice cap would undergo any significant changes in the short or long term.[6]

Scientists working for the U.S. military argued that they would be able to learn much more about climatic conditions particular to the Arctic in the past, present, and perhaps even the future if they drilled down into the ice sheet to the greatest possible depth. Their argument was scientifically sound, as the permanent ice sheet is one huge archive of past climate conditions, where the snow deposited in individual years can be identified in the same way as annual growth rings in a tree trunk. They reasoned that the thickness of the individual layers and their content of air bubbles, dust, radioactivity, and so on would speak volumes about climate variations in Greenland over the past few hundred years or more. And with such knowledge, one might, with some degree of certainty, be able to predict changes in the future. These were the thoughts brewing in the American military establishment around 1950, when two individuals who would have a huge impact on climate research for the remainder of the twentieth century arrived on the scene.

NEW IDEAS ABOUT ICE

In a frequently quoted article from 1949 entitled "Trends in Glaciology in Europe," the Swiss glaciologist Henri Bader lamented the sad state of his research field, a state that at the time had prevailed for several decades.[7] Researchers, particularly from Switzerland and Sweden, had long been studying how Alpine and Scandinavian glaciers advanced and receded, enabling them to observe how ice constantly shapes the landscapes that surround it, partly by eroding the substrata and partly by depositing materials transported in or by the ice. This had led researchers toward a theory—today the general consensus—that over the past couple of million years Earth has undergone dramatic changes in its climate, with successive ice ages (glacial periods) covering large regions of the planet in a thick mantle of ice alternating with interglacial periods when much of the ice melted away. However, as Bader noted in his article, the problem was that such empirical observations could not tell scientists anything about the internal structure of the ice, nor could they explain why and how glaciers moved. Passing his harsh judgment on glaciology in 1949, Bader explained:

> The first quarter of our century saw an orgy of hypothesizing on con-
> ditions prevailing inside glaciers and on the mechanism of glacier flow
> based on quite insufficient observational and experimental data. Pub-
> lished observations on firn [glacial snow too fresh to have been com-
> pressed into ice] and ice petrography during this period are amazingly
> few. One can browse through volume after volume of *Zeitschrift für
> Gletscherkunde* without finding any reference to grain size, air bub-
> bles, etc., of the ice of countless glaciers otherwise described in detail.[8]

The root cause of this deplorable situation, according to Bader, was that no scientists specializing in the numerous new disciplines that had solidified during the preceding century—physics, chemistry, biology, geology, petrology, mineralogy, and meteorology—regarded ice as a significant part of their research field. The situation now called for an interdisciplinary effort that would see numerous scientists, each specializing in their own field, collaborating to generate new knowledge within a field Bader found it appropriate to call "physical glaciology." He concluded his paper by outlining a large-scale research project he wished to see realized, promising "results of theoretical significance and practical importance" if his wish came to pass.[9]

The U.S. Army seems to have agreed with Bader's point of view. The following year, in 1950, the U.S. Army Corps of Engineers established a new science institute called the Snow, Ice, and Permafrost Research Establishment (SIPRE), which was dedicated to interdisciplinary research. One of its leading scientists was Henri Bader. SIPRE's mission was, of course, military in nature: "to provide the military establishment with data which can be used as a basis for increasing the efficiency of military operations in an environment dominated by the presence of snow, ice, seasonally frozen ground and permafrost."[10] However, the body of fundamental facts and experience regarding ice and snow was so full of holes that many of the problems facing the military had to be approached as basic scientific research. As the next section will show, Bader made the most of the opportunities that presented themselves in 1954 during preparations for the International Geophysical Year of 1957–1958.

Even as Bader was beginning to carry out his ideas of a new interdisciplinary research program financed by the U.S. military, on the other side of the Atlantic another scientist had begun to think deeply about ice. His name was Willi Dansgaard, and he was a Dane. He had earned his master's degree in physics in 1947, specializing in biophysics at the University of Copenhagen, then spending a year at the Magnetic Observatory in the town of Godhavn (today, Qeqertarsuaq) in Greenland before getting a job in 1948 at the Meteorological Institute in Copenhagen. He was therefore well versed in biophysics and geophysics when he

FIGURE 7.1 Willi Dansgaard's simple experiment from 1952, set up on his lawn in Herlev, northwest of Copenhagen, during sustained precipitation from a warm front passing over the area on June 21–22. In his book *Grønland—i istid og nutid*, Dansgaard describes this experiment as a "miracle" that "kick-started forty years of intriguing work": "The miraculous aspect is that I began by chance to collect rain under these unusually propitious circumstances." What made the circumstances so remarkably favorable was the unusually large and consistent weather system that had developed precisely in those two days during which Dansgaard—serendipitously—decided to set up the beer-bottle sample-collection array in his garden.

returned to his old stomping grounds at the university's Biophysical Laboratory in 1949 to help the lab set up and use a new mass spectrometer for nuclear-physics analyses of various gas samples. Funding for the expensive apparatus had been allocated by the committee tasked with distributing Denmark's share of the Marshall Aid program the United States had sent to Western Europe in the wake of World War II.[11]

It soon turned out that the demand for nuclear-physics analyses on the mass spectrometer was not as large as the funding body had expected. This gave Dansgaard ample occasion to use the new apparatus to test out a wild idea that had come to him on the afternoon of June 21, 1952, as he sat looking through the window into his suburban garden, where rain had just begun to pour down. What started as showers gradually developed into solid rainfall, thanks to a heavy low-pressure system, a "warm front," that took more than twenty-four hours to pass. To while away the rainy hours, Dansgaard brought out an empty beer bottle, inserted a funnel into the bottleneck, and placed his arrangement in the garden. At roughly one-hour intervals he went out and emptied the bottle's contents of rainwater into a fresh glass or pot, continuing to do so until it stopped raining.

Most people know that water—rainwater included—consists of oxygen atoms (O) and hydrogen atoms (H) that hook up into water molecules (as H_2O). The interesting detail in our context is that oxygen atoms come in two varieties, or isotopes. The lighter of the two (O^{16}) is by far the most common; the heavier isotope (O^{18}) is quite rare. Using a mass spectrometer it is possible to separate the two isotopes and thereby measure the concentrations of O^{18} and O^{16} isotopes and the ratio between them.[12] The gist of Dansgaard's wild idea was to use the mass spectrometer at the Biophysical Laboratory to measure whether this ratio in his collected rainwater samples changed as the weather front passed overhead. Based on the meteorological principles he had learned while working at the Meteorological Institute, he knew that the rain precipitating first in a warm front had normally condensed at the highest altitude, where the temperature is lowest. He therefore guessed that his first samples would contain relatively fewer heavy O^{18} isotopes than the rain falling later from the lower, warmer cloud layers. That proved to be exactly what the spectrometer measurements of his rain-water samples showed. In other words, Dansgaard concluded, by measuring the relative concentrations of O^{18} and O^{16} in a raindrop it is possible to determine the temperature in the mass of air where the drop was formed.

In 1954, after a couple of years spent studying precipitation in the form of rain, snow, and ice collected in many different locations around the globe, Dansgaard was so convinced by his research that he dared to publish his findings in a British journal called *Geochimicha et Cosmochimica Acta*.[13] The main result cited in his paper was that the relationship between the concentrations of O^{18} and O^{16} in a given unit of precipitation (its $O^{18}:O^{16}$ ratio) can be used as a temperature indicator, at least in regions with temperate or polar climates. Extrapolating this idea: since an ice sheet was a product of precipitation that fell untold ages ago, it would be possible to "read" the temperatures and thus to "read" the climate changes occurring across many millennia, if only one could measure the $O^{18}:O^{16}$ ratio down through the Greenland ice cap or the Antarctic ice cover. Such was Dansgaard's hypothesis in 1954. As he wrote many years later: "I was absolutely sure this was a good idea, perhaps the only really good one I've ever had. On the other hand, I've been able to suck on this idea for the rest of my life."[14]

Dansgaard would have liked nothing better than to get to work on the idea immediately, but he realized a project like his would require such enormous resources that he would have precious little chance of making it happen in any foreseeable future—unless he got incredibly lucky. Still, he boldly concluded his article by optimistically predicting: "An investigation will be undertaken as soon as an opportunity [presents itself]."[15]

THE EARLY ICE CORES FROM GREENLAND

Generally speaking, scientific and military interests in the geophysical disciplines, including ice-core research, had a remarkable tendency to

FIGURE 7.2 Willi Dansgaard at Camp Century in the summer of 1964, extracting snow samples from the wall of a tunnel between the reactor and railway tunnels. "It was unpleasantly cold, –22°C," as he wrote in his scientific autobiography from 2000. "The mean annual temperature here is –22°C. I sliced 48 samples for isotope measurement along a vertical line, which, according to Steve Mock [of CRREL] represent the annual layers, running top down, from 1959 up to and including 1953."

coincide in the early years of the Cold War. Willi Dansgaard and some of the other scientists who became involved in such work had no military connections at all, while others like Henri Bader were directly employed by military research institutions and cultivated fields and disciplines that were benefiting civilian research as well as the military community. Yet others attempted to play down or conceal their military objectives.

A good case in point is the International Geophysical Year (IGY) of 1957–1958, which in many contexts was touted as a purely scientific project.[16] The IGY initiative was backed by international scientific associations, and its research projects had been prepared by scientists working together internationally, sometimes even across the Iron Curtain separating East and West. Behind the scenes, however, the U.S. military had brought its interests to bear right from the start, bolstering the IGY's scientific façade.[17] Many of the scientific projects conducted under the auspices of the IGY were spinoffs of or follow-ups to specifically military projects—including the ice-core drilling program in Greenland and the Antarctic, originally proposed by Henri Bader and others and accepted by the American selection committee as an IGY project.[18]

The ice-core project was run by SIPRE, part of the U.S. Army, and headed by Bader. It could therefore avail itself of logistic and technical support from the army, but in practice it received help from all three branches of the U.S. Armed Forces, and the help was sorely needed. The first ice-core drilling operations in Greenland were planned to take place at Site 2, a small military radar station located some 350 km (217 miles) east of Thule Air Base, in the same area where Camp Fistclench had been built in 1957. The site was so far inland that in practice the U.S. military was the only organization capable of transporting the necessary personnel and equipment to the remote location high on the ice cap. The actual drilling operations, led by the project's leader Robert Lange and lead driller Jack Tedrow and assisted by a group of students from Dartmouth College in New Hampshire, used a commercial rock-drilling rig that had been equipped with a drill head designed for cutting ice. Using this equipment, in 1956 the team had already reached a depth of 305 meters (1,000 feet) and extracted an ice core of that length, although in sections that were just a few meters long and had a diameter of about 10 cm (4 inches). The following year, they succeeded in bringing to the surface a core that was 411 meters (1,348 feet) in length. Like the 1956 core, this new core was marked and stored in a specially constructed subsurface ice tunnel. Because the 1957 core was longer than its predecessor and also superior in quality, its material was used for most of the analytical work done in the years that followed.[19]

The person responsible for registering, storing, and analyzing the ice core was Chester C. Langway Jr., a specialist in glaciology. The analytical work was much like examining a tree trunk, and it began straightaway, in 1957. The process consisted in investigating the annual variations in the snow/ice core's "year rings": determining mass, analyzing the air in the air bubbles, analyzing crystal formations, measuring the number of dust particles in the ice, among many other factors, all stated as a function of depth. Running the full range of analyses was an enormous task, and although partial findings were regularly published, the final results were not available until 1967, a decade later.[20] By that time, ice-core researchers had access to a much longer specimen: the core from Camp Century.

DRILLING OPERATIONS AT CAMP CENTURY, 1960–1966

The construction of Camp Century in 1959–1960 gave the American scientists a research station that was more easily accessible, better equipped, and more comfortable than Site 2. As soon as Camp Century was operational, most of the research projects at Site 2 were moved there, including the ice-core project. The actual drilling at Camp Century was done under the leadership of the physicist and chief of technical services Lyle Hansen, with the assistance of the drilling engineers Herbert T. Ueda (mentioned in chapter 5, by the Boy Scouts) and Donald E. Garfield, all associated with the Cold Regions Research and

Engineering Laboratory (CRREL). Langway, mentioned earlier, handled the registration and analytical work.[21] When Hansen and his team began drilling at Camp Century in 1960, they used a newly designed thermal drill that had been tested at Camp Tuto, near the edge of the ice sheet. The mechanism in the new drill replaced the customary diamond drill bit with two electrically heated, ring-shaped pole shoes that simply melted their way down through the ice. Progress was fairly good for the first hundred meters or so, roughly corresponding to the firn layer, where densification has not yet closed all pores in the material. But below that depth the ice was so solidly compacted that the meltwater collecting in the circular hole could no longer penetrate the ice and diffuse. It had to be collected in a purpose-built container in the drilling array while the drilled-out ice core was transported to the surface in a metal cylinder. For every 10 feet, the entire drilling array, which weighed a good 400 kg (900 pounds), had to be hoisted to the surface, emptied, then reinserted and lowered into the drill hole.

This was an arduous, time-consuming process. Twice the team was forced to abandon a drill hole and start from scratch because the drill bit froze solid and the cable ruptured when attempts were made to hoist the array to the surface. The first time this happened, in 1961, the team had reached a depth of 186 meters (610 feet). Their second attempt in 1962 went slightly better, as they reached 238 meters (781 feet) before losing the drilling array. They embarked on a third attempt in 1963, and when the summer season ended they had reached 264 meters (866 feet). Before leaving the site, to counteract compression the team filled the drill hole with a fluid that had the same density as ice (a mixture of diesel and trichloroethylene), then sealed the hole until drilling could resume.[22]

At the very same time, Vagn Buchwald, then the Danish scientific adviser to Denmark's liaison officer at Thule Air Base, was visiting Camp Century for briefings about the American experiments going on there. In his report about the visit, Buchwald gave a detailed description of the difficulties that had beset the ice-core project, concluding with a somewhat pessimistic prediction: "The hole was temporarily sealed off for the summer, but the plan was to continue either in the

autumn of 1963 or the spring of 1964 (which now, after Century's closure, seems to be long way off)."[23] Fortunately, his prediction did not
come to pass. Although in autumn 1963 Camp Century was closed for
the winter, it opened again as a summer camp in 1964. This meant that
Lyle Hansen and his team could continue drilling in the same hole,
moving on from the depth they had reached in August 1963. Working
on through the 1964 summer season and the spring of 1965, they
reached a depth of 535 meters (1,755 feet) in mid-1965. At this point, they
still had another 800 meters (2,600 feet) to go—and an unknown number of months or years before they would reach the bottom of the ice
sheet. The situation was untenable. The ice-core team would have to
make some radical changes for the better if it wanted to turn a looming
fiasco into the success everyone was anticipating.[24]

Why was progress so slow? The reasons were many and varied. All
sorts of problems, large and small, kept cropping up and requiring
solution. The main factors were probably the difficulty in removing the
copious amounts of meltwater from the drill hole and the way the mixture of diesel oil and trichloroethylene continuously corroded the ever-
lengthening cable holding the whole drilling array. These conditions
resulted in the leaching of significant quantities of matter and substances, which accumulated as a thick layer of insulating sludge around
the drill head, rendering its ice-melting mechanism ineffectual. To
make matters worse, the built-up sludge had a tendency to clog the
pump installed to remove the meltwater. All these complications
reduced drilling speed at depths below the upper firn layer to about an
inch per minute during active drilling time—and much of the time the
drill was not active at all: each time a ten-foot section had been drilled

FIGURE 7.3 The drill rig in Tunnel 12 at Camp Century. Willi Dansgaard and two
other Danish scientists stayed at Camp Century in the summer of 1964, but they were
not allowed to see the drilling operation. As Dansgaard drily remarked in one diary
entry (also included in his abridged English autobiography): "Sounds as if some military secrets are involved. What a shame, because the ice core must be very interesting
for measuring stable isotopes. What the Americans are going to do with the ice core is
unknown."

out, the team had to haul the drilling array up to the surface, empty out the ice-core section and meltwater, then lower the array back down into the hole.[25]

Consequently, in July 1965, the worn-out thermal drill head was replaced by an electrically powered mechanical drill with rotating drill blades that operated at 225 rpm. From there on, the work proceeded as a standard fluid drilling operation, a technique often applied with good results in oil drilling. At Camp Century, however, the lower part of the drill hole was not filled with oil but with glycol, a substance able to dissolve the ice chips sheared away. The fluid was hoisted to the surface for emptying every time the drill had descended another 4.5 meters (15 feet) into the ice, pressing an ice core of equal length into the extraction cylinder fitted above the drill head. Once the new drill's teething troubles had been resolved, the electromechanical array lived up to its full potential, drilling as much as 15–20 centimeters (6–8 inches) per minute. This meant that on July 2, 1966, after just one more year of drilling, the team reached the bottom of the ice sheet, a depth of 1,390 meters (4,560 feet).[26]

This was a milestone for the American ice-core project, as the Danish scientific advisers for that year—Børge Fristrup and Svend E. Bendix-Almgreen—reported to the Danish liaison officer at Thule Air Base in August 1966. Indeed, in their opinion the completion of the Greenland ice core was probably the most momentous achievement of all the scientific projects at Camp Century. And truth be told, the American team had spent six long years on an endeavor fraught with disappointments and beset with problems, working hard and living ensconced in one of the most isolated places on Earth before finally achieving their ambitious goal: extracting the first entire ice core from the ancient Greenland ice sheet. Two years later, the same team, using the same electromechanical drill head, successfully reached the bottom of the Antarctic ice sheet at Byrd Station, complementing the 1,390-meter ice core from the Arctic with a 2,164-meter (7,100-foot) sister core from the Antarctic. In 1966–1967, both ice cores were transported to a large frozen-storage facility at CRREL headquarters, located on the

U.S. Army base in Hanover, New Hampshire, where Chester Langway would be heading the analytical work that lay ahead.[27]

ANALYZING THE CAMP CENTURY ICE CORE

The drilling has been carried out as a core-drilling operation, and they now have a virtually continuous series of drill samples from top to bottom. In connection with the drilling itself, the density of the ice has been determined and a macroscopic description made, but otherwise the drilled core has been scrupulously preserved for later analysis. . . . Thus far no analyses have been conducted of [the Camp Century ice core], the intention being first to discuss which analyses and analytical methods will be most appropriate. Considering the fact that this is the only complete drill sample from the ice sheet in existence, it is important to make the utmost of the drill sample.[28]

This is what Fristrup and Bendix-Almgreen wrote about the Camp Century ice core in their August 1966 report, succinctly summing up the challenge facing Chester Langway at this point. Theoretically, the scientists could subject the samples to a multitude of tests, but Langway did not have unlimited funds at his disposal. Nor did he have the necessary scientific equipment or, indeed, enough specialists to conduct the countless tests other ice-core researchers might desire. With these problems in mind, Langway decided to delegate as much work as possible to scientific institutions in the United States and abroad who were eager to handle one or more of the desired tests and who could document the expertise their task would require.[29]

There was certainly no lack of tasks. As early as 1962, Bader had drawn up a list of all the potential ways in which he would like to examine and test ice cores. Then, four years later, in September 1966, the U.S. Army made a summary of the points it considered most important. These included the examination of "volcanic dust index horizons, cosmic dust

FIGURE 7.4 Chester C. Langway Jr., the leading ice-core expert at CRREL, conducting a preliminary examination on a light table of a section from the newly completed (and ultimately successful) ice-core drilling operation at Camp Century. Seen here in Tunnel 12; the year is 1966.

concentrations, atmospheric pollution studies, stable isotope investigations, compositional analysis of fossil atmospheres [in air bubbles in the ice] and climatological correlation of ice core data with historically recorded events."[30]

This was just the sort of "opportunity" Willi Dansgaard had been waiting for. He seized the chance that presented itself, later coming to play a key role in the investigation of the Camp Century core. From the project's inception, Dansgaard had taken a keen interest in the ice-core drilling in Greenland, and as a recognized expert in measuring ratios of concentrations of O^{18} and O^{16} in rain, snow, and ice, he had already received some samples in 1958–1959 of a 411-meter (1,348-foot) ice core from Site 2. Even though the samples were not long enough for him to determine conclusively the temperature variations dating back to the time when the lower part of the Site 2 core had been formed, they still enabled Dansgaard and his scientific team to develop further the technical equipment at their laboratory in Copenhagen. This in turn enabled them to determine, with great accuracy and certainty, the seasonal variations in the $O^{18}:O^{16}$ ratio, even in the bottommost and therefore extremely compressed portions of the ice core. One of Langway's employees, the American isotope expert Samuel Epstein, carried out corresponding measurements on certain sections of the Site 2 ice core, which Langway had prepared for study. Somewhere along the way, however, the two Americans disagreed on how to interpret the results, and so their findings were not published in full until 1967.[31] We do not know whether the disagreement (or potential dispute) between Langway and Epstein precluded Epstein from being considered when the time came to carry out a corresponding analysis on the entire Camp Century core or whether he was not interested in the job. At any rate, the enormous undertaking ended up with Willi Dansgaard and his group in Copenhagen.

As soon as Dansgaard learned that the American drilling team at Camp Century had reached the bottom of the Greenland ice sheet in July 1966, he contacted Langway, with whom he had corresponded several years earlier. The Dane offered to conduct a complete analysis of the $O^{18}:O^{16}$ ratio for the full Camp Century core, working from his Copenhagen laboratory and, not least, with Danish funding. This was an offer that Langway could not, and did not, refuse. For one thing, he could hardly have imagined that an assignment of that magnitude could be completed anytime soon. For another, he was soon convinced that the scientists at Dansgaard's laboratory in Copenhagen were up to the task. Throughout the 1960s, Dansgaard had succeeded in building a geophysics research group in which each member was a specialist in their own field while at the same time supplementing the others, creating a close-knit constellation that had earned international recognition as providers of reliable isotope analyses. In this way, the positive international trend in the geophysical disciplines had also come to Copenhagen, a location where influence from military funding was practically nonexistent. By virtue of his fine reputation and his good relations with various funding bodies, first and foremost the Carlsberg Foundation, Dansgaard was also able to obtain the considerable amounts of money necessary for his group to undertake the enormous task.[32]

Back in the United States, Langway was doing the painstaking job of preparing the specimens on his own, so it was slow work getting the ice-core slivers ready for dispatch to Copenhagen. To expedite the process, Dansgaard sent a few of his people to Langway's laboratory in Hanover. So it was that in 1967, the Danish chemist Jørgen Møller spent several months in New Hampshire, helping cut specimens. He was later followed by Sigfus Johnsen and Henrik Clausen, both experts in mass spectrometry and also key members of Dansgaard's research group. Their visits to the United States not only speeded up the transfer to Copenhagen of the physical specimens from the Camp Century ice core, compared to the original plan. The personal interaction also built trust, respect, and friendship across the scientific cultures on the two sides of the Atlantic—the significance of which can hardly be overestimated in light of the decades-long collaboration that followed between Langway and Dansgaard.[33]

Although the first Camp Century ice-core specimens did not reach Dansgaard's laboratory until January 1968, the Danish scientists were able to present their first preliminary results in August of that year. What is more, because the team was completing their analytical work almost as fast as the specimens from the United States were arriving, they were able to publish a widely cited article in *Science* as early as October 7, 1969, featuring a temperature graph that went 100,000 years back in time.[34] Based on mass-spectroscopy measurements of the respective concentrations of O^{18} and O^{16} isotopes in the ice in each of the roughly 1,600 samples—which represented the entire 1,390-meter-long Camp

Century core, top to bottom—Dansgaard and his colleagues were able to determine the average temperature in each of the time periods during which the snow in the samples had precipitated. The results were remarkable, showing temperature variations of up to 10 degrees Celsius, or 18 degrees Fahrenheit.

One of the great challenges was establishing the correlation between the layers from which the specimens originated and their age. Down to a depth of a few hundred meters it was easy enough to study the annual seasonal variations in the O^{18}:O^{16} ratio and determine the specimen's age with a high degree of certainty. Based on this, the research team had been able to work out a temperature curve for the last millennium, and it was highly consistent with more traditional sources on historical climate information, such as studies of tree rings, pollen analyses from ancient bogs, and carbon-14 analyses of wood and other organic materials. However, at much greater depths, meaning in much older samples, there was a problem: it was no longer possible to distinguish seasonal variations in the O^{18}:O^{16} ratio, making it impossible for the scientists to determine the age of the ice using this straightforward method.

Dansgaard and his team were therefore obliged to apply a model that calculated the age of the ice as a function of depth—a model that, obviously, had to be in accordance with all of the empirical facts, notably the well-established correlation between sample age and depth in the upper few hundred meters of the ice sheet. Taking the lead on this part of the job was Willi Dansgaard's long-time colleague Sigfus Johnsen, who took his cue from a model of glacier movement elaborated by the British physicist John Nye. According to Nye's model, every part of the ice moved horizontally at a constant speed, even as it was slowly compressed downward as a result of the ever-increasing weight and pressure from the overlying layers. Johnsen modified Nye's model to take into account the fact that the bottommost *central* part of the ice cap logically must be compressed directly against the bedrock and therefore must be horizontally immobile. Johnsen therefore assumed that the various layers in the lower ice strata would have varying speeds of horizontal movement, which decreased toward the bottom center, where eventually there would be no movement and hence a speed of

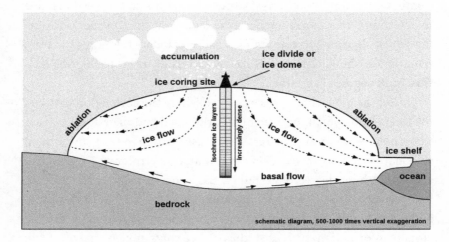

FIGURE 7.5 Sigfus Johnsen's "sandwich model" illustrates a vertical cross-section through the ice sheet, from west to east. Arrows running from the top indicate the direction of movement, downward and outward. Only from the topmost point is the ice movement vertical. Around the vertical central line ("the ice divider"), horizontal lines indicate ice layers gradually stretching and thinning as they descend. Near the bottom of the ice sheet each annual layer is just fractions of a millimeter thick, whereas in the upper layers of the firn they are some 0.5 meters (18 inches) thick. This means the vast majority of annual layers are densely packed deep down in the ice. The ablation zone is the coastal region where there is a net loss of ice, while accumulation typically takes place at the upper part of the ice sheet.

zero. Johnsen's "sandwich model" allowed him to estimate correlations between the depths of the ice-core specimens and their age. In his estimation, the very deepest portions of the ice sheet around Camp Century were some 120,000 years old.[35]

The publication of the Camp Century temperature graph confirmed results from similar cores extracted from deep below the seabed, which also enable scientists to reconstruct temperature variations far into the distant past. Both methods showed that ice-age cycles lasting tens of thousands of years have followed a saw-toothed curve, indicating relatively rapid heating followed by the gradual return to a cooler climate. From a geological-chronology perspective, the warmer interglacial periods (like the one we now live in, which gave rise to human civilization) are

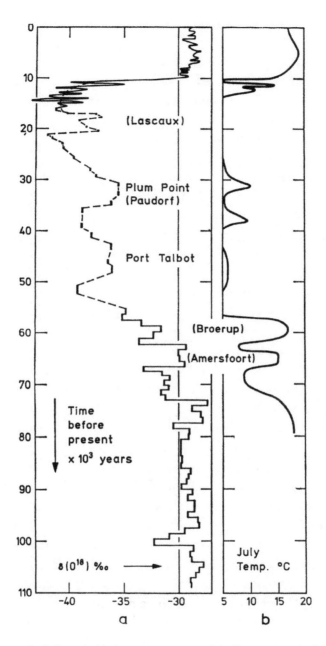

FIGURE 7.6 The left graph (a) shows variations in δ (O¹⁸)—a measure of the O¹⁸:O¹⁶ ratio—in the Camp Century ice core, indicating temperature variations for more than 100,000 years back in time. The other graph (b) shows historical temperature variations calculated from Dutch pollen studies. European names of abrupt warm and moist periods, so-called interstadials, are given in parentheses. These graphs appeared in the article by Dansgaard et al. published in *Science* in 1969.

short-lived phenomena. Some scientists emphasized that despite John-sen's sandwich model, there was still some uncertainty in dating the deeper layers of the Greenland ice core. As a result, well into the 1970s, deep-sea sediments were still yielding the most reliable results on Earth's changing climate in prehistoric times.[36]

Nevertheless, the results from the Camp Century ice core were hugely important to climate research because they substantiated climate variations occurring in a period much closer to our own time. Examples are the Little Ice Age (c. 1400–1700); the preceding, warmer Medieval Climate Optimum around the turn of the last millennium (c. 900–1200); and the cold period during the Iron Age, a few centuries BCE. People were also impressed at how science was now able to describe certain climatic variation for which dating had previously been highly uncertain—including the many longer and shorter periods of milder weather during the most recent Ice Age—with a degree of detail that few had even dared to imagine.

The fruitful collaboration between Langway's and Dansgaard's research teams continued over the ensuing years. Furthermore, they later began to work with a Swiss group headed by Hans Oeschger, whose carbon-14 laboratory was able to measure the CO_2 content of the bubbles, which were tiny pockets of air captured in the ice cores. This allowed them to correlate temperature variations in bygone eras with the atmospheric content of carbon dioxide at the time, an important part of assessing the scope and impact of manmade climate change. It is also worth mentioning that in the 1970s and 1980s they were able to secure funding for a number of new ice-core drilling projects in Greenland (referred to as DYE, GISP, and GRIP) that were partially carried out with a Danish-developed lightweight drill (ISTUK) that proved extremely well suited to the task. These projects took place at various locations closer to the ice cap's north-south dividing line, where the ice is thickest. The resulting ice cores enabled researchers to confirm all their analytical results from the Camp Century core. What is more, scientists could now distinguish climate variations even further back in time and also link certain variations to cataclysmic prehistoric volcanic eruptions.[37]

FROM COLD WAR TO CLIMATE RESEARCH

Taking a broader historical view, it is ironic that the Cold War, which suddenly made planet-wide devastation a real possibility because of the huge stockpiles of nuclear weapons in the East and West, also directly facilitated the founding of modern climate research, the object of which is to understand Earth's climate in order to protect the planet as we know it. Paul N. Edwards, an American historian of technology, has described the surprising links between atmospheric nuclear testing in the 1950s and early 1960s and modern-day climate models and climate-surveillance systems.[38] Immediately after the first experimental nuclear detonation ever, the Trinity Test on July 16, 1945, in the New Mexico desert, it was clear that radioactivity had spread across a huge area via the atmosphere. Increasingly powerful nuclear devices set off at higher altitudes increased the spread of radioactivity, which was one of the reasons the U.S. military chose to move its testing to small, remote islands in the Pacific Ocean. But here, too, the dispersal of radioactive fallout was much greater than expected, motivating the United States to initiate a global monitoring network at its military bases across the globe—a network, incidentally, also seen as an opportunity to track nuclear testing by the Soviet Union.[39]

One of the earliest and most striking results of the U.S. monitoring initiative was the discovery that the circulation taking place in the upper layers of the atmosphere (the stratosphere) was much greater than anyone had imagined. This meant that emissions into the atmosphere of radioactive material and gases like carbon dioxide can spread globally, going far beyond local or regional impact. As a result of this, in the 1950s researchers seeking a better understanding of global circulation patterns began developing computer models to describe the dynamics of the atmosphere. Meanwhile, numerous meteorologists and data specialists were using that era's new, albeit by modern standards very primitive, computers to forecast the weather. A leading figure in these efforts was John von Neumann, a Hungarian-American mathematician and computer scientist who envisioned computers someday being able

FIGURE 7.7 From left to right, Willi Dansgaard, Chester C. Langway Jr., and Hans Oeschger celebrating a new triumph in 1981: the successful extraction of a complete ice core (of 2,037 meters/6,683 feet) from the Greenland ice sheet at the DYE-3 radar station. The drilling operation was part of the comprehensive Greenland Ice Sheet Project (GISP), a long-term initiative cofunded by research councils in the United States, Denmark, and Switzerland.

FIGURE 7.8 Today, many of the ice cores from the Greenland ice sheet are kept at the Niels Bohr Institute, part of the University of Copenhagen. This section is from the DYE-3 ice core, near the very bottom of the ice sheet. Note the thin layers, reminiscent of the annual rings in a tree trunk. Each layer holds information about climate conditions in the distant past.

to make "an infinite forecast."[40] Although we have not realized Neumann's dream yet, there is no doubt that scientists pursuing climate research would never have made as much progress as they did had it not been for the extensive efforts in the field of geophysical research during the Cold War.

Another conspicuous irony is that research into the environmental effects of potential nuclear warfare gave rise to the idea of a "nuclear winter," which in turn opened many eyes to the ways that human activities and behavior can inadvertently affect the climate of the entire planet. A "nuclear winter" is the hypothetical scenario that will arise if multiple nuclear devices of a certain size are detonated at the same time. In addition to the catastrophic damage caused by the blasts and by the subsequent radioactive fallout, the scenario envisions the injection of so much soot into the atmosphere that it would block the rays of the sun and lead to the rapid and significant cooling of Earth's surface. Here, too, some of the early climate models—which were in fact models of global atmospheric dynamics—were used to produce various shocking and hotly debated scenarios for a planet-wide nuclear winter. Scientific research into nuclear winters ended along with the Cold War, around 1990, but by that time it had already played a part in forming our perception of humankind's potential for affecting Earth's climate.[41]

The story of the Camp Century ice core is another good example of how the Cold War and climate research coincided. Initially, the ice-core project was a military endeavor aimed at improving operational

capabilities in the exceptional environmental conditions of the Arctic, based on descriptions of long-term variations in the region's weather and climate. It ended up making significant contributions to our understanding of temperature variations over extensive time spans and of the correlation between human carbon emissions and climate changes. In one sense, the 1966 ice core marked a turning point in geophysical research in Greenland and a shift in our understanding of Greenland. In scientific terms, from the late 1960s onward the research done in Greenland gradually began to change from serving almost exclusively military objectives to comprising a wide range of scientific projects, including a heightened focus on prioritizing environmental issues.[42]

Greenland also gained a new status during this period. Early in the Cold War, the United States mainly regarded Greenland as a critical piece of the puzzle of U.S. security policy and technological infrastructure—in the military parlance of the late 1940s, it was "the world's largest . . . stationary aircraft carrier." Throughout the 1970s, it became increasingly common to think about Greenland as a fragile and finely tuned ecosystem that had to be protected rather than exploited. That particular shift in mindset is one reason why the story of Camp Century would soon take on an entirely new dimension, as discussed at length in our final chapter. But let us first move on to chapter 8, where the world, at least for a time, would bid farewell to "the city under the ice."

8

LEAVING THE ICE SHEET

A Lingering Farewell

BREAKING NEWS ON JUNE 7, 1964

"U.S. will remove reactor in Arctic. . . . After spending millions of dollars to install a nuclear reactor inside the Greenland ice sheet and operating it for less than three years, the Army has decided to haul it out." These were the introductory lines by the well-known *New York Times* journalist Walter Sullivan, who on June 7, 1964, broke the news in the U.S. media that Camp Century had been slated for removal. Since 1960, the newspaper-reading, television-viewing public had heard time and again about America's immensely important nuclear-powered military camp in the Arctic and about the colossal efforts it had taken to build it. Now, lo and behold, the army was going to bring the reactor out and decommission the entire facility! Many Americans found this message surprising, almost shocking, and demanded an explanation. The remainder of Sullivan's article was dedicated to explaining the necessity behind the change of plans: "The immediate reason for the decision, which was announced several days ago, is that the reactor is being squeezed out of existence. The inexorable compression of Arctic snows, heaped one upon the other, turns the snow to ice and is shrinking the reactor tunnel."[1]

Sullivan presented the story as a perplexing scoop, but the facts were not new at all. As early as 1961 in Walter Cronkite's televised reporting from Camp Century, allusions had been made to the ice tunnels' tendency to shrink, and the *Popular Science* article published in 1960 (described in chapter 4) referred to tunnel maintenance as the camp's greatest operational challenge by far. Probably the majority of viewers and readers had taken little note of these remarks, instead feeling confident that the undaunted, innovative engineers of the U.S. military would find a solution to the problem.

By the same token, the announcement that the nuclear reactor at Camp Century had completed its tour of duty in Greenland and earned an honorable discharge could hardly qualify as a sensational news flash. The removal of the reactor had already been decided the previous year. While we cannot say whether it had been communicated to the wider American public, the decision had certainly been mentioned in Danish newspapers as early as the spring of 1963, at which time it was also disclosed to professional circles interested in commercially exploiting nuclear power. On April 5, 1963, the Danish daily *Berlingske Tidende* asked the question: "Atomic Oven to Be Dismantled?" Their reference for the question was that "many Americans now believe this part of the project has yielded the desired insights."[2] Further, in November 1963 the North Jutland broadsheet *Aalborg Stiftstidende* reported: "World's Most Northerly Nuclear Reactor Goes Cold." As the newspaper described it, the Americans had realized that "the continuing battle against the formidable forces of nature would require an effort that did not tally up with the scientific gain."[3]

Even though news of the reactor's decommissioning and the ensuing winter shutdown of the camp had already leaked, Sullivan's brief article still held some value as news. He went beyond stating that the reactor was being removed because of the ice sheet's relentless movement and resulting tunnel deformation and beyond affirming that the army had already harvested the results it intended to obtain when installing the reactor there in the first place. Both these conclusions were too facile for a veteran of critical journalism like Sullivan, who also worked at one of the world's most well-reputed newspapers. Cutting to the chase, he concluded: "Camp Century has largely served its purpose. . . . Today such bases seem less necessary. Polaris submarines that can keep constantly on the move beneath the polar ice appear far more reliable. Furthermore, the only large ice-covered region in the North is Greenland, which is Danish territory. The Danes are very sensitive about American activities there."[4] In these few sentences Sullivan hints at and sums up several conclusions reached by later and far more deeply probing investigations into the whole Camp Century project. Camp Century was an integral part of the American strategy for the northern polar region, the aim of which was to defend the North American continent against Soviet attacks across the Arctic by setting up American defense positions in Greenland, among other measures. The development of Polaris missiles, armed with nuclear warheads and launchable from submarines—a technology the United States also offered to share with the United Kingdom—meant that the polar-based strategy of launching nuclear devices from Greenland, as envisioned in Project Iceworm, had become redundant. In addition, the Danish "sensitivity" about Camp Century and "the concept of atoms" in Greenland had shown that perhaps it would not be quite so easy to convince Denmark to make the Greenland ice sheet available for the installation of "such bases," as Sullivan put it.

THE ICEWORM MELTDOWN

As explained in chapter 3, Project Iceworm had originally been developed by the U.S. Army think tank in the late 1950s as the army's pitch for a nuclear missile system that could strike targets in the Soviet Union from launching ramps concealed in tunnels embedded in the ice cap. The same think tank was also working to better understand the consequences of a potential nuclear war, which proved to be even more horrific than many analysts and civilians had envisaged in the early 1950s. Among other points, the think tank's analytical work proved that the advent of the hydrogen bomb and intercontinental missiles

would make it virtually impossible to limit or contain a nuclear conflict. In all probability, any nuclear war would develop exponentially
and result in rampant destruction or even global annihilation, not
least in the form of vast, uncontrollable clouds of radioactive fallout,
which would also hit America's heartland. According to the American
military historian William Baldwin, the U.S. Army think tank was
one of the first research institutions to analyze thoroughly the consequences of the American policy of massive retaliation. Nevertheless,
later assessments and analyses have largely confirmed its conclusion:
that nuclear retaliation by the Americans would be tantamount to
suicide.[5]

Shortly after John F. Kennedy was sworn in as president of the United
States in January 1961, the new administration in Washington decided
to scrutinize and reconsider the nation's entire atomic strategy thoroughly. Kennedy and his closest advisers had grown skeptical of how
much "security" actually lay in the New Look strategy laid down by
Eisenhower and Dulles, according to which the USSR risked immediate and total nuclear retaliation for any Soviet aggression directed at a
NATO member country or even any aggression against a country that
was "merely" nonallied. Their reassessment was partly motivated by
findings like those of the U.S. Army think tank—the very same body
that had conceived and developed Project Iceworm and was now issu-
ing words of warning.

To avoid throwing the world into nuclear holocaust by mistake, or as
a result of what might be a serious but limited provocation on the part
of the Soviet Union, Kennedy felt the need for a more flexible strategy,
one that would give a more balanced response to such provocation. In
other words, he wanted the U.S. president (also the commander-in-
chief of the armed forces) to have other options than being forced to
choose all-out nuclear retaliation. Such thoughts were already built
into Eisenhower's New New Look strategy from the mid-1950s, which
nevertheless still included the option of massive retaliation. Kennedy's
new "flexible response" doctrine made it quite clear that U.S. defense
policy would primarily be based on an adaptable retaliation system that
also required the military to be able to defend the United States using

conventional weapons. Nuclear retaliation was no longer an option, except as the very last resort.[6]

Kennedy's doctrine had the potential to occasion a steep rise in military expenses, calling upon leaders to prioritize existing and planned nuclear-arms programs. The fact of the matter was that all three branches of the U.S. Armed Forces were working on their own missile deployment systems: Minuteman (under the air force), Polaris (under the navy), and Iceworm (under the army). In 1961 and 1962, all three programs were exhaustively evaluated by a special Pentagon-appointed committee, which ordered studies of the respective technical and financial pros and cons. One small "study group" was led by Henry C. Ramsey, who was a member of the Policy Planning Council, an influential body under the U.S. Department of State. In February 1962, Ramsey and his group submitted a thirty-four-page report about the Iceworm system entitled "Deployment of NATO MRBM's in the Greenland Icecap." The authors concluded—probably based on the early optimistic results of tests conducted at Camp Tuto and Camp Century—that there were no technical problems relating to the project. They also stated that Iceworm offered several military and political advantages. First, the missile-launching system would be difficult if not impossible for the Soviet Union to destroy in a surprise attack, partly because the far-flung network would lie concealed beneath the surface of the ice sheet and partly because the ice would provide a certain amount of protection. Second, high-precision medium- or intermediate-range missiles (IRBMs) had already been developed, whereas intercontinental ballistic missiles (ICBMs) were not yet fully reliable. And third, according to the preliminary project outline the Iceworm network would be installed in an uninhabited area far from U.S. soil—more precisely, in northern Greenland's ice sheet. From there, Iceman IRBMs would be capable of reaching 90 percent of all important targets in the Soviet Union.[7]

Ramsey forwarded the study group's finished report to Deputy Secretary of State Foy Kohler, accompanied by a letter in which he concluded "that Iceworm has very attractive possibilities as a NATO system and that it is potentially possible to obtain Danish acquiescence and association in the system if further evaluation confirms that the military

FIGURE 8.1 Minuteman missile in 1963, shortly after a test launch from a reinforced underground silo, somewhere in the continental United States.

FIGURE 8.2 Corresponding test launch of a Polaris missile from a nuclear submarine in 1960. The U.S. Air Force's Minuteman system and the U.S. Navy's Polaris system prevailed in the internal rivalry among the three branches of the U.S. Armed Forces. The U.S. Army's project, known as Iceworm, was never realized.

premiums are as high as they now appear to be."[8] The letter went a step further than the report, which actually stated that the greatest difficulty facing Project Iceworm would probably be Denmark's "subjective aversion to all matters nuclear." If and when the project became public knowledge, the report reasoned, it would not be inconceivable that "the full force of neutralist and pacifist attitudes, which are latent in Denmark and Scandinavia, would be summoned against the concept" and that consequently the Danish government would have a difficult time harmonizing its acquiescence with its well-known policy of not permitting nuclear weapons in its "metropolitan area in peacetime." Still, as the report reassuringly added, "Denmark, however, might not apply this policy to Greenland." And its final conclusion: "If it could be clearly demonstrated that Iceworm would contribute materially to the survival of Denmark and her NATO allies, the Danes might take the plunge."[9]

The study group behind the report also made clear something that Walter Sullivan would later mention in his news article on the dismantling of Camp Century's nuclear reactor, namely, that considerable Danish opposition to Project Iceworm ought to be anticipated. As for the report, it attempted to show several strategies that might plausibly make the project more palatable and convince the Danes of its merits. If, for instance, the Danes could be brought to accept that Project Iceworm was an essential precondition for the joint kingdom's very survival, they might "take the plunge" despite their ingrained aversion to all things atomic. Another recommendation for overcoming Danish hesitation on this point was to have someone discreetly encourage Danish support for the view that Project Iceworm was necessary to guarantee the security of the entire European continent and to avoid the nuclear arming of West Germany. The study group also speculated on who this "someone" ought to be, in the event its recommendation was followed: it might be best if the United States exerted her influence in secret, then left the initiative to her European allies—while at the same time linking the proposal of Project Iceworm with Denmark's wish to join the European Economic Community.[10]

The report, released in forty copies, was part of the federal government's final decision-making process, which was headed by Defense

Secretary Robert McNamara. We know of no sources that shed light on how the decision was reached, but we do know the result of the process. Sometime in late 1962 or early 1963, McNamara made the final decision to shelve Project Iceworm and rely solely on Minuteman and Polaris. There is no doubt that factors such as technical problems, rivalry among the three branches of the U.S. military, and financial issues played an important role in the decision-making process. On the first count, technical problems with tunnel deformation were presumably a crucial aspect. They certainly had a strong negative impact on the financial profile of Project Iceworm, as the cost of ensuring tunnel integrity beneath the ice sheet's surface would be very high—an argument surely welcomed by the project's opponents in the navy and the air force.

On the other hand, the Danish historian Nikolaj Petersen, who has made important contributions to our knowledge about Project Iceworm, points out that Denmark's sovereignty over Greenlandic territory must also have been an argument that tipped the balance heavily to the "con" side when the project was weighed and found wanting. Petersen has argued that if Iceworm had been chosen as a high-profile American deterrence project, Denmark's position on it would have been enormously important. Even though Denmark may have had no prior knowledge of the project at all, when it was made public the small country would find itself between at least two rocks and a hard place, squeezed by its obligations to NATO, its wary nuclear policy (precluding nuclear weapons on Danish soil in the given circumstances), and its established propensity to back proposals supporting détente in the Baltic region and the Arctic. In Petersen's assessment, there is an extremely high probability, verging on certainty, that any Danish government coalition would have ended up saying "no" to a proposal that would turn northwestern Greenland into a NATO base with nuclear weapons. So, unlike the study group that analyzed the project, Petersen does not believe Denmark would have been prepared to "take the plunge" on Project Iceworm. He further assesses that the U.S. administration must have realized that their country could find themselves in a confrontation with a small but important NATO ally if it attempted to cajole or coerce Denmark into accepting the project.[11]

No official public announcements were made when Project Ice-worm was scrapped in early 1963. This was only to be expected, since officially the project did not exist at all. But because Camp Century must be seen as an important step along a Project Iceworm trajectory, it is logical that the scrapping of the project meant change for Camp Century. In terms of timing, it is unlikely that the summer 1963 decision to remove the reactor—heralding the facility's gradual shutdown—occurred at that time by chance.

GOING PUBLIC

Another thing that was only to be expected was the army's low-key handling of the impending closure of Camp Century. It was, after all, a prestigious project, and the army had gone to great lengths to convince large segments of the public in America, Denmark, and elsewhere that the camp effectively demonstrated its unmatched engineering prowess. But the army also had other factors to consider, including commercial interests in developing mobile nuclear reactors. This may be one reason for the following small-print news item, which appeared on February 21, 1963, in *Nucleonics Week*, the professional journal for commercial stakeholders and engineers in the nuclear-power business:

PLANS TO DISPOSE OF THE PM-2A REACTOR AT CAMP CEN-TURY, Greenland, have been disclosed by the Army Material Command. The Navy, it is understood, has expressed some interest in acquiring the 1500-kwe unit for relocation at an Antarctic base. AMC's decision to dispose of the reactor may be confirmation of reported plans for limiting use of Camp Century to the summer seasons or possibly closing it down. Also AMC has indicated that the two-year-old reactor has become too costly to operate in relation to the value of the data now being derived.[12]

These few lines show that tunnel maintenance was not the only costly aspect of running the camp. Operating the PM-2A reactor was expensive, too—and it may have been one of the three most important reasons why Project Iceworm was abandoned (besides the anticipated Danish opposition and the American need to reduce funding for

Low-level radioactive liquid discharge (volumes and radioactivity)
fed into the Greenland ice sheet in 1962

Date	Discharged volume (gallons)	Discharged activity (millicuries)
January 3	2,755	1.115
January 22	2,613	1.790
February 9	3,025	1.525
February 25	2,850	1.240
March 11	1,812	0.118
April 2	2,205	0.227
April 26	2,350	0.267
May 26	3,250	1.530
June 8	3,460	1.310
June 24	2,400	0.605
June 28	2,325	0.214
July 11	1,950	0.064
August 1	2,375	0.037
August 28	1,850	0.330
September 24	1,950	0.012
October 10	2,050	0.410
October 26	2,000	0.016
November 14	1,850	0.126
December 4	1,625	0.105
December 18	2,375	0.562
Total	**47,078**	**11.333**

Source: Clark (1965), 50.

nuclear missiles). The news must have reached Risø Nuclear Research Laboratory in Denmark soon after *Nucleonics Week* appeared, as the journal was always laid out on the appropriate shelf at Risø's in-house library. Naturally, the management and leadership at Risø were notified at once, as were the employees who, at regular intervals, had visited Greenland to inspect the Camp Century reactor: Robert Kayser and Frederik List (August 15–24, 1961), Povl L. Ølgaard (August 13–23, 1962), and Cecil F. Jacobsen (July 21–30, 1964).[13] During these inspection visits, the Danish scientists checked radiation levels at a number of measuring points in and around the reactor to verify that international threshold values were not being exceeded. They also checked to make sure the Risø-approved discharge of low-level radioactive liquid waste into a sinkhole in the ice (created specifically for that purpose) did not exceed the preset upper limit of 1.9 GBq (50 millicuries) per year.[14] The first set of measurements were not difficult to conduct and rarely gave rise to any comments at all. Meanwhile, the second part of the Risø-based inspectors' mission, checking the discharge into the ice-sheet cavity, was a complicated task, since wastewater was not discharged only when the Danish inspectors were present. Discharges took place at irregular intervals, typically spaced about two weeks apart, and discharge amounts could vary from some 7,500 liters to almost 38,000 liters (with amounts shown in gallons in the discharge table included here). In practice, the Danish inspectors had to trust that the American reactor team at Camp Century was meticulous in its record keeping for each individual discharge operation. We have no reason to believe otherwise, since the reactor operators were professionals and the team was large enough to double-check and verify data entries.

Further news of the PM-2A reactor's fate reached the relevant authorities in Denmark in September 1963, when Vagn Buchwald, the serving scientific adviser to the Danish liaison officer at Thule Air Base, submitted his report on U.S. testing and experimental activities in Greenland that summer. Here, he stated that "Camp Century will be closed down, at any rate for the coming winter."[15] According to Buchwald, the problem lay in the gradual collapse of the tunnel ceilings, which was especially conspicuous in the reactor tunnel. The weight of the layer atop the large metal roof arches was constantly growing as new snowfalls added at least a meter each year to what was already there. In addition, the heat radiating from the camp's buildings, human bodies, and machinery speeded up the gradual narrowing of the tunnels as moisture and steam condensed on the interior surfaces and froze there. As Buchwald wrote:

> In 1962 the roofs had to be renewed on tunnels 2, 3, 4, and 5, where the reactor plant and the diesel equipment are located. This was an extensive task that was completed without accidents, but it had cost almost 20,000 man-hours and it gradually became clear that other tunnels, too, were in need of a thorough overhaul. . . . At this point the risk that the roof above the reactor might cave in was so great that Major Meeken decided to shut it down. This was done on July 9, 1963. . . . However, the situation in other tunnels was such that on July 30 a decision was made that the reactor would not be put into operation again, and that Century had to be closed for the winter.[16]

This information, which Buchwald had obtained during his visit to Camp Century in August 1963, was more precise than previous reporting, and at the time of his visit the PM-2A had already been shut down. By means of remote-controlled equipment, the exhausted and highly radioactive fuel rods had also been removed from the reactor chamber and placed in a water-filled spent-fuel tank in the ice next to the reactor. The most complicated part of the process was bringing the rods to the surface of the ice sheet. Before this could happen, they had to be placed inside several ten-ton, lead-lined steel drums to prevent members of the work crew from being exposed to deadly doses of radiation. Success nevertheless seemed within reach after the Army Corps of Engineers built a supportive structure known as a "Bailey bridge" with a span of 21 meters and a crane section capable of hoisting ten tons. Wrapping up the section on Camp Century's PM-2A reactor in his 1963 summer report, Buchwald concluded that "in the course of September the 32 fuel elements will be placed, one by one, in their drums and be transported by heavy swing to Camp Tuto."[17]

REMOVING THE REACTOR—
AND THE ANXIETY

Buchwald's information was largely confirmed by the report the U.S. Army Corps of Engineers sent to the Danish embassy in Washington in January 1964. Corresponding reports were also presented to the authorities for the years 1961 and 1962, but the one for 1963 is the most noteworthy, being rich in details about the reactor's final year at Camp Century. In 1963, the reactor had operated for 3,815 hours, corresponding to just under 90 percent of the time, before shutdown; during that time it produced 3,314,400 kWh of electrical energy; no one at Camp Century had received more than the permitted radiation dose; and the aggregate amount of liquid radioactive material discharged into the ice sheet totaled 1.4 GBq (38 millicuries) for the entire three-year period of operation. This last figure was significantly less than the annual 1.9 GBq (50 millicuries) originally agreed with the Danish foreign ministry as the upper threshold for the discharged liquid radioactive waste.

The U.S. Army report also stated that the reactor was shut down on July 9, 1963, to enable necessary repair work on the roof of the reactor tunnel, a task estimated to last a month. However, on August 1 (note that Buchwald stated it was July 30), what had been communicated as a "temporary" shutdown was altered to a permanent shutdown, "due to extensive structural failure in the arches of all trenches." The fuel rods were thus removed from the reactor, placed in the spent-fuel water tank, maneuvered into seven lead-lined steel drums, and transported to Camp Tuto. There they were left to "cool off" for the winter of 1963/1964 before being shipped to the United States the next summer.[18]

Official American notification regarding the shutdown and removal of the Camp Century PM-2A reactor arrived at the Danish Ministry of Foreign Affairs in a letter that was dated January 22, 1964, signed by the U.S. Department of Defense, and addressed to the Danish embassy in Washington, DC. The contents show that several factors—some anticipated, others not—played a role in the decision. One was the fact that, as expected, the fuel rods in the reactor core were almost exhausted. Another was that the camp was literally caving in, which, although expected at some point, was happening faster than predicted. The authorities had therefore decided that, going forward, it would be adequate to open a small section of the camp during the summer, when diesel engines could handle the camp's energy needs. The Department of Defense further stated that, as originally agreed, the reactor and all solid radioactive material would be removed from Greenland over the 1964 summer season, although as a contingency plan in case of bad weather or other unforeseen events the removal operation would be completed in 1965 at the latest. The remaining liquid radioactive waste would first be stored in an appropriate container, then diluted and discharged into the ice sheet.[19]

The reactor and its ancillary components were moved in the summer of 1964, nearly a year after its decommissioning. The last parts of the plant left Camp Century on June 30 on a special caterpillar transport, arriving at Camp Tuto on July 4, and a few days later they were loaded onto two transport vessels docked at Thule Air Base: the USNS *Greenville Victory* and the USNS *Robinson*, leaving Greenland and heading for the United States on July 27 and August 1, 1964, respectively.[20]

The PM-2A reactor's final movements on Greenlandic soil were overseen by the Danish Atomic Energy Commission, represented by Professor Cecil F. Jacobsen of the Chemistry Department at Risø Nuclear Research Laboratory. The decision to have Jacobsen supervise the operation was a natural extension of the many previous visits by Risø staff to Camp Century. What is more, the Americans had conveyed to the Danish Ministry of Foreign Affairs that they would very much like to have Danish experts present to observe the process and confirm that everything was being done in a proper, orderly fashion. Jacobsen, who was in Greenland from July 21 to 30, 1964, and visited Thule Air Base and Camp Century, clearly felt able to sanction the process wholeheartedly. Before leaving Thule Air Base for the ice-sheet crossing to Camp Century, Jacobsen inspected one of the navy vessels and her cargo. He was greatly impressed:

> It was interesting to note that the stowing of the components and
> the containers apparently were performed with very little hindrance

FIGURE 8.3 The PM-2A reactor was shut down in 1963 and had already been removed when, in the summer of 1964, the reactor tank was transported from Camp Century to Camp Tuto and from there to the harbor at Thule Air Base.

from the radioactive nature of the cargo. A careful planning of the operation with consideration of the health physics aspects, and the presence of a capable crew on the ship and on the dockside was obviously all that was needed to make the stowing differ very little from that of a conventional cargo stowing.[21]

Satisfied with what he had seen on the vessel, Jacobsen went inland to Camp Century, where he spent July 24 and 25. Here, too, he observed that everything was in order. According to Jacobson, the measuring instruments that registered various types of radioactive emissions in the tunnel spaces where the reactor, the heat exchanger, the steam turbine, and the generator had been located until just a few days before indicated values that were significantly below the permitted levels. Even so, his English-language report does not mention any concrete numbers. It seems odd that Jacobsen does not mention—and possibly contradicts—a problem specifically noted in the U.S. Army's final report on Camp Century:

> Residual radiation levels around the primary unit (i.e. reactor and hot waste tank) were considerably higher than had been expected. Hence, daily permissible exposure of crew members disassembling these components was shorter than had been calculated, and, as a result, more personnel were required to accomplish the task in time to meet scheduled shipping dates than was planned originally.[22]

The Dane noted just a single event that had not gone according to plan. In Tunnel 4, which had housed the reactor, an unspecified amount of radioactive water had seeped out onto the tunnel floor, causing a radioactive spill that exceeded the permitted limits. However, the officer in charge of removing the reactor had immediately realized that the snow would have to be dug away down to a considerable depth to eradicate the problem entirely—which was either impossible or simply deemed a disproportionately arduous task. Therefore the officer, of his own accord, had decided to remove only the uppermost layer of the contaminated snow and subsequently pile a thick layer of fresh snow on top of the seepage site. This proved adequate to reduce radiation to a level significantly lower than the critical threshold value, so the officer was satisfied with the course he had chosen, and Jacobsen fully concurred:

> Being strictly formal, one might object that the contaminated snow should have been disposed of in the hot waste well. However, I find no objections to the method used to reduce the radioactive level, as the amount of radioactivity must have been extremely small—this can be seen from the amount retained in the removed flooring, and as a proposal for two auxiliary wells for minute amounts of radioactivity undoubtedly would have been acceptable. I did not mention the formal point of view, as I did not want to give the impression that my thoughts had even lingered at the idea that the very conscientious and

FIGURE 8.4 The spent fuel rods were highly radioactive. They were ensconced in large, lead-lined drums and also returned to the United States in the summer of 1964. This is described in various sources, including first-hand accounts from the Danish professor C. F. Jacobsen, of the Risø Nuclear Research Laboratory.

efficient radiological clearance should have been carried on into the ridiculous for the sake of formalities.[23]

To sum up, Jacobsen gave a thoroughly positive, almost effusively enthusiastic assessment of the way the Americans had demonstrated that it was indeed possible to install a mobile nuclear reactor in a remote location, run it for a number of years, then remove it again without the process causing any significant environmental problems. Nevertheless, as he reflected in his conclusion, "It is, of course, no surprise that a job is well done, when the people in charge have very high professional qualifications."[24] Furthermore, in a private letter addressed to the officer in charge of the dismantling operation, reproduced in the official book about the U.S. Army's Nuclear Power Program, Jacobsen added:

I have emphasized the extremely high quality of the job done under adverse conditions, both the running of the reactor and the dismantling and the clearance. Actually, I have proposed that we use your work as propaganda for atomic energy, as you have proven that reactors can be used and taken apart without danger to anybody even without the use of highly specialized equipment which one would use if a permanent plant should be dismantled. It shows that highly qualified leaders with a sense for "good housekeeping" is what is needed. Maybe it will help in removing the anxiety about nuclear reactors, which corresponds to the [requirement in former times] that a man with a red flag [had to walk in front of all] railway trains.[25]

The U.S. Army's reactor experts could hardly have dreamed up a finer endorsement of their activities at Camp Century.

THE CRUSHING OF CAMP CENTURY

After the decommissioning of the PM-2A, there were rumors at Camp Century that the reactor would be sent all the way to the Antarctic, where—if the rumors were true—it would be installed in another year-round camp on the opposite side of the globe. In actual fact, attempts were made to persuade units in the army, navy, and air force to take over the reactor, but in the end no one was really interested. Hence, upon their arrival in the United States, the reactor tank and other radioactive components were loaded onto eight railway cars and transported to the army's test facility for nuclear reactors in Idaho. Here, scientists set about studying whether the intense neutron bombardment the reactor tank had undergone for three years had made its walls brittle and, by consequence, made the reactor potentially dangerous to operate. From April to December 1966, they subjected the travel-worn veteran of a tank to a series of rigorous tests, although the scientists' attempts to break it down were not successful until they had induced deep cracks and drenched them with hydrochloric acid.[26] There was clearly no danger that the reactor tank would have ruptured, and it could have remained operational for many more years at Camp Century or some other location. But instead, the once-celebrated tank ended its life as radioactive scrap metal in Idaho.

Camp Century continued to function even after losing its nuclear power source. From 1964 to 1966, it served as a summer base for a variety of tests and experiments initiated while the camp was still operating

year-round, but no new experiments were begun. Late in the summer of 1966, activities at Camp Century were definitively over when the ice-core drilling that would later gain such renown was completed after the drill touched bedrock at the bottom of the ice sheet. Materials and equipment regarded as valuable were transported back to Thule Air Base and from there back to the United States. Materials deemed worthless

FIGURE 8.5 A solitary caterpillar vehicle crawling away from the camp entrance, among the tracks of countless other vehicles. A striking visual image of the final shut-down of Camp Century. Presumably late summer 1966.

were left behind in the tunnel systems, which continued to shrink and each year sink further beneath the ice cap's white surface.

In 1969, representatives of the U.S. Army once again visited the site and returned with photo documentation of the tunnels. The images plainly show that all the tunnels had more or less collapsed, with residential units and other installations reduced to piles of warped metal and splintered wood.[27] The state of decline was indisputable then, and it has since continued to deteriorate. Today, there are no visible traces of the camp on the surface. The remains of Camp Century, including its liquid waste and solid detritus, are now encased deep beneath the pristine and perpetually frozen surface of the ice sheet, leaving one of the most remarkable symbols of Cold War defense innovation dead and buried forever. Or so an overwhelming majority of the stakeholders involved in this story thought. Then, in 2016, a new and very different scenario was brought to light.

9

THE LEGACY OF CAMP CENTURY

CAMP CENTURY REVISITED—YET AGAIN

When the Americans left Camp Century in 1966 they assumed it would lie dead and buried forever, deep in the perpetual ice. They were wrong. "The city under the ice" has continued to play a role in Danish domestic and foreign policy up to the present day. What is more, it now seems the camp will have political and environmental impacts far into the future.

This final chapter begins by describing and discussing three events that took place in 1980, 1995–1997, and 2016–2018. After Camp Century's closure, these events reawakened debates about the facility while at the same time yielding deeper insights into its purpose, daily life, research, press coverage, and further issues beyond the scope of this book. This analysis also scratches the surface of what seems to be an extremely well-kept secret only recently disclosed.

Each of these three events in their own way shaped the ongoing relations between the United States, Denmark, and Greenland. For a time, the most recent of these seemed poised to profoundly affect the long-standing relationship of Greenland and Denmark within the framework of the joint realm. The ultimate outcome of this and past events will only become clear many years from now, although one thing is certain: Camp Century will continue to stimulate debate and dispute. One source that makes this claim is a scientific paper published in August 2016 in the distinguished American journal *Geophysical Research Letters* by the Canadian glaciologist William Colgan and his research colleagues.[1] Based on climate models that predict net annual melting on the stretch of the ice sheet overlying Camp Century over the next seventy-five years, Colgan and his coauthors warned that we must expect to see the camp—and whatever environmentally hazardous waste it may contain—reemerge some time in the twenty-first or twenty-second century.

The revelation that Camp Century will plausibly resurface within the foreseeable future dropped like a bombshell on the diplomatic relations between Greenland and Denmark, shaking the very foundations of the centuries-old construction we know as *Rigsfællesskabet*, the community of three nationalities in the unified Kingdom of Denmark, Greenland, and the Faroe Islands. The resulting cracks in the mortar of the kingdom's walls and ramparts seemed to be significantly deeper than those caused by the unveiling in 1980 and 1996 of hitherto unknown facts about Camp Century. In fact, the release of this third, most recent finding has put Dano-Greenlandic relations under such pressure that the underlying problems might be irresolvable within the framework of the joint kingdom. Based on the current situation, posterity may someday see this as Camp Century's heaviest legacy.

RADIOACTIVE WASTE LOCKED IN THE ICE CAP

By the time Camp Century was shut down in 1966, the tension between the world's two superpowers had relaxed considerably. The leaders of the United States and the Soviet Union seemed to have realized that the world did not dare, once again, to step up to the brink of a global apocalypse, where it had stood for several nerve-wracking days and nights during the height of the Cuban Missile Crisis in late October and early

November 1962. This period of détente between East and West lasted until around 1980, but even in this less treacherous landscape of superpower diplomacy, both sides still sought to undermine the other's position in former colonies in Asia and Africa. One example was the Vietnam War. Beginning in 1954–1955, the conflict dragged into the 1960s and 1970s and was eventually televised, reaching viewers in living rooms around the world. Many regard the Vietnam War as one of the key factors behind the counterculture hippie movement among certain youth groups in the Western world in the late 1960s.[2] University students were particularly active in confronting "the Establishment" and generally challenging accepted norms and existing social structures. Scholars and scientists began questioning the wisdom of sustained economic growth, and a global environmental movement gradually took shape.[3] Besides opposing the Vietnam War, another commonality in the complex mosaic of protest movements and revolutionary trends was the opposition to nuclear weapons and nuclear power. The first Danish protest march against nuclear weapons, inspired by similar events in the United Kingdom, took place on October 21–22, 1960. It began in the town of Holbæk, about 65 km west of Copenhagen, where American Nike missiles were located; passed an Honest John missile battery near Roskilde, some 30 km west of the capital; and ended up at Copenhagen City Hall Square with a gathering of roughly five thousand protesters.[4]

The youth movement was closely linked to the emergence of a counterexpertise community, consisting mainly of young researchers who sought in their work to challenge "experts" and disprove "accepted wisdom." For one thing, the circles opposing nuclear weapons evolved into a widespread "No Nukes" peace movement whose peace-study scholars challenged the existing security policy rationale, which was built on nuclear deterrence and winning the arms race. One such academic group, coalescing in New Zealand in the late 1960s, counted such prominent members as Owen Wilkes, Robert Mann, Phil Howell, and Murray Horton. Among their exploits, earning them renown in their native country, was the discovery that some of the activity going on in the Antarctic during and after the International Geophysical Year

(IGY, 1957–1958) was actually military based and not simply "civilian research" as the official statements purported.[5]

Owen Wilkes holds particular relevance for the history of Camp Century. From 1976 to 1982, he was a resident academic at the international centers for peace studies in Oslo and Stockholm, and while in Scandinavia he studied the extent of American military research in Greenland—simply by typing the word "Greenland" into search engines to find relevant titles and abstracts in accessible U.S. databases. Using this straightforward approach, he was able to identify hundreds of reports about research projects in Greenland, all funded by the military and all clearly interesting to the military. A small part of Wilkes's findings appeared in 1980 in the Danish-language journal *Forsvar* (Defense), a critical, independent, research-based periodical on military topics. Here, based on his studies of the final report on Camp Century prepared and published by the U.S. Army's Cold Regions Research Engineering Laboratory (CRREL),[6] Wilkes concluded:

> Besides heat and electricity, the reactor [PM-2A] also generated radioactive waste. The high-level radioactive waste was collected in a tank, which was occasionally emptied over into lead-encased drums that were transported by ship to the United States. Additionally, there were much larger amounts of low-level radioactive water, and the US military had permission from the Danish government to lead this warm radioactive water out into a cavity in the permanent ice sheet. This cavity was kept open, and it became larger as the warm water melted the ice. The Army had permission to discharge up to 50 millicuries per year in this way. The US Army conducted measurements and publicized numbers to show that the thresholds were not exceeded.[7]

The setup certainly looked reassuring. But could the numbers be trusted? Wilkes had his doubts. Two years before, in 1978, he had coauthored and published a paper with the New Zealand biochemist and peace researcher Robert Mann that described, in detail, the problems the U.S. Army had encountered in Antarctica with the reactor it had operated there, a PM-3A incongruously nicknamed "Nukey Poo." The

PM-3A, a successor of the PM-2A reactor at Camp Century, was not installed until 1962, allowing the reactor experts to learn from their initial experience operating the PM-2A.[8] The PM-3A plant was built on bedrock in an environment that was less harsh than Camp Century's. Continuous operations commenced in 1963, but the PM-3A was beset by misfortune. In 1972, it was decommissioned for good because of suspected damage to the pressure tank. Its numerous problems also included radioactive contamination of the environment, leading Wilkes and Mann to conclude, even while hinting that a U.S. cover-up might be brewing, that

> sometime soon the U.S. Navy will have to find some place to quietly dispose of 12,200 tons of radioactive dirt, an embarrassing by-product of 10 years of operating a small military power reactor in Antarctica. . . . When the entire 12,200 tons is finally covered over, it will be probably the last episode in the story of Nukey Poo, Antarctica's only nuclear reactor—a story that illustrates just how bad a nuclear reactor can be, even if nothing as spectacular as a core meltdown occurs.[9]

Having thus documented that the PM-3A reactor at McMurdo Sound, Antarctica, had caused the Americans enormous operational problems, what about its polar predecessor, the PM-2A in Greenland, which had also operated in such a region but under conditions far more taxing than those of the PM-3A? The question was all the more pressing because the Antarctic Treaty precluded any military secrecy about the PM-3A. Wilkes thus reasoned that perhaps the available information given about the PM-2A in Greenland was not complete. In violation of the Antarctic Treaty, low-level radioactive waste had been discharged into the PM-3A's surroundings, meaning that over the next two to three years, thousands of tons of slightly radioactive soil had to be transported back to the United States—an operation that followed the drawn-out, difficult, and very costly dismantling and removal of the highly radioactive PM-3A reactor. Based on this knowledge, in his 1980 Danish-language article, Wilkes asked a question that would have wide repercussions: "Given that all this transpired in Antarctica, what might we guess went on in Camp Century under cover of the military secrecy surrounding that base?"[10]

Wilkes's speculations provoked a reaction in the Greenlandic press, being accessible to the often Danish-savvy and Greenlandic-speaking population. In April 1980, the Nuuk-based, bilingual national newspaper *Atuagagdliutit/Grønlandsposten* [*AG, The Greenland Post*] ran an article, simply signed "-h.," summarizing the Wilkes article in *Forsvar*. Nevertheless, the article's rather chilling heading, "Vældigt område af indlandsisen svagt radioaktivt" ("Huge region of the ice sheet slightly radioactive"),[11] evidently gave rise to little debate. Likewise, we have found no indications that, at the time, the newly formed Greenlandic Home Rule government posed any critical questions about Camp Century. In other words, no Greenlandic demands were presented to Denmark or the United States asking for further reports on Camp Century, nor were any demands made that the alleged contamination be removed.

However, Wilkes's work also spurred Margrete Auken—today one of Europe's veteran Green MEPs, back then a member of the Danish parliament for the Socialist People's Party—to follow up on the matter on June 25, 1980. She therefore submitted an official question to the minister of the environment, Erik Holst of the Social Democratic Party, requesting information about "the environmental security measures in connection with the sudden shut-down of the American nuclear reactor PM-2A on July 9, 1963 (removed in summer 1964) at Camp Century in the American military base east of Thule."[12] After consulting the Danish Environmental Protection Agency (EPA), on July 3, 1980, Holst was able to present a reassuring response to Auken's question. He explained that the Danish authorities, including persons with special expertise from the Danish Atomic Energy Commission (AEC), had received the plant's security documentation for their review and approval, besides which they had been kept informed about the plant's operation, including the depositing of small amounts of radioactive wastewater. The environment minister was thus able to conclude that "for the entire period of operation, the radioactivity in the deposited material amounted to 70 millicuries in all (maximum permitted deposit: 50 millicuries per year in operation)."[13] In plain language, this meant contamination was significantly lower than what the Danish authorities had permitted the Americans to dump. What is more, Danish experts had also inspected the PM-2A on several occasions, both during installation and while it was running. In this context, the ministerial response specifically referred to "a representative of the AEC [Professor C. F. Jacobsen, introduced in chapter 8, who] on July 27, 1964 [inspected] Camp Century. During the inspection it was found that all reactor equipment had been removed from the location, and a control measurement showed compliance with the above-mentioned measurements."[14]

We do not know whether the response reassured Auken. The message from the environment minister was that the Danish authorities had consistently monitored Camp Century and its nuclear reactor and that "nothing in the existing information about measurements in the vicinity and measurements in the facility itself, or about the registration of waste deposited in liquid form, indicates that radioactive substances have been left behind at Camp Century to such an extent that, now or in the future, it might be expected to lead to health or environmental risks."[15] At any rate, Auken did not pursue the case any further, and Wilkes's work was not followed up. Interestingly, three years later, Wilkes's Danish article from 1980 was part of the background material for a little-known Danish book bearing the ironic title *Grønland— Middelhavets perle* (Greenland—pearl of the Mediterranean).[16]

ATOMIC BOMBS IN THE ICE CAP

Another fifteen years passed without any noteworthy news about Camp Century. Meanwhile, momentous things were happening in the wider world. The Cold War had intensified in the first half of the 1980s, as hundreds of intermediate-range ballistic missiles (IRBMs) were stationed in Eastern and Western Europe. Then came the surprisingly rapid development of détente, propelled by the fall of the Berlin Wall in

1989, German reunification in 1990, and the collapse of the Soviet empire in 1991. As it turned out, this was not "game over" in the sense of total victory for Western capitalism, as the well-known American writer and professor of political science Francis Fukuyama optimistically predicted in 1992—even though for some years in the 1990s it did look like such a scenario might come to pass.[17]

In Denmark, a conservative government (led by Prime Minister Poul Schlüter) was succeeded by a Social Democratic–Social Liberal coalition government in 1993 (with Prime Minister Poul Nyrup Rasmussen from the former party and Foreign Minister Niels Helveg Petersen from the latter). One political concern that would soon shoot to the top of the new government's agenda was the "Thule Affair," a disastrous incident in northwestern Greenland in 1968, in which a B-52 Stratofortress from the U.S. Air Force carrying hydrogen bombs crashed on the ice-covered surface of Wolstenholme Fjord, seven kilometers from Thule Air Base. This incident gave rise to a lengthy diplomatic crisis between the United States and Denmark, even while a large-scale cleanup operation was initiated in the grueling Arctic conditions around the crash site. Several hundred people from the United States, Denmark, and Greenland spent months collecting snow and ice contaminated with plutonium and depositing it in large containers that were subsequently transported to the United States. The operation was described in a joint Danish-American report, which concluded that the "radio-ecological investigations have shown that the plutonium levels in the collected samples in no instances were such that they can be considered harmful to man or to higher animals in the Thule district or in any part of Greenland."[18]

Despite the unambiguous message from the scientific team, the late 1980s still brought renewed focus on the 1968 crash incident and on U.S. military activities in Greenland. The underlying reason was that a number of Danes and Greenlanders who had helped in the cleanup operation had long complained of ill health. Many developed cancer, which they attributed to radiation exposure during the cleanup. To investigate this in detail, the Danish Health Authority collected the data accessible from U.S. and Danish sources and proceeded, from 1986 to 1991, to conduct a variety of studies and tests on all those who had been at or near Thule Air Base during the relevant period. Based on the investigation, the Danish Health Authority did not feel justified in confirming the suspected link proposed by the group that came to be known as the "Thule workers" between their higher prevalence of illness and premature death and their involvement in the cleanup and contact with the radioactive contamination caused by the crash.[19] It is also worth noting that in 2010–2011 the Danish Health Authority did a follow-up investigation and reached largely the same conclusions as in the first investigation.[20]

Story after story about cancer-stricken Thule workers nonetheless continued to appear, chipping away at public trust in the Danish authorities. This atmosphere of distrust produced a series of accusations in the press, claiming that information was being withheld and the truth suppressed. Poul Brink, an investigative journalist with the Danish Broadcasting Corporation (DR), championed this campaign, and in 1997 he received a Cavling Award—the most prestigious prize in Danish journalism—for his efforts. The following year, Brink published a Danish-language book with the evocative title *Thule-sagen—Løgnens Univers* (The Thule affair: a universe of lies).[21] Brink's accusations against the authorities were not limited to the 1968 crash and cleanup or to the harm allegedly inflicted on the Thule workers. He also claimed there had been a deliberate Danish hush-hush policy about American aircraft crossing Greenlandic airspace carrying nuclear devices and about the clandestine storage of such weapons at Thule Air Base, a location where unwitting employees might also have been exposed to radiation. A feature film by the Danish director Christina Rosendahl, based on Brink's book and titled *Idealisten* (subtitled in English as *The Idealist*), was released in 2015. The film was generally well received, but like Brink's book it was criticized by historians for its conspiracy-theory approach to the subject matter. Both book and film lean toward interpreting the affair as a huge conspiracy aimed at shrouding the nuclear aspects of U.S. military engagement in Greenland in a veil of secrecy.

However, they ignore the fact that the vast majority of elements in the American nuclear polar strategy were well known and widely accepted in Denmark and the other NATO countries.[22]

By 1995, partly as a result of Brink's diligent digging, the Thule Affair had become so convoluted and confusing that Denmark's sitting Social Democratic–Social Liberal coalition government was obliged to submit a report to the Danish parliament about Denmark's nuclear policy from the 1950s onward. The report was presented on June 29, 1995,[23] publicly revealing for the first time that U.S. ambassador Val Peterson had contacted Danish prime (and foreign) minister Hans Christian "H.C." Hansen in November 1957 (as described in chapter 2), resulting in Hansen's tacit acceptance of U.S. nuclear weapons at Thule Air Base.

This caused great dismay, exacerbated by another disclosure: Sitting prime minister Poul Nyrup Rasmussen and his government had known about Hansen's reply to Val Peterson since March 1994. During the opening session of the Danish parliament that year, held on October 5, 1995, and during the opening session of the Greenlandic national assembly in Nuuk a week later, Greenlandic politicians delivered scathing speeches about how the Greenlandic population, particularly the people of the Thule area, had been deceived by Denmark and the United States. Naturally the Danish newspapers threw themselves into the fray, led this time by the reporter Per Kanstrup, from the Danish tabloid *Ekstra Bladet*, whose piece under the heading "Dommedagsbrag i Thulesagen" (Judgment Day boom in the Thule Affair) referred to the new information as "shocking revelations."[24] The political opposition smelled blood, and the Danish government felt compelled to submit a formal inquiry to the U.S. government to clarify the scope and timing of the actual presence of nuclear weapons in Greenland. Just two weeks later, they received a statement from the American authorities declaring that, during two intervals, nuclear weapons had been stationed at Thule Air Base: for eight months beginning in February 1958 and from December 1959 until the summer of 1965. The statement also indicated that all nuclear weapons had been withdrawn from Greenlandic territory in the summer of 1965 and that the United States had not had any nuclear weapons stationed in Greenland after that time.[25]

On August 8, 1995, prompted by the heated parliamentary and press debates in the wake of these disclosures, the government asked the independent research institution DIIS (Danish Institute for International Studies) to prepare a "historical report in the form of a 'White Paper' [an investigative report] about the United States' flyovers of Greenland with nuclear weapons and the role of Thule Air Base in that connection."[26] The researchers were promised as much access as was possible to all available materials, both in the United States and in Denmark—everything that might shed light on the questions their mandate authorized them to investigate. Originally the white paper was to be submitted in the spring of 1996, but because the task proved to be quite extensive it was not delivered to the Danish government until December 17, 1996. The delay was inconvenient, but when the two-volume white paper report (incidentally bound in blue) was finally made available to the public on January 17, 1997, the quality of the work was deemed very high. By academic standards, the DIIS report, mentioned in chapter 3 and bearing the full title *Grønland under den kolde krig. Dansk og amerikansk sikkerhedspolitik 1945–68* (Greenland during the Cold War: Danish and American security policy, 1945–1968), was worthy of the near-unanimous approval it received.

The DIIS report contained even more answers than the government had sought, the most remarkable of which related specifically to the topic of this book: Camp Century. As the scholarly work was proceeding apace, several journalists and historians had succeeded in uncovering a wealth of previously published but long-forgotten details about the subsurface facility. Then came the sensational news: Camp Century had actually been a pilot project for an American nuclear deterrence project of mind-boggling dimensions. Aided by Dutch colleagues, the Danish historians had located a document in the American archives that outlined the essentials of a top-secret U.S. Army project called Iceworm. This document also showed that high-level U.S. military officials had wondered how the United States could best persuade Denmark to agree to the excavation and construction of an enormous network of rail-equipped tunnels within the ice, spanning several thousand square kilometers across the northern expanses of the Greenland ice sheet—the aim being to enable the hidden transportation, by train, of 600 missiles equipped with nuclear warheads capable of directing a first-strike or second-strike attack against key military and civilian targets in the Soviet Union.[27]

The day after the DIIS report was published, it was widely quoted in Danish newspapers, many of which mentioned the highly controversial Iceworm document. As the newspaper journalists Simon Andersen and Jesper Larsen, from *Jyllands-Posten*, put it: now, finally, here was proof that since the early 1950s leading Danish politicians had known that Thule Air Base, and hence Greenland, was "a stepping stone for massive attacks against the Soviet Union."[28]

In another broadsheet, *Berlingske Tidende*, the journalists Troels Mylenberg and Ask Rostrup went through "Operation Iceworm" (the headline of the article) in considerable detail.[29] They described the gist of the plan, its ultimate aim, the arguably obvious purpose of Camp Century as a test site for key elements in the greater plan, and the difficulties that finally put an end to the project. As they summarized: "And even though nowadays [Project Iceworm] seems like some monstrous figment of the imagination that could have been featured in an early James Bond film, it serves today as an extreme but clear-cut illustration of what the world looked like just 35 years ago. It was, indeed, an ice-cold war."[30]

A third large Danish newspaper, *Politiken*, had their staff journalist Ib Faurby write about the story, and he largely presented the same details as his colleagues at *Jyllands-Posten* and *Berlingske Tidende*. But toward the end of his piece Faurby made a point presumably meant to suggest that, generally speaking, the Danes have been incredibly naïve for a very long time. "And why?" he asked. Because as early as the 1960s,

in the July edition of *Det Bedste* [the Danish version of *Reader's Digest*], [they had been able to] read the following about Camp Century: "Five years of experiments have preceded the construction of this town. The work areas are dominated by scientific laboratories, but should it become necessary to put the main focus on military installations—for instance, launch ramps for intercontinental missiles or remote-controlled projectiles—all plans and installations are ready, and all equipment."[31]

Faurby offered no thoughts on why Danish readers did not react to this information in 1960. Perhaps he was at a loss to provide convincing arguments and answers, just as we are. From a historian's perspective, however, we find it fair to point out that in Denmark the more well-educated circles would often shrug off *Det Bedste* and its contents as trivial. Seeing the publication's pieces on technological innovations as habitually sensationalist, many spurned its coverage of new inventions, which were always presented as being on the cusp of reality, ready to revolutionize our lives and improve the lot of humankind at large. In that light, perhaps it is less surprising that the comments in *Det Bedste* about the future prospects of Camp Century–style installations embedded in the ice cap were not taken very seriously in 1960. On the other hand, it is possible that, at the time, major Danish newspapers understood all too well how explosive the topic could be. That may have made them willing to desist, in the interest of not putting the Danish government and parliament in an untenable situation. Certainly, as explained in chapter 4, for a number of years the Danish foreign ministry did its best to prevent the Danes from being exposed to too much disquieting news of this sort.

RADIOACTIVE WASTE RESURFACES
IN THE MEDIA

After the press had spent a few weeks delving into the DIIS report and dealing with its revelations about Project Iceworm, the topic of Camp Century once again faded into the background in the media landscape. Unlike the public exposure in 1995 of H. C. Hansen's internal memo, the 1997 exposure of the Iceworm–Camp Century connection does not seem to have roused much public interest in the Greenlandic community. At the time, it did not give rise to any major debates in the country's parliament or cause any widespread polemical debate in the Greenlandic media. That still lay in the future.

Besides the uncovering of Project Iceworm during the 1995–1997 stage of the Thule Affair, this period brought renewed focus on potential radioactive contamination in and around Camp Century. The publication of Owen Wilkes's article in 1980 had not caused much debate, beyond the official question the left-wing Danish MP Margrethe Auken put to the minister for the environment. Fast-forwarding to the summer of 1995, however, we find Otto Steenholdt entering the picture, a Greenlandic MP who held one of Greenland's two seats in the 179-member Danish parliament. Steenholdt had become aware of Wilkes's article, now fifteen years old, and he took the opportunity to ask Foreign Minister Niels Helveg Petersen (who was already hard pressed in handling matters concerning Greenland) about his assessment of the shutdown of Camp Century. As Steenholdt wrote in the motivation for his question: "It is becoming more and more certain that the American nuclear reactor had been built with the permission of the Danish government. Therefore the Danish government must also be able to inform me as to whether the radioactive fuels and residues have been removed in a responsible manner, and under the supervision of the Danish government."[32]

Berlingske Tidende brought news of Otto Steenholdt's parliamentary question on July 14, 1995, along with a statement from Povl L. Ølgaard, a professor of reactor physics at the Technical University of Denmark (DTU). Ølgaard, like a number of other employees at the Risø Nuclear Research Laboratory, had been sent to Camp Century by the Danish AEC between 1959 and 1964 to inspect the PM-2A reactor and conduct test measurements to check the surrounding radioactivity levels. He was therefore one of the experts whose assessment could carry quite a bit of weight in a matter such as this. In Ølgaard's view, there was no doubt: "During the time the reactor was operating, the Americans only discharged 72 millicuries, and that is so little that it would be a waste of the taxpayers' money to drill down to get it."[33] Steenholdt later received much the same answer from Foreign Minister Helveg Petersen, although worded more diplomatically, so according to the Danish foreign minister and the prominent Danish reactor expert, the situation

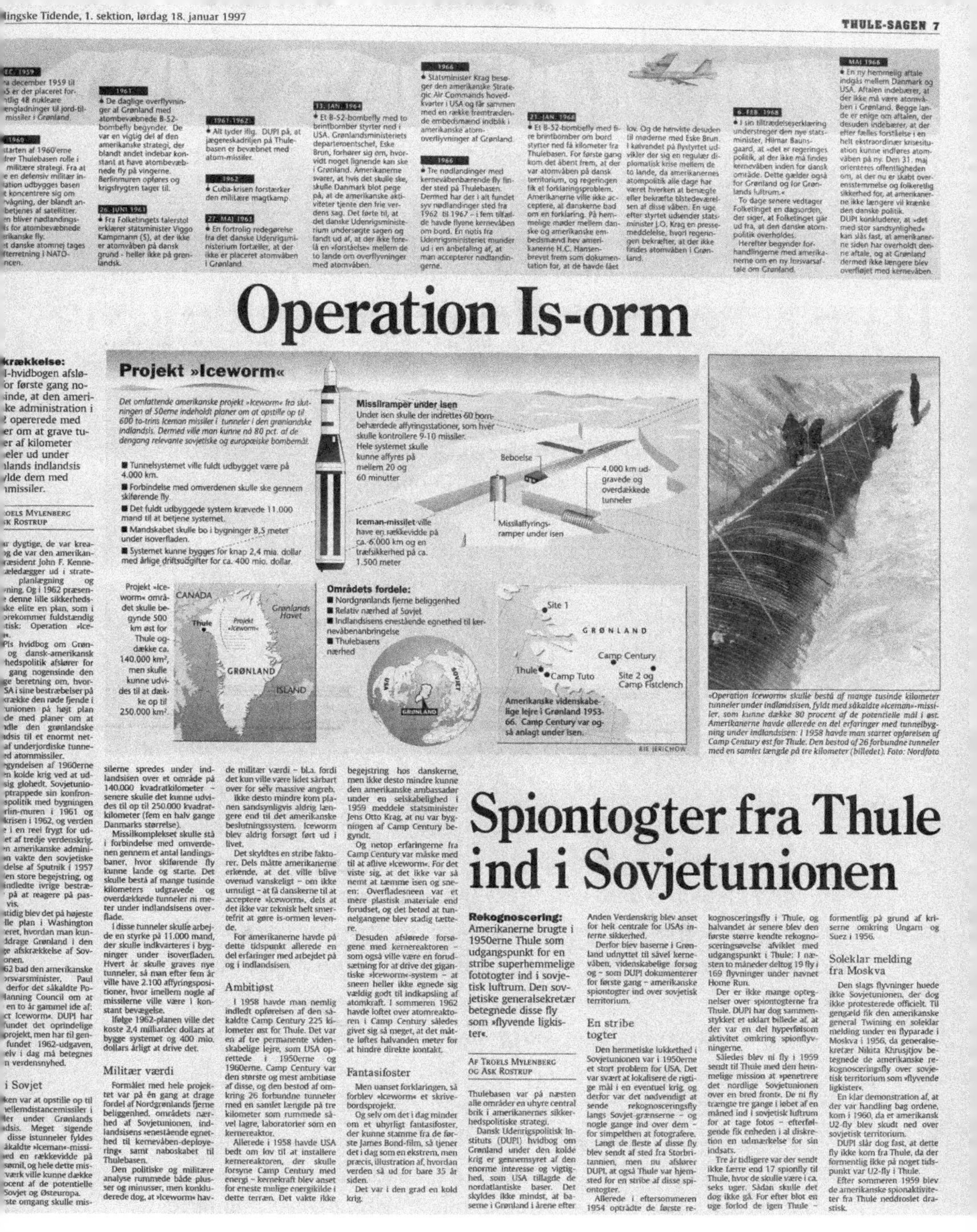

Berlingske Tidende, 1. sektion, lørdag 18. januar 1997

THULE-SAGEN 7

Operation Is-orm

Projekt »Iceworm«

Det omfattende amerikanske projekt »Iceworm« fra slutningen af 50erne indeholdt planer om at opstille op til 600 to-trins Iceman missiler i tunneler i den grønlandske indlandsis. Dermed ville man kunne nå 80 pct. af de dengang relevante sovjetiske og europæiske bombemål.

- Tunnelsystemet ville fuldt udbygget være på 4.000 km.
- Forbindelse med omverdenen skulle ske gennem skiførende fly.
- Det fuldt udbyggede system krævede 11.000 mand til at betjene systemet.
- Mandskabet skulle bo i bygninger 8,5 meter under isoverfladen.
- Systemet kunne bygges for knap 2,4 mia. dollar med årlige driftsudgifter for ca. 400 mio. dollar.

»Operation Iceworm« skulle bestå af mange tusinde kilometer tunneler under indlandsisen, fyldt med såkaldte »Iceman«-missiler, som kunne dække 80 procent af de potentielle mål i øst. Amerikanerne havde allerede en del erfaringer med tunnelbygning under indlandsisen: I 1958 havde man startet opførelsen af Camp Century øst for Thule. Den bestod af 26 forbundne tunneler med en samlet længde på tre kilometer (billedet). Foto: Nordfoto

Spiontogter fra Thule ind i Sovjetunionen

Rekognoscering: Amerikanerne brugte i 1950erne Thule som udgangspunkt for en stribe superhemmelige fototogter ind i sovjetisk luftrum. Den sovjetiske generalsekretær betegnede disse fly som »flyvende ligkister«.

AF TROELS MYLENBERG OG ASK ROSTRUP

Thulebasen var på næsten alle områder en uhyre central brik i amerikanernes sikkerhedspolitiske strategi.

Dansk Udenrigspolitisk Institut (DUPI) hvidbog om Grønland under den kolde krig er gennemsyret af den enorme interesse og vigtighed, som USA tillagde de nordatlantiske baser. Det skyldes ikke mindst, at baserne i Grønland i årene efter Anden Verdenskrig blev anset for helt centrale for USAs interne sikkerhed.

Derfor blev baserne i Grønland udnyttet til såvel kernevåben, videnskabelige forsøg og – som DUPI dokumenterer for første gang – amerikanske spiontogter ind over sovjetisk territorium.

En stribe togter

Den hermetiske lukkethed i Sovjetunionen var i 1950erne et stort problem for USA. Det var svært at lokalisere de rigtige mål i en eventuel krig, og derfor var det nødvendigt at sende rekognosceringsfly langs Sovjet-grænserne – og nogle gange ind over dem – for simpelthen at fotografere.

Langt de fleste af disse fly blev sendt af sted fra Storbritannien, men nu afslører DUPI, at også Thule var hjemsted for en stribe af disse spiontogter.

Allerede i eftersommeren 1954 optrådte de første rekognosceringsfly i Thule, og halvandet år senere blev den første større kendte rekognosceringsøvelse afviklet med udgangspunkt i Thule: I næsten to måneder deltog 19 fly i 169 flyvninger under navnet Home Run.

Der er ikke mange optegnelser over spiontogterne fra Thule. DUPI har dog sammenstykket et uklart billede af, at der var en del hyperfølsom aktivitet omkring spionflyvningerne.

Således blev ni fly i 1959 sendt til Thule med den hemmelige mission at »penetrere det nordlige Sovjetunionen over en bred front«. De ni fly trængte tre gange i løbet af en måned ind i sovjetisk luftrum for at tage fotos – efterfølgende fik enheden i al diskretion en udmærkelse for sin indsats.

Tre år tidligere var der sendt ikke færre end 17 spionfly til Thule, hvor de skulle være i ca. seks uger. Sådan skulle det dog ikke gå. For efter blot en uge forlod de igen Thule – formentlig på grund af kriserne omkring Ungarn og Suez i 1956.

Soleklar melding fra Moskva

Den slags flyvninger huede ikke Sovjetunionen, der dog ikke protesterede officielt. Til gengæld fik den amerikanske general Twining en soleklar melding under en flyparade i Moskva i 1956, da generalsekretær Nikita Khrusjtjov betegnede de amerikanske rekognosceringsfly over sovjetisk territorium som »flyvende ligkister«.

En klar demonstration af, at der var handling bag ordene, kom i 1960, da et amerikansk U2-fly blev skudt ned over sovjetisk territorium.

DUPI slår dog fast, at dette fly ikke kom fra Thule, da der formentlig ikke på noget tidspunkt var U2-fly i Thule.

Efter sommeren 1959 blev de amerikanske spionaktiviteter fra Thule neddroslet drastisk.

FIGURE 9.1 Article by the Danish investigative journalists Troels Mylenberg and Ask Rostrup, which appeared in the Danish daily *Berlingske Tidende* on January 18, 1997—the day the DIIS report *Grønland under den kolde krig* [Greenland during the Cold War] was made available to the public.

was a nonissue. When faced with this massive rebuttal of a potential problem in the form of dangerously high radiation levels in and around Camp Century, Otto Steenholdt refrained from pursuing the matter. With that, what could have escalated into a perfect storm in 1980 and again in 1995, in the wake of Camp Century's swift shutdown in the mid-1960s, never rose above the level of a few moderate gusts, which did not shake the apparent certainty and conviction underlying all official statements from the Danish government on the matter.

Over the next twenty years, the old news stories would pop up again at irregular intervals in newspapers and popular magazines and later on various websites. The angle would usually be the insanity of the Cold War era, a time when rational people could conjure up projects like Camp Century and Iceworm. However, the contamination issue was also raised again in 2014 by another Greenlandic MP in the Danish parliament, Doris Jacobsen, who on January 14 of that year posed an official question on the topic to the parliament's Greenland Committee. A follow-up came in May 2014 when Aleqa Hammond, premier of Greenland, reminded Foreign Minister Martin Lidegaard of the outstanding question during her visit to Copenhagen. The minister responded in a letter dated May 26, 2014, explaining the sequence of events surrounding the installation and operation of Camp Century's PM-2A reactor. Among other things, Lidegaard wrote that "final approval of the American use of the nuclear reactor to supply the camp with energy was given by relevant, competent Danish authorities on January 10, 1960," concluding:

> In connection with the final approval, a number of preconditions for American use of the reactor had been laid down, including, for instance, that the United States remove all of the radioactive components from Greenland after use. . . . Danish representatives [followed] the activities in the camp throughout the entire period, and no objections were made by Denmark's sitting Atomic Energy Commission against the American plan for disposing of radioactive waste and taking down the reactor. . . . [The] average concentration of radioactive substances in the wastewater at Camp Century was, by way of comparison, significantly lower than the Danish Health Authority's established

maximum concentration of radioactive substances in the water discharged to public sewer systems from, for instance, a hospital or a
research department. . . . [The above] factors are certainly part of the
explanation why, to the best of our knowledge at the Ministry of Foreign Affairs, it has not been deemed necessary to subsequently supervise the camp.[34]

Not long after, when Foreign Minister Lidegaard paid a return visit to
Greenland in August 2014, Hammond requested more documentation
regarding Camp Century. Therefore, shortly after his return to Copenhagen, Lidegaard sent a new letter, dated August 21, 2014, containing
two attachments he believed would fulfill Hammond's request.[35] One
attachment was the report from the Danish AEC dated October 2, 1964,
and written by C. F. Jacobsen, from the Risø Nuclear Research Laboratory. The other was the official American report about the construction
and operation of Camp Century.[36] The correspondence between Hammond and Lidegaard and the two attached reports clearly show that a
Danish-American agreement dated 1960 did exist, in which Denmark
granted the United States permission to have a nuclear reactor at Camp
Century and to discharge a small, rigorously described amount of
radioactive wastewater into the ice sheet. In return for this, the United
States undertook to remove all radioactive components from Greenland upon closure of Camp Century. Jacobsen's report also testified
that the last condition had been met to the letter.

Once again the blustery discussions about Camp Century settled
down for almost two years. Then came the summer of 2016, which flung
open a new and dramatic chapter in the history of the city under the ice.

CLIMATE CHANGE AND THE UNCOVERING
OF CAMP CENTURY

August 2016 witnessed an event that suddenly and unexpectedly
transformed Camp Century from a rusty, splintered remnant of an

FIGURE 9.2 The Canadian glaciologist William Colgan dressed for summer work in the Arctic. Colgan headed the international science team that revealed, in August 2016, that because of climate change, waste from Camp Century may give rise to new environmental problems in the vulnerable Arctic region some time in the next century.

ever-more-distant Cold War era into a hot topic and a modern-day political and environmental dilemma that is currently rocking the very foundations of the joint Kingdom of Denmark, Greenland, and the Faroe Islands. On August 4, 2016, the journal *Geophysical Research Letters* published William Colgan's scientific article about Camp Century's anticipated future in light of climate change. In normal circumstances, such an article would only be read by a relatively limited group of experts.[37] In this instance, however, "normal" did not apply. The publishers of the journal, the American Geophysical Union, issued a press release under the heading "Melting Ice Sheet Could Release Frozen Cold War–Era Waste." The press release made it clear that the question of responsibility for the cleanup would be of crucial importance but that it had so far been, and remained, undecided.[38]

On that very same day, the award-winning daily news site of the journal *Science* ran the story of the new Camp Century findings. When one of this book's authors got a telephone call from the American journalist Julia Rosen asking for comments on the matter, he explained: "It plays into a discussion about the United States and Denmark using Greenland for their own purposes, and then the Greenlandic people have to deal with it afterward."[39] Many other international journals, news media, and social media latched on to the story, which soon became one of the hottest breaking-news items around the globe that day. The research team behind the original article was "totally overwhelmed by all the interest," as an article in *Politiken* rendered the reaction from William Colgan, who was head of the team.[40] Colgan drew attention to the fact that the article had previously been rejected by two other journals that considered it "too esoteric."[41]

The story behind the article began back in the summer of 2010, when William Colgan was walking on the ice cap around the location of the long-buried Camp Century. Colgan and his team of geophysicists and other specialists had come to that particular spot to supplement the ice core drilled in 1966 with a core covering the period 1966–2010. While preparing the drilling site for the new core, he found himself wondering about the waste pockets containing the remains of Camp Century. How big were they? How far down in the ice? And might they conceivably resurface within the foreseeable future as a result of the global warming currently under way? After obtaining the supplementary core and seeing the team's ice-core results published, Colgan assembled a group of glaciologists and climate researchers who wanted to answer the questions Colgan had asked himself back in 2010.[42]

The first question, regarding the dimensions and volumes of waste, was relatively easy to answer—but only if one trusted the nearly fifty-year-old military reports describing all aspects of the experiments and studies taking place at Camp Century. It was a natural choice for Colgan to trust the material, since most of the military experts had been scientists educated and trained in reporting measurements, quantifiable results, and calculations as precisely and exhaustively as possible.

Camp Century may have been a military project, but that in itself was no reason to doubt the scientific records. Using these records, Colgan and his colleagues arrived at a figure for physical waste left behind totaling some 9,200 metric tons of buildings, rails sections, electrical radiators, and the like. In terms of chemical waste, they could expect to find about 200 metric tons of diesel oil and waste oil, as well as an unknown but certainly not negligible amount of polychlorinated biphenyls (PCBs), chemicals that belong to a group of environmentally persistent organic compounds that already constitute a significant problem in the vulnerable ecosystems of the Arctic.[43] In the article, Colgan and his colleagues assert that PCBs in particular are the most worrying group of potential pollutants from the Camp Century site.

As for the biological waste, the researchers estimated there would be roughly 24 million liters (6.3 million gallons) of raw sewage, which at the time had been dumped into an unlined discharge cavity in the ice in close proximity to the camp's personnel tunnels, as described in chapter 3. Last but certainly not least, the camp had discharged batches of slightly radioactive water with an aggregate radioactivity of 2.7 GBq (72 millicuries) at the time of discharge, in 1960 through 1966. These had been deposited in another likewise unlined cavity in the ice. The scientists mentioned that although the total radioactivity from Camp Century is "nontrivial," it is small in comparison to the radioactivity caused by the Thule incident in 1968, when a plane crash spread approximately 4,000 times more radioactivity.[44]

After the Colgan group's article, two Danish experts—the senior scientist Sven Poul Nielsen, from the Center for Nuclear Technologies at DTU, and the former DTU professor Povl L. Ølgaard (mentioned earlier), both of whom had visited Camp Century in 1962 to inspect the reactor and also made statements about the issue to the press in 1995—confirmed to Kalaallit Nunaata Radioa (KNR, the Greenlandic Broadcasting Corporation) that the total radioactivity left behind in the ice at Camp Century was limited. Ølgaard repeated his assessment from 1995, that "there aren't very large amounts of radioactivity down there," while Nielsen stated that "there must have been some very strict discharge requirements to that reactor, up there on the ice cap."[45] In

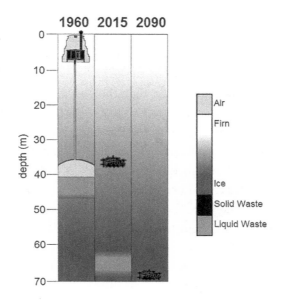

FIGURE 9.3 Figure 2 from the scientific paper by Colgan et al. (2016) showing the estimated depth of Camp Century's solid waste (indicated in black) and liquid waste (brown) in 1960, 2015, and 2090.

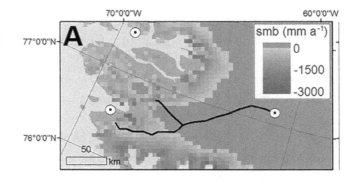

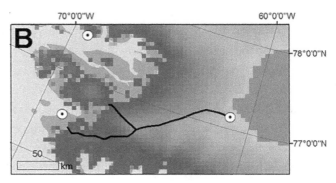

FIGURE 9.4 Figure 4 from Colgan et al. (2016) showing areas in northwestern Greenland around Thule Air Base with ice-sheet melt-off in 1960 and projected for 2090. Areas with no melt-off are marked in blue; melt-off areas are marked in red. The location of Camp Century is indicated by a circle on the right-hand portion of each map, and the models indicate that this area may well be subject to melt-off in 2090.

comparison, the threshold value for radioactivity in wastewater from the last nuclear reactor at the Risø facility (fed directly into Roskilde Fjord) is 200 times higher than the Camp Century threshold.

Besides waste volumes and hazard levels, in order to assess future risks it is important to know the depth of the various types of waste. There are two ways to determine depth. One is to use standard models to calculate how quickly solid and liquid materials move downward in ice. The other is to use radar techniques capable of identifying small cavities in the ice to indicate the current positions of the once spacious tunnels. Colgan and his team applied both methods, finding in 2015 that most of the solid waste was located about 36 meters below the surface, whereas most of the originally liquid, now-frozen waste had probably reached a depth of at least 65 meters.[46]

The reason this new research gained attention internationally was the group's projection showing what would happen to the Camp Century waste in light of the changing climate. By using existing climate models that describe how the ice sheet will develop in a future climate with unchanged levels of greenhouse gases, the scientists were able to project that the waste from Camp Century will become visible and seep out of the ice in just under a century. The solid waste will reappear on the future surface of the ice sheet sometime during the second half of the twenty-second century. The liquid waste will seep down through the ice along with meltwater runoff and eventually reach areas beyond the margin of the ice sheet. Although the latter processes are far more difficult to predict, the scientists conclude they may cause the liquid waste to become a problem decades before the solid waste resurfaces.[47]

The results are highly uncertain, obviously, given that they predict events foreseen to occur many decades from now. But as the senior scientist Dirk van As, who works for GEUS (the Geological Survey of Denmark and Greenland) and was Denmark's participant in the project, underscored in a newspaper interview with *Information*: "It's not a question of whether it will happen. It's more a question of when it will happen. That's one of our main conclusions: If climate change continues—and we know it will continue—this waste is not going to remain enclosed in the ice forever. If climate change goes on long enough, this waste will reach the surface of the ice and be led out into the ocean."[48] But is that a major problem? And will it "just" be a question of local pollution and contamination? "To be honest," Dirk van As said, "we really don't know."[49] The volumes of waste are sizeable, and the processes that transport them to the ocean will definitely be very slow. Some of the substances, especially the very persistent organic compounds (like PCBs), will accumulate in the food chain, a problem that is already grave because the unique climatic conditions in the Arctic have a tendency to "trap" such substances in the ecosystems there.[50] As for whether the waste can be removed at the present time, van As replied that such an operation would pose an enormous logistic challenge, which might in itself cause contamination, concluding: "I think the only conceivable way is to wait until the ice above has melted, and then move in as fast as possible to capture the waste."[51]

CRACKS IN THE MORTAR THAT BINDS THE UNIFIED REALM

The conclusion Dirk van As reached was pragmatic and prudently watchful, but these were by no means the two attitudes most visible in the subsequent debate. The often intense deliberations continued throughout the autumn of 2016, led by Greenlandic politicians who wanted clarity in allocating the responsibility for cleaning up after Camp Century. Briefly, in mid-December, there even seemed to be a risk that the contentious issue would jeopardize the unity and viability of the tripartite structure of the joint realm. At the crux of the matter lay the insecurity about future pollution and contamination from the Camp Century site, combined with the responsibility for carrying out the actual cleanup operation. As Aaja Chemnitz Larsen, one of the two sitting Greenlandic MPs to Denmark, explained to the newspaper *Information*: "This is a worrying topic, but also difficult because we don't have the full picture of who bears responsibility. The only clear thing is: It's Greenland that's going to feel the consequences if the waste gets out and impacts the environment."[52]

Aaja Chemnitz Larsen was supported by Vittus Qujaukitsoq, a member of Greenland's government, Naalakkersuisut, and its appointed minister for business, the labor market, trade, and foreign affairs. Qujaukitsoq pointed out that on previous occasions Naalakkersuisut had attempted to make Denmark clarify responsibility not only for Camp Century but for all of the military installations that, over the years, have been transferred from the United States to Denmark and that are now (or may someday become) the cause of extensive environmental pollution on Greenlandic soil. Danish politicians, too, including the former foreign minister (and Social Liberal) Martin Lidegaard, have encouraged sitting Danish governments to raise the issue of allocating responsibility in discussions with the United States. "It's clear," said Lidegaard, "that Greenland shouldn't be left holding the responsibility for this." He was supported by Karsten Hønge (of the Socialist People's Party), who remarked that in this matter the "polluter pays" principle must be invoked.[53]

Besides the question of responsibility, the issue also quickly came to revolve around waste volumes. The group behind the scientific article that had ignited the whole affair had toned down the radioactive contamination, pointing out instead that the environmentally persistent organic compounds were presumably the greatest potential problem hidden in the ruins and refuse of Camp Century. Nevertheless, the Greenlandic politicians were particularly preoccupied with the radioactive wastewater. On September 27, 2016, Aaja Chemnitz Larsen again posed an official question, this time addressed to the Danish parliament's Greenland Committee and specifically to Minister of Foreign Affairs Kristian Jensen. She wanted to know: Did Jensen intend to maintain what he had previously told the committee with reference to the AEC report from 1964 and the assessment of the Danish Health Authority, namely, that the level of radioactivity and the remaining wastewater cannot be expected to cause damage to people and the environment?[54]

Kristian Jensen submitted his response a little less than a month later. He referred once again to the report from 1964, which concluded that the level of radioactivity in the remaining wastewater was below the threshold values set. He additionally referred to the earlier environment minister's written response (dated July 3, 1980) to MP Margrethe Auken's "Section 20" question, which on the same basis had reached the same conclusion. He further mentioned that Larsen's question (and his own response) had been presented to the Danish Health Authority's radiation protection unit, which handles all matters for government bodies and authorities concerning radiation protection and Danish radioactivity legislation. This process had failed to yield any further information the minister could pass on.[55]

The Greenlandic politicians did not feel they had received a full and satisfying answer to their questions about the scope of radioactive contamination at Camp Century or about the responsibility for cleanups at former U.S. base sites in Greenland. Essentially, all they had seen was the same information presented first to the Danish government in 1964, then to the Danish MP Margrethe Auken in 1980, and finally to Greenland's premier, Aleqa Hammond, in 2014. Furthermore, the Greenlanders saw not the slightest opening or potential goodwill to renegotiate the 1951 Defense Agreement between the United States and Denmark, which stipulates, in Article 11: "It is understood that any areas or facilities made available to the Government of the United States of America under this Agreement need not be left in the condition in which they were at the time they were thus made available."[56]

In a feature article appearing on October 13, 2016, in *Berlingske Tidende*, Vittus Qujaukitsoq underscored that Camp Century was just one of many abandoned U.S. military bases on Greenlandic soil where too little cleanup work had been done and that a particular concern was the unresolved question of environmentally persistent organic solvents present at such sites. This was the same argument Larsen had advanced, but Qujaukitsoq went one step further, writing that international treaties and conventions obliged Denmark to cooperate with the Greenlanders to implement measures that would protect the environment and also to

FIGURE 9.5 Before tensions ran high. Photo from the Isfjord, taken in the summer of 2016 in Greenland. Left to right: Foreign Minister Kristian Jensen; Premier of the Greenlandic Government Kim Kielsen; U.S. Secretary of State John Kerry; and Greenlandic Minister for Business, Labour Market, Commerce, and Foreign Affairs Vittus Qujaukitsoq. They met to see for themselves the effects of climate change, which are particularly noticeable in and around the Isfjord.

pay Greenland compensation for areas that are ruined or "nonusable." Thus far, Qujaukitsoq concluded, Denmark had not wished to comply with its obligations to Greenland under international law.[57]

Later in October 2016, Qujaukitsoq sent a letter to Foreign Minister Kristian Jensen, setting out Greenland's demands for Denmark's cooperation in establishing environmental protection measures and potentially paying compensation to Greenland. As he phrased it: "If there is no willingness on the part of Denmark to take steps to accommodate our wishes, Greenland will be forced to bring the case before the relevant international bodies."[58] Qujaukitsoq had not used precise wording in his letter, and as later pointed out by Rasmus Gjedssø Bertelsen, a professor of social sciences at the University of Tromsø under the Arctic University of Norway, Greenland is unable to take legal action against Denmark before the International Court of Justice in The Hague because the country is not a nation-state. However, that by no means precludes Greenlandic politicians from mobilizing considerable discontent with Denmark by referring to the International Labour Organization and ILO Convention Number 169, which deals with the rights of indigenous peoples.[59]

Early in November 2016, Foreign Minister Kristian Jensen and Minister of Environment, Food, and Fisheries Esben Lunde Larsen were summoned to an open consultation meeting in the Danish parliament's Greenland Committee. In this forum, Jensen acknowledged that no clear agreements exist as to who is responsible for cleaning up in and around former U.S. bases and installations, causing further frustration among the committee's Greenlandic members. Aaja Chemnitz Larsen was far from content with the failure to allocate responsibility, and she emphasized that under no circumstances should Greenland be responsible for cleaning up after Camp Century.[60]

From this point, the tone on the Greenlandic side of the acrimonious debate became much sharper. The most prominent voice was that of Vittus Qujaukitsoq, who has family roots in the hunting and fishing community of Qaanaaq, near Thule Air Base. In an interview in one of Greenland's two national newspapers, *Sermitsiaq*, Qujaukitsoq expressed that he was "profoundly shocked" at the Danish ministerial responses on the issue of Camp Century during the parliamentary consultation meeting, asserting that he suspected the Danish authorities of suppressing new information about extensive pollution and contamination not just at the Camp Century site but also at Thule Air Base and other abandoned American installations in the area.[61] Then, in a high-profile newspaper interview featured in the Danish daily *Politiken* on December 13, 2016, Qujaukitsoq expressed that he had lost trust in the Danish authorities.[62]

And that was not all. Even though the modest-sized Greenlandic party, Demokraterne (the Democrats, then part of the opposition), was "shocked at the tone in Qujaukitsoq's criticism of Denmark,"[63] the entire Greenlandic parliament, Inatsisartut, shared his view that Denmark had not been forthcoming enough in treating Greenland's request to have the whole matter thoroughly reviewed. In November, a unanimous Inatsisartut had adopted an official statement that the 1951 Defense Agreement was to be renegotiated, such that Greenland would receive compensation for making the area around Thule Air Base available to the United States. What is more, on December 1, 2016, Vittus Qujaukitsoq had a personal meeting, in private, with the secretary general of NATO to explain Greenland's position and its difficulties in reaching an agreement with Denmark.[64] "For us, this is 75 years of pent-up frustration," Qujaukitsoq declared, describing a clear perception in his country that Denmark was not taking Greenland seriously and predicting how that very arrogance might ultimately break the unity of the joint realm. According to Qujaukitsoq, the most important issue for the Greenlanders was achieving the right to codetermine what the United States would be asked to do—and what it would be asked to pay—for its presence on Greenlandic territory.[65]

THE DEBATE ROLLS ON

The pressure Greenland exerted on the Danish government came around the time Donald Trump became president, bringing a new uncertainty about U.S. foreign policy and about the American position on Thule Air Base. Statements by President Trump indicated that he intended to strengthen the nation's defense capabilities, including its missile defense and warning system. Importantly in this context, Thule Air Base—with its advanced land-based radar and satellite systems and an airstrip long enough for large bombers—is the most crucial American hub in the Arctic, making it a likely candidate for the president's bolstering of U.S. military efforts.[66] In the summer of 2016, an American appeals court ruled that a seven-year contract for servicing Thule Air Base, valued at some 2.4 billion Danish kroner (about 350 million U.S. dollars) could rightly be awarded to the American company Exelis

FIGURE 9.6 Resurgent interest in Camp Century in 2016 made the Danish government decide to set up permanent monitoring where Camp Century once lay. A new scientific expedition visited the location in the summer of 2017, where for the first time the Greenlandic and Danish flags flew over the "city under the ice" buried deep below.

Services, rather than to three Danish companies—Per Aarsleff, Copenhagen Arctic, and Greenland Contractors (the last with Greenlandic co-ownership)—a constellation that had previously held the contract and serviced the base. If the American ruling is the last word in the legal proceedings, which is uncertain at this time, Greenland's public news provider, KNR, estimates it will cost the nation some 200 million Danish kroner (about 30 million U.S. dollars) in lost income for each year the contract runs.[67]

On the matter of cleanups and responsibility, the pressure from Greenland worked. On February 9, 2017, the government of Greenland approved a Danish proposal that the Danish state would take steps to further investigate environmental, health, and pollution issues in the area where the remains of Camp Century lie buried. The task of carrying out the investigation and testing regime—officially named "The Camp Century Climate Monitoring Programme"—will be handled by people from multiple scientific organizations, including GEUS and Asiaq (Grønlands Forundersøgelser, the Greenland surveying body). Their scientific work and results are freely available to all interested parties at the website www.campcenturyclimate.dk.

Arriving in mid-July 2017, the team began setting up an automatic weather station to monitor air temperature, sunlight, and ice temperatures down to a depth of 50 meters, preparing plans for ice-core drilling and radar mapping of the waste pockets. The program's aim is to remain vigilant in the area and to shed more light on the scope of the problem. Commenting on the new initiative to KNR in 2016, William Colgan, head of the investigations that revived and renewed the discussions about the remains of Camp Century, explained: "We expect that most of the waste deposits will be 35 meters down in the ice. But we're not sure. Some of the waste may be deeper down than that if liquid was dumped. And some may be higher up if it was dumped on the surface in the 1960s instead of down below. It's important to know how far down the meltwater has to go in the future before it turns into a problem."[68] Even so, the mere prospect of a new and comprehensive monitoring initiative was not enough to satisfy Greenland. The problem was that the issue of attributing responsibility for a potential cleanup had not yet been addressed. The Greenlandic authorities were adamant in their position that either the Danes or the Americans would have to assume responsibility for cleaning up. While the United States has not yet made any public statements, in the spring of 2017 Denmark expressed its willingness to handle such an operation in collaboration with the government of Greenland, Naalakkersuisut.[69]

The whole affair also revealed that rifts in Greenland's own political landscape ran deep, even affecting the way Naalakkersuisut approached the handling of Greenland's unresolved issues with Denmark and the United States. Greenland's premier, Kim Kielsen, preferred a more conciliatory position toward Denmark, not wishing under any circumstances to see Greenland threaten to withdraw from the unified realm—a position that caused Vittus Qujaukitsoq to step down as foreign minister on April 24, 2017.[70] Figuratively slamming the door as he left, Qujaukitsoq also threatened in no uncertain terms that he would be seeking the chairmanship of Siumut, the governing party in Greenland—the very position Kielsen had held since 2014. At the same time, Qujaukitsoq lodged an official complaint about the Danish government with the United Nations, claiming that Denmark had not

assumed sufficient responsibility for cleaning up after military installations in Greenland and that Denmark had not seen to it that Greenland
received a reasonable financial outcome from accommodating Thule
Air Base.[71] Naalakkersuisut later retracted the complaint.

Qujaukitsoq's challenge may have motivated Kielsen to raise the
topic of military facility cleanups in Greenland during the leaders'
summit for the unified realm held in June 2017. We do not know. But
what does seem clear is that after the Faroe Islands promised, shortly
before the summit meeting, to clean up a number of abandoned fishing
stations along Greenland's west coast, Kielsen was "hungry for more,"[72]
and Denmark ended up accepting Greenland's demands. At the summit meeting, Premier Kielsen and Prime Minister Lars Løkke Rasmussen
signed a letter of intent stating that from 2018 the Danish government
will seek appropriation of a fixed annual sum of 30 million Danish kroner (roughly 4.5 million U.S. dollars) over a five-year period "to clean
up after the former American military presence in Greenland."[73]

Along with the already initiated monitoring program on the ice
sheet, the letter of intent resolves the most recent affair involving Camp
Century—at least for the time being. In the future, the facility will
doubtless be revisited again as part of Cold War history and as an environmental problem. "The city under the ice" was constructed at the
peak of the Cold War, becoming an icon for American security policy
and the extensive network of American military installations in Greenland. Equipped with a mobile nuclear reactor, the camp was also a possible beachhead for the peaceful exploitation of nuclear energy in the
High North, even while posing an enormous challenge to the Danish
government, which would have preferred to see all mention of the "concept of atoms" in the context of Greenland kept to a minimum. In this
connection, the Danish authorities made it clear that although they did
take a positive view of the American presence in Greenland with the
building of a network of scientific bases, they still had certain reservations about overt mention of the United States' large-scale missile plans.
Later, after the Americans pulled out of Camp Century, the complex
was transformed into a slumbering giant, a potential environmental
predicament in the making. As early as 1980, concerned scientists and

politicians were focusing on the residual radioactivity in the ice, and since then a variety of scenarios have been envisioned and discussed, with increasing intensity. Chronicling the aftermath of Camp Century shows that its legacy and the physical remains it left behind have still not been entirely put to rest.

THE MAN WITHOUT A SHADOW

As recently as the spring of 2018, another intriguing angle was added to the story of Camp Century, already a convoluted labyrinth full of surprising twists and turns that have only gradually emerged from obscurity since the camp's final abandonment in 1966. This new angle was revealed in a Danish-language podcast series entitled *The Man Without a Shadow*, broadcast on Danish public radio in April and May 2018.[74] The pivotal character in the podcast was a man named Tuk Erik Jørgen-Jensen (born 1935), who was able to document that he had been employed by the Danish Defense Intelligence Service (DDIS) and stationed in Greenland from March 1960 to August 1963 at Thule Air Base and the three American research camps Tuto, Century, and Fistclench. In his account, the Americans had called him "the man without a shadow," alluding perhaps to the fact that he was not on an official mission but operated outside the established diplomatic channels between Denmark and the United States. His job description was simple: "Observe and report." He was there to keep his eyes peeled and pass on information about notable activities and events at the American bases in northwestern Greenland, reporting directly to DDIS headquarters in Copenhagen—but with no precise instructions on how to do this and without any idea how the intelligence he provided would be used. He pretty much had to invent his own job on the spot, in Thule and elsewhere in the region.[75]

For the purpose of the podcast, the two Danish journalists, Jacob Grosen and Thomas Vinther Larsen, interviewed former captain Leon E. McKinney, who was responsible for operating the nuclear reactor at

FIGURE 9.7 Tuk Erik Jørgen-Jensen at Thule Air Base, presumably in 1961, boarding a helicopter bound for Camp Century. Here, in accordance with his instructions, he would be observing and reporting notable or unusual events to the Danish Defense Intelligence Service in Copenhagen.

Camp Century from 1962 to the winter of 1963, encompassing its shutdown. In this interview, McKinney confirms having met Tuk Erik Jørgen-Jensen at Camp Century. He also talks about the radiation levels and the cleanup work associated with dismantling the reactor, explaining that although there is always radiation in a nuclear reactor, the lead cladding provides protection. The radiation levels were quite a bit higher than expected, he concedes, but sums up by confirming that they "removed all radioactive material and left the place in as good shape as [it was] before we were there."[76]

According to Jørgen-Jensen, the reason he chose to come forward in 2018, more than fifty years after he was stationed in Greenland, was twofold: first, the topicality in the Danish media of these events and (potential) cleanup of the Camp Century site in 2016–2018, and second, the desire to tell his side of the story and contribute by bringing what he could to light. But Jørgen-Jensen's mission in northwestern Greenland is still mysterious: we have been unable to find any information in Danish archives that sheds light on his role or even mentions his name. One explanation for this could be that—according to Jørgen-Jensen—he was on a secret mission, acting more or less independently and only reporting directly to the DDIS. It does seem remarkable, though, that at the time the Danish defense authorities needed this type of operative in northwestern Greenland—and that the Americans evidently agreed to Denmark having such an operative. Ever since the 1951 Defense Agreement between Denmark and the United States came into force, laying down the terms for Greenland's defense, a Danish military liaison officer from Greenland Command (now Joint Arctic Command, a special division of the Danish armed forces) has been stationed at Thule Air Base. The duties of the officer appointed as liaison at any given time consist partly in making the cooperation between Danish and American authorities as smooth as possible and partly in keeping an eye on changes in the numbers of military personnel and aircraft and on various defense installations, research projects, and so on not just at Thule Air Base but also beyond base terrain, outside the Thule defense area proper. To help with this huge task, beginning in the summer of 1954 the liaison officer had a scientific adviser, often called the "scientific liaison officer," who was usually appointed for one year at a time. Readers of this book will have come across this role and the various people who held it numerous times. This raises the question: Given that the arrangement had become a set practice and had apparently been working to everyone's satisfaction since the early 1950s, why, in 1960, was another person sent to the region with tasks that were partly overlapping, but without the official status of a liaison officer?

The lack of such status is evident in the apparent absence of any official mention, anywhere, of a person named Tuk Erik Jørgen-Jensen in the wealth of archival material from the Ministry of Foreign Affairs—an absence confirmed by the Danish foreign minister Anders Samuelsen, who attended a parliamentary consultation meeting on May 29, 2018, with the Greenland Committee. On this occasion, the minister stated that the ministry had once again reviewed "old archival packets with documents and microfilm," concluding: "In the reviewed material, the Ministry of Foreign Affairs has not found information about Erik Jørgen-Jensen, or from Erik Jørgen-Jensen about this information."[77] At the same time, however, the foreign minister passed the ball to the Danish defense ministry, which "is investigating the historical circumstances concerning liaison officers at Thule Air Base. This also goes for any terms of employment for the individual in the radio program, Erik Jørgen-Jensen. We await the result of that investigation."[78] But here the trail goes cold. Besides acknowledging that Jørgen-Jensen served as a conscript recruit in the Danish military in 1957–1958, the Ministry of Defense has subsequently stated that it "cannot touch upon any further circumstances regarding Tuk Erik Jørgen-Jensen."[79] In other words, there is unbreakable confidentiality in the matter from the two Danish ministries that dealt with Jørgen-Jensen's stationing in Greenland.

Jørgen-Jensen believes the most probable explanation is that—from a Danish point of view—the arrangement based on military and scientific liaison officers had not been satisfactory.[80] As described in chapter 2, the Danish foreign minister at the time, Jens Otto Krag, was extremely surprised if not shocked when, on August 18, 1959, the American ambassador to Denmark, Val Peterson, informed him that the U.S.

Army Polar Research and Development Center had already begun building Camp Century, even though the Danes had not yet given permission for the project. Krag's surprise may have been replaced by chagrin at not knowing more about the projected camp and its nuclear reactor. Reports from the scientific and military liaison officers about the groundwork at Camp Century were making their way through the authorized information channels, including news that the nuclear reactor would not be installed in the summer of 1959 but would instead arrive the following summer. Meanwhile, the liaison information may not have reached the foreign minister at the time, and it is quite likely he found what information he received to be inadequate.

It may seem strange to modern readers that in the summer of 1959 the foreign minister of Denmark had not been informed that hundreds of tons of building materials destined for Camp Century had landed as cargo at the harbor near Thule Air Base, been transported on various vehicles to Camp Tuto at the edge of the ice sheet, and then been moved on heavy swings across the ice sheet to the Camp Century site. In other words, the construction of Camp Century was in full swing. The weekly dispatches from the Thule-based liaison officer at the time, Lieutenant Commander Knud Alexander Edvars, to his superiors at Greenland Command did not emphasize the many heavy transports that arrived at Thule harbor in July 1959 and were immediately sent on to Camp Tuto.[81] The dispatch from Edvars dated August 11, 1959, containing his reporting for the month of July also contains an American "weekly progress report" from the U.S. Army Polar Research and Development Center (which handled the many American scientific activities), and this report stated the size of the transports to Camp Century. It shows that from July 12 to 18, 1959, shipments amounting to 43 metric tons were moved from Camp Tuto to Camp Century.[82] The dispatch Edvars sent in August also contained a report from the scientific adviser, Helge Larsen, who had just paid a visit to Camp Century in July, writing in his report about "Camp Century, 220 km from Thule, a 'camp' that is under construction and, as far as I could understand, will be very large in extent, being, among other things, the location where the reactor is to be built."[83]

It is reasonable to hypothesize that Foreign Minister Jens Otto Krag found the information flow from Thule Air Base lacking and that high-ranking people in the Danish defense administration wanted to make sure similar situations could be avoided in the future. It is also reasonable to assume that the Danish authorities did this by stationing an agent who was independent of the military liaison officers. In other words, a "man without a shadow," with permission to move freely around the defense area of Thule Air Base and the scientific camps associated with it (Tuto, Fistclench, and Century), an agent whose mission was to report all unusual incidents directly to the DDIS. Supporting this hypothesis, we also have Jørgen-Jensen's own accounts describing how he was initially contacted by the DDIS in late November 1959, shortly after the informal meeting between Krag and Peterson, and how in early 1960 he attended three meetings at which his tasks and authorization were discussed. The first such meeting took place at the American embassy in Copenhagen in early February 1960. Here, Jørgen-Jensen was informed that he would have access to all locations in and around Thule Air Base. He then received a passport with the necessary stamps, as well as a military ID card. The second meeting took place at the Danish Ministry of Foreign Affairs, in Krag's ministerial office, and the third at Krag's own home on a quiet residential street in Frederiksberg, close to central Copenhagen. Besides the minister and the agent-to-be, these meetings were attended by civil servants from the foreign ministry, the U.S. ambassador to Denmark, and a person from the DDIS. At the last meeting in Krag's home, the parties concluded that the United States and Denmark agreed that Denmark could send a person (Tuk Erik Jørgen-Jensen) to Thule, with access to camps associated with Thule Air Base; that the parties would not inform the American or Danish press about sending this person; that as far as possible, Jørgen-Jensen was to avoid contact with the Danish liaison officers and scientific advisers, so as not to risk the Danish press getting wind of the new initiative; and that Jens Otto Krag was confident that with the new arrangement he would not be subjected to any more unpleasant surprises—like learning that the construction of Camp Century had begun without the necessary Danish permissions in place.[84]

Immediately after this final, very private meeting in the foreign minister's home, Jørgen-Jensen got ready to leave. He was given his ticket and travel money at the DDIS headquarters in Copenhagen, and on March 19, 1961, he climbed aboard an SAS DC-7B propeller plane to travel from Copenhagen Airport to Søndre Strømfjord (Kangerlussuaq) in Greenland. Bad weather grounded him at Kangerlussuaq Airport for three days, but on March 22 he was able to find passage to Thule Air Base on board an American C-124 military aircraft. At the base, he was met by the "Air Police," who drove him to an officers' barracks near base HQ. There he found himself with a two-room apartment at his disposal, plus a Jeep, an ID card, and various Arctic gear. This was to be

FIGURE 9.8 During his stay in Greenland, Tuk Erik Jørgen-Jensen was driven to Camp Century in a "polecat"—seen here during the 220-km journey. Note the sledge in tow, presumably packed with lightweight goods.

FIGURE 9.9 The SAC (Strategic Air Command) pass, which—in conjunction with the American embassy's visa notations in Tuk Erik Jørgen-Jensen's Danish passport—gave him unlimited access to all facilities at Thule Air Base, Camp Tuto, and Camp Century.

his home for the next three years. It was his starting point for visits to Thule Air Base, to missile batteries in the surrounding terrain, and to the scientific camps—not least Camp Century—where, in accordance with his instructions, he would "observe and report" conspicuous, noteworthy news and events back to his superiors at DDIS.[85]

Unfortunately, the authors of this book have been unable to access the reports Jørgen-Jensen sent to the DDIS in Copenhagen. With one exception, we have similarly had no access to the private diary Jørgen-Jensen kept while he was in Greenland, so we cannot document which specific events he reported or the contents of such reports. However, it is by no means impossible or implausible that, at the time, some of his reports had political consequences in Denmark or affected relations between Danish and American authorities in Greenland. Be that as it may, the four observations Jørgen-Jensen has chosen to emphasize in our conversations and correspondence as the most notable from his time in Greenland are the following:

1.   Once, in the winter of 1962, he watched as an American B-52 bomber made a dramatic emergency landing at Thule Air Base. As described in the 1997 DIIS report *Grønland under den kolde krig* (Greenland during the Cold War), the Danish liaison officer stationed at the base (O. W. Lorentsen) had also reported to his superiors at Greenland Command, notifying them that a landing of this sort had taken place on February 28, 1962—one of seven emergency landings occurring between 1962 and 1967, referred to as "Broken Arrow" incidents.[86]

2.   Once, in 1961, Jørgen-Jensen visited the missile batteries around Thule Air Base, observing the storage there of "12 nuclear warheads for rockets . . . in a storage room that was drilled into the bedrock."[87] He reported this to DDIS headquarters, but the Danes at home never got back to him on the issue. Not that this surprised him: before he left for Greenland, the intelligence service's people had told him that "the base had been allowed to have just a few nuclear warheads as a last-ditch resistance measure against attack. So there was nothing illegal in it."[88] Yet actually it was illegal, since the Danish parliament had never been

asked to grant permission for the storage of nuclear weapons at Thule Air Base. And had they been asked, the reply would undoubtedly have been a resounding "No." Permission, such as it was, rested solely on the assent of the Danish prime minister, H. C. Hansen, given in his confidential memo to the U.S. ambassador, Val Peterson, in November 1957, as detailed in chapter 1. The most interesting aspect of Jørgen-Jensen's account of visiting the missile batteries around the base in 1951 is its revelation that even though the DDIS had, in all likelihood, not seen Prime Minister Hansen's confidential memo, obviously they had nonetheless been informed that the Danes had given the Americans some sort of "permit" to store nuclear warheads at Thule Air Base. It was only in 1995 that the United States officially admitted that nuclear ammunition for the Nike batteries had, indeed, been present at Thule Air Base "from December 1959 till the summer of 1965."[89]

3. On several occasions during visits to Camp Century in 1961, Jørgen-Jensen had had the opportunity to meet up with a certain Captain Page, who worked at the PM-2A reactor. Page gradually came to look more and more ill, and suddenly he had left the camp. Jørgen-Jensen is convinced that Page had been subjected to an excess of radiation when the reactor was started in October/November 1960 and there were problems with radiation levels above the reactor exceeding the permitted limits, as remarked in chapter 3. At the same time, however, Jørgen-Jensen does grant that Page never mentioned anything to him about this, conceding that he has no professional medical background to justify such an opinion. The official American report about Camp Century explicitly states that no personnel received more than the permitted dose of radiation, which is also in line with the statements made to the Danes immediately after the incident.[90] We have not subsequently been able to determine whether Jørgen-Jensen's supposition about Captain Page was correct or whether the official version of the story holds true.

4. During a visit Jørgen-Jensen paid to Camp Fistclench in 1963, he observed railway tracks in a subsurface tunnel. He found this so surprising that he reported the facts to his Danish employers, but this did not elicit a response either. As recounted in chapter 6 of this book, the

observation cannot have been particularly surprising back in Copenhagen, as similar tests were also going on near Camp Century in 1962 and 1963 and were described in great detail by the serving scientific adviser. What is more, as early as 1960, Danish and Greenlandic newspapers were writing about the Americans' grand plans to install a railway line beneath the ice, running from Thule Air Base to Camp Century and from there on to Søndre Strømfjord (Kangerlussuaq)—plans that never came to fruition, as later years would show.

As for the story of "the man without a shadow," the last word has hardly been said. There may be other surprises in store for those interested in learning more about Camp Century and the lesser-known aspects of its history.

THE HISTORICAL SIGNIFICANCE OF CAMP CENTURY

Danes and Greenlanders were taken aback when suddenly, in August 2019, U.S. president Donald Trump announced that he was interested in buying Greenland. The offer sparked strong reactions and even aversion, following comments from the president that he perceived the potential American purchase of Greenland as "strategically interesting" and "essentially a large real estate deal."[91] Asked to comment on the proposal in an interview on Danish national television, Mette Frederiksen, the country's recently elected prime minister, called the whole discussion "absurd."[92] Frederiksen joined Kim Kielsen, the premier of Greenland, in asserting that Greenland was not, and is not, for sale. Nevertheless, beneath Trump's awkward bid for Arctic real estate lies a variety of growing strategic and economic interests in the region. Russia already has an ambitious program to secure its foothold in the Arctic, which includes new military bases and infrastructure facilities to support and secure polar shipping routes now becoming navigable as a result of global warming. China laid out its Arctic policy in early 2018, wishing to explore the region's natural resources and work with Russia to develop a "Polar Silk Road" that would facilitate global shipping. In contrast, the United States has so far remained relatively inactive and provided little response to the new geopolitical, environmental, and economic challenges emerging in the Arctic. However ill-conceived, President Trump's tentative bid for Greenland was one attempt to deal with the stagnation in U.S. policy on the Arctic.[93]

The modern-day predicament of small Arctic nations such as Denmark and Greenland bears some resemblance to the situation just after World War II, when the events in this book began. Given a perceived lack of strategic military mobilization in the polar region, the United States aspired to build an "Arctic fortress" in Greenland to protect U.S. territory from attacks launched by the Soviet Union. This coincided with the beginning of the Cold War, so named not only because the conflicts never led to direct military engagements between the two superpowers but also because many of its underlying conflicts came to play out across the frigid North. Then, in a bid to simplify the situation all round, the United States offered to buy Greenland from Denmark— and was quite surprised when the offer was squarely rejected. Danish politicians already had their own vision for Greenland, prepared in collaboration with prominent members of the Greenlandic nation: to create a modern Greenlandic society that was on an equal footing with Denmark. The intention was not (merely) to have Greenland serve as a military base for the United States. The 1951 Defense Agreement— which pertained to Greenland but was signed by Denmark and the United States and based on the terms of the North Atlantic Treaty Organization (NATO)—was signed on April 27, 1951, and it granted America the right to have military bases in Greenland. Two years later, an amendment to the Danish Constitution formally made Greenland part of the unified Kingdom of Denmark, putting the country on an administrative par with a Danish county.

The history of Camp Century began a little later, in the ice-cold political climate of the Cold War in the late 1950s. "Nuclear deterrence" and "massive retaliation" were the phrases most often used to describe the tense geopolitical situation, but the U.S. "polar strategy" was also an important factor, not least for Denmark and Greenland. The polar strategy envisioned that a potential strike, and potential retaliation, would take place across the Arctic region. It was the polar strategy that motivated the United States to set up the still-operational Thule Air Base in 1951 and that lay behind the profusion of American research projects in Greenland, which aimed to understand the environment and climate on the ice sheet, thereby enabling the United States to better establish and secure its northernmost defense positions.

As a preliminary study to the enormous conceptual project known as Iceworm, Camp Century was an offshoot of the polar strategy's role in deterrence and mass retaliation. But besides that, the camp was also part of a more or less subtle American propaganda campaign aimed at convincing the United States, and the world at large, of American supremacy not only in the fields of research, technology, and military exploits but also—and no less importantly—in political ideology, resolve, and the capacity to act. Camp Century was part of an all-out war game in which any and every pawn was exploited, even guileless scouts and modern communication technology, all in the interest of winning a moral victory while avoiding actual combat. The large amounts of information about Camp Century that were made accessible to the undoubtedly astonished public may have made the Cold War even more frigid. Now everyone was able to see that the Cold War could also be waged in the dark, inhospitable world beneath the very surface of the ice. In chapter 6 we also referred to the historian Janet Martin-Nielsen's term the "other cold war," meaning the battle against the eternal ice. Perhaps the stories about Camp Century, many of which portrayed the camp as a sort of science-fiction scenario come true, made the Cold War seem more unreal. In any case, in his acclaimed 1997 novel about the United States during the Cold War, bearing the suggestive title *Underworld*, the American writer Don DeLillo reflected that "maybe Greenland was just a delicate piece of war-gaming played in some defense institute, with hazelnut coffee and croissants."[94]

To the Danish authorities, Camp Century was much more than a sophisticated diplomatic game. Information about the American plans to build Camp Century did not reach Denmark until late 1958, at a time

when Danish nuclear weapons policy was still embryonic. Only a handful of people knew that the previous year the country's prime minister,
H. C. Hansen, had announced in public that "under the current circumstances" Denmark would refuse to receive nuclear weapons on
Danish soil, while at the same time having secretly intimated to the
Americans that they could position nuclear bombs and missiles in
Greenland. Only a few more people than that knew about the American plans for Camp Century. One of these few individuals, numbering
perhaps three in total, who at that time had full insight into such matters (Project Iceworm excluded) was the Danish foreign minister Jens
Otto Krag. According to a diary entry he wrote shortly after it became
clear in August 1958 that the Americans were *not* going to place Camp
Century in Alaska, as the Danes had proposed, Krag had second
thoughts about the whole matter of American nuclear weapons in
Greenland. He had also voiced to the prime minister that things ought
to be put in order, meaning that the Danish parliament and its foreign
policy council ought to be informed.

The American plans for Camp Century put the Danish government
in something of a tight spot not because the Americans had any intention of installing nuclear weapons in their tunnel town in the ice but
because mentioning "the concept of atoms" (referring to the camp's
proposed nuclear reactor) in a Greenlandic context might call attention
to the issue of nuclear weapons in Greenland and perhaps also to the
issue of the deeper reasons behind the existence of Camp Century.
Around this time, the United States was actively attempting to introduce
the world to the idea of "the peaceful exploitation of the atom." This
approach was also applied when offering the Danish people "the concept of atoms" in Greenland, linking Camp Century's nuclear reactor
to the opportunities embodied in introducing peaceful nuclear power
to far-flung regions of the realm. Then, when the Danish authorities
also realized that the Americans intended to invite numerous journalists to visit the new camp—not to mention two Boy Scouts, who would
live and work in the camp courtesy of the U.S. Army—civil servants in
the Danish ministries found themselves asked to comment on and pro-
pose modifications to the large number of manuscripts that were sent

to Copenhagen, pursuant to the 1953 Press Agreement. Was it censorship? Many American journalists thought so, even while Denmark seemed bent on doing what they could to minimize references in the press to Camp Century's military significance.[95]

The Danish nuclear arms policy of the late 1950s had been formulated to ensure "the greatest possible flexibility."[96] The Danish authorities certainly treated all things Camp Century with extreme flexibility, reflecting the special Danish tightrope walk made up of hesitation and agility when dealing with nuclear weapons and an American military presence in Greenland, as detailed in chapter 1. On the one hand, Denmark was forthcoming and amenable when it came to American requests for research-based activities outside the defense areas in Greenland. This approach was also extended to the construction of a military camp beneath the ice, complete with its own nuclear reactor— and the ensuing difficulties when it came to explaining to the Danish public what on earth "the concept of atoms" had to do with Greenland anyway. On the other hand, the Danes made it clear to the Americans there was a limit to what they were willing to accept. It is particularly striking how quick the Danes initially were to reject the whole idea of locating the Camp Century project in Greenland, communicating this in late November 1958, followed by a friendly recommendation that the Americans test out their idea of a major subsurface military installation under the Alaskan ice instead. This demonstrates Danish reservations when considering certain types of American military activities outside the designated defense areas. The Danish comments to draft articles about Camp Century, sent to Copenhagen for review before their publication, also demonstrate that the Danes had reservations about any mention of building expansive missile-defense systems in Greenland. Finally, the American evaluation of Project Iceworm, which Danish historians discovered while working on the investigative DIIS report *Grønland under den kolde krig* (Greenland during the Cold War), clearly indicates that Washington was counting on the likelihood of Denmark feeling considerable opposition were such a plan to be carried out.[97]

Camp Century was abandoned just as the Cold War was exhibiting, for the first time, nascent signs of détente between the superpowers. The link between these coinciding events cannot have been widely realized, given that Camp Century had for the most part been represented as a purely scientific project. This is also why the Danish broadsheet *Berlingske Tidende* was able to announce on May 2, 1964, that despite the closure of Camp Century, the United States still had grand plans in Greenland.[98] As the article went on, its readers learned that the nature of these plans was scientific, not military, and that one of them involved drilling ice cores with Camp Century serving as the project base. In many circles the ice-core project later became one of the activities Camp Century is best remembered for hosting. This shows that in the decades that followed, environmental and climate-related topics increasingly came to define the public understanding of this many-faceted facility. And although as historians we look more into the past than into the future, we feel fairly confident in predicting that Greenland—and Camp Century—will continue to play a role as history unfolds.

NOTES

1. FORTRESS GREENLAND

1. *Time* (1947).
2. Arnold (1946). Quoted in Farquhar (2014), 36.
3. DIIS (1997), 112.
4. Farquhar (2014), 37.
5. Farquhar (2014), 37.
6. *Time* (1947).
7. Olesen (2013), 121n9.
8. Danish National Archives (2017); A. K. Sørensen (2015).
9. DIIS (1997), 1:79.
10. DIIS (1997), 1:50–53.
11. DIIS (1997), 1:79.
12. Jensen, Knudsen, and Andersen (2000), 20.
13. DIIS (1997), 1:83.
14. Beukel, Jensen, and Rytter (2010); A. K. Sørensen (2006).
15. K. H. Nielsen (2013); Nielsen and Kjærgaard (2015).
16. Grønlandskommissionen [Greenland Commission] (1950), 1:18.
17. A. K. Sørensen (2006).
18. Hansen (2000).
19. DIIS (1997), 1:92–98.
20. Denmark's relations with NATO from 1949 to 1961 have been described in detail in Villaume (1995).
21. DIIS (1997), 1:104. The authors of the DIIS report have stated that this was the first time "the Greenland card" was played in the context of NATO. They also wrote that "the Greenland card" as a phrase later took on an alternative meaning, when NATO

allies criticized Denmark's efforts in the defense alliance. In this context, Danes would often argue that, as everyone well knew, Denmark made Greenland available as a highly significant part of the Danish contribution.

22. DIIS (1997), 1:105–6.
23. Petersen (2011), 92–93.
24. The U.S. interest in uranium deposits in Greenland has been described in Knudsen and Nielsen (2016).
25. Quoted from Archer (1988), 129.
26. Gaddis (2005).
27. Petersen (2011), 98–99.
28. DIIS (1997), 1:159–70.
29. DIIS (1997), 1:169.
30. Yale Law School (2008).
31. Taagholt (2002), 50.
32. Wright (1986), ii.
33. Taagholt (2002).
34. Ross and Ancker (1977).
35. H. K. Nielsen (2004); Walsøe (2003).
36. Petersen (2011); Ross and Ancker (1977).
37. DIIS (1997), 1:309–11.
38. DIIS (1997), 1:356–60; Martin-Nielsen (2012); K. H. Nielsen (2013).
39. Taagholt (2002), 60–66.
40. Taagholt (2002), 54.
41. Taagholt (2002), 57–60.
42. Petersen (2011), 111–13.
43. Buderi (1996), 411–14; Spinardi (2007).
44. Gaddis (2005), chap. 6.
45. Brodie (1959); Gaddis (2005); Huntington (1961); O'Gorman (2012).
46. Quoted after Agger and Wolsgård (2001b), 402.
47. Quoted in Villaume (1995), 17.
48. Olesen and Villaume (2005), 301–13.
49. DIIS (2005), 1:293–332.
50. Udenrigsministeriet [Danish Ministry of Foreign Affairs] (1968), append. 156. Quoted from the English translation of Bulganin's letter found in NATO's archives, see NATO Online Archive, Executive Secretariat (1952–1970), Item RDC(57)156, http://archives.nato.int/uploads/r/null/3/8/38124/RDC_57_156_ENG.pdf.
51. Udenrigsministeriet [Danish Ministry of Foreign Affairs] (1968), append. 156.
52. Udenrigsministeriet [Danish Ministry of Foreign Affairs] (1968), append. 157. Quoted from the English translation of Hansen's letter found in NATO's archives, see NATO Online Archive, Executive Secretariat (1952–1970), Item RDC(57)177, http://archives.nato.int/uploads/r/null/3/8/38154/RDC_57_177_ENG.pdf.
53. Olesen and Villaume (2005), 315.
54. Agger and Wolsgård (2001a).

55. DIIS (1997), 1:333–36.
56. Lidegaard (2001), 600.
57. DIIS (1997), 1:431.
58. DIIS (1997), 1:432.
59. DIIS (1997), 1:279.

2. "THE CONCEPT OF ATOMS" IN GREENLAND

1.   Peterson's informal contact with Krag is described in two separate documents, each of which sheds light on different aspects of what transpired without contradicting the other document: Minutes of meeting, August 20, 1959, Item 27, "Joint Archive of the Permanent Secretaries," Ministry for Greenland, Danish National Archives; and Minutes of meeting on the establishment of a nuclear reactor near Thule, August 20, 1959, UM 105.F.2.b/2, Archive for the Ministry of Foreign Affairs, Danish National Archives. Camp Century has previously been described in some detail in DIIS (1997), 1:357–60; Nielsen and Nielsen (2015, 2016); Petersen (2008); Weiss (2001).

2.   K. Krag to J. O. Lindberg, August 19, 1959, UM 105.F.2.b/2, Archive for the Ministry of Foreign Affairs, Danish National Archives.

3.   Krag to Lindberg, August 19, 1959.

4.   "Etablering af en atomreaktor i nærheden af Thule-forsvarsområdet" [Establishment of a nuclear reactor near the Thule defense area], August 19, 1959, UM 105.F.2.b/2, Archive for the Ministry of Foreign Affairs, Danish National Archives.

5.   Helge Larsen, "Foreløbig rapport fra den videnskabelige rådgiver til den danske forbindelsesofficer ved Thule Air Base" [Preliminary report from the scientific adviser to the Danish liaison officer at Thule Air Base], July 20, 1959, UM 105.F.8., Archive for the Ministry of Foreign Affairs, Danish National Archives.

6.   Larsen, "Foreløbig rapport."

7.   Helge Larsen and Anker Weidick, "Afsluttende rapport fra de videnskabelige rådgivere for forbindelsesofficeren ved Thule Air Base for sommeren 1959" [Final report from the scientific advisers to the Danish liaison officer at Thule Air Base for the summer of 1959], February 16, 1960, UM 105.F.8., Archive for the Ministry of Foreign Affairs, Danish National Archives.

8.   Minutes of meeting, August 20, 1959, Item 27, Joint Archive of the Permanent Secretaries, Ministry for Greenland, Danish National Archives.

9.   Lidegaard (1996), 189.

10. Minutes of meeting, August 20, 1959, Item 27, Joint Archive of the Permanent Secretaries, Ministry for Greenland, Danish National Archives.

11. DIIS (2005), 1:207–9, 308.

12. Minutes of meeting regarding the establishment of a nuclear reactor near Thule, August 20, 1959, UM 105.F.2.b/2, Archive for the Ministry of Foreign Affairs, Danish National Archives.

13. Minutes of meeting, August 20, 1959, Item 27, Joint Archive of the Permanent Secretaries, Ministry for Greenland, Danish National Archives. A handwritten note to the conclusion of these minutes reads: "Før vi hører nærmere fra indenrigsministeriet og udenrigsministeriet" [Before we hear details from the ministry for the interior and the foreign ministry].

14. Internal memo, November 19, 1958, UM 105.F.2.b/2, Archive for the Ministry of Foreign Affairs, Danish National Archives.

15. Internal memo, November 19, 1958.

16. m- (1958a). This "m-" and similar initials in our notes are journalists' signatures used when authors' bylines were still rare in the Danish press.

17. m- (1958b).

18. m- (1958b).

19. P (1958).

20. n- (1958a).

21. n- (1958b).

22. Internal memo, November 19, 1958, UM 105.F.2.b/2, Archive for the Ministry of Foreign Affairs, Danish National Archives.

23. Internal memo, November 19, 1958.

24. Embassy of the United States of America, N° 273, February 16, 1959, UM 105.F.9.a, Archive for the Ministry of Foreign Affairs, Danish National Archives.

25. Ministry for Greenland, "Notits om Paul Siples besøg" [Internal memo on Paul Siple's visit], November 3, 1958, UM 105.F.9.a, Archive for the Ministry of Foreign Affairs, Danish National Archives.

26. Embassy of the United States of America, N° 273, February 16, 1959, UM 105.F.9.a, Archive for the Ministry of Foreign Affairs, Danish National Archives.

27. Comment concerning an American note dated February 20, 1959, February 25, 1959, UM 105.F.9.a, Archive for the Ministry of Foreign Affairs, Danish National Archives.

28. Comment concerning an American note dated February 20, 1959.

29. Embassy of the United States of America, N° 382, May 29, 1959, UM 105.F.2.b/2, Archive for the Ministry of Foreign Affairs, Danish National Archives.

30. Hans Christensen, "Notits om forsøg med atomreaktor i nærheden af Thule Forsvarsområde" [Internal memo on experiments with nuclear reactor near Thule Defense Area], June 1, 1959, UM 105.F.2.b/2, Archive for the Ministry of Foreign Affairs, Danish National Archives.

31. Christensen, "Notits om forsøg."

32. Christensen, "Notits om forsøg."

33. Atomic Energy Commission, Denmark, "Notat vedrørende et fra amerikansk side fremsat projekt om indretning af en videnskabelig station under isen ca. 120 miles øst for Thule" [Memorandum on a project, presented by the Americans, concerning the outfitting of a scientific station beneath the ice approx. 120 miles east of Thule], June 25, 1959, UM 105.F.2.b/2, Archive for the Ministry of Foreign Affairs, Danish National Archives.

34. Torben Rønne, "Notits. Installation og drift af lille varme- og kraftreaktor ved Thule" [Internal memo. Installation and operation of small heat and power reactor

near Thule], August 4, 1959, UM 105.F.2.b/2, Archive for the Ministry of Foreign Affairs, Danish National Archives.

35. "Notits. Etableringen af en atomreaktor i nærheden af Thule Forsvarsområde" [Internal memo. Establishment of a nuclear reactor near Thule Defense Area], August 25, 1959, UM 105.F.2.b/2, Archive for the Ministry of Foreign Affairs, Danish National Archives.

36. *Berlingske Tidende* (1959); *Politiken* (1959).

37. Mikkelsen (1987).

38. Minutes of meeting in the Foreign Policy Committee, September 7, 1959, UM 105.F.2.b/2, Archive for the Ministry of Foreign Affairs, Danish National Archives.

39. Nils Svenningsen, "Note Verbale" [Verbatim note], September 14, 1959, UM 105.F.2.b/2, Archive for the Ministry of Foreign Affairs, Danish National Archives.

40. Torben Rønne, "Notits. Presseforespørgsel vedrørende atomreaktoren på Grønland" [Internal memo. Press inquiry relating to the nuclear reactor on Greenland], November 13, 1959, UM 105.F.2.b/2, Archive for the Ministry of Foreign Affairs, Danish National Archives.

41. Rønne, "Notits."

3. THE CITY UNDER THE ICE

1. DIIS (1997), 2:315–48; Petersen (2008); Weiss (2001).

2. Baldwin (1985), 53–56; DIIS (1997), 1:319–25, 2:315–48.

3. U.S. Army Polar Research and Development Center (1958).

4. Baldwin (1985), 49.

5. Heefner (2012).

6. Spinardi (1994).

7. Baldwin (1985), 41.

8. Divine (1993); Roman (1995).

9. Baldwin (1985), 53; Petersen (2008), 79.

10. Baldwin (1985), 56.

11. Minutes of meeting regarding the establishment of a nuclear reactor near Thule, August 20, 1959, UM 105.F.2.b/2, Archive for the Ministry of Foreign Affairs, Danish National Archives; Helge Larsen, "Foreløbig rapport fra den videnskabelige rådgiver til den danske forbindelsesofficer ved Thule Air Base" [Preliminary report from the scientific adviser to the Danish liaison officer at Thule Air Base], July 20, 1959, UM 105.F.8., Archive for the Ministry of Foreign Affairs, Danish National Archives.

12. Taagholt (2002), 68; Wager (1962), 52.

13. United States Army (1961a).

14. Clark (1965); Evans (1961); Wager (1962).

15. Clark (1965), 31–38.

16. Clark (1965), 29.

17. Clark (1965), 38, 42.

18.   Clark (1965), 57–58.

19.   Clark (1965), 23–24.

20.   Clark (1965), 42.

21.   Clark (1965), 41–44.

22.   Verbatim note from the director of the Danish Ministry of Foreign Affairs, Nils Svenningsen, to the U.S. Embassy in Copenhagen, October 14, 1959, UM 105.F.2.b/2, Archive for the Ministry of Foreign Affairs, Danish National Archives.

23.   Suid (1990).

24.   Danish Atomic Energy Commission (1960), "Referat af møderne i Washington, DC, med repræsentanter for U.S. Army angående PM-2A reaktoren på Grønlands indlandsis" [Minutes of the meetings in Washington, DC, with representatives of the U.S. Army regarding the PM-2A reactor on Greenland's ice cap], January 2, 1960, Material concerning PM-2A, Camp Century, Thule, Miscellaneous correspondence 1960, 1963, Box 101, Risø National Laboratory, Executive Committee, Danish National Archives.

25.   Danish Atomic Energy Commission (1960), "Referat af møderne," 2–6.

26.   Danish Atomic Energy Commission (1960), "Referat af møderne," 13, 17.

27.   Danish Atomic Energy Commission (1960), "Referat af møderne." One gram of the radium isotope Ra^{226} represents roughly 37 billion radioactive decay events per second. This magnitude of activity was originally referred to as 1 curie, and this was also the unit used while Camp Century was a functional facility. Today, the unit Becquerel (Bq) is used to measure the activity of a radioactive source, 1 Bq corresponding to one decay event per second. Hence, 30 millicurie is the same as 1.1 billion Bq, or 1.1 GBq ($G = giga = 10^9$).

28.   H. Gjørup, O. Kofoed-Hansen, and P. L. Ølgaard to the Danish Atomic Energy Commission, "Ang.: Den amerikanske ansøgning om tilladelse til opførelse af PM-2A reaktoren i Camp Century på Grønlands indlandsis" [Re: The American application for permission to construct the PM-2A reactor in Camp Century on Greenland's ice cap], January 11, 1960, Material concerning PM-2A, Camp Century, Thule, Miscellaneous correspondence 1960, 1963, Box 101, Risø National Laboratory, Executive Committee, Danish National Archives.

29.   Gjørup, Kofoed-Hansen, and Ølgaard to the Danish Atomic Energy Commission, January 11, 1960.

30.   Verbatim note dated February 10, 1960, from the Danish Ministry of Foreign Affairs to the U.S. embassy in Copenhagen, UM 105.F.2.b/2, Archive for the Ministry of Foreign Affairs, Danish National Archives. In the copy of the note kept in the Danish National Archives, an unknown person has underlined the first condition in pencil.

31.   W. B. Taylor to T. Dahlgaard, economic adviser, Danish Embassy, Washington, DC, February 29, 1960, UM 105.F.2.b/2, Archive for the Ministry of Foreign Affairs, Danish National Archives.

32.   H. Gjørup, O. Kofoed-Hansen, J. Thomas, and P. L. Ølgaard to the Danish Atomic Energy Commission, April 20, 1960, Material concerning PM-2A, Camp Century,

Thule, Miscellaneous correspondence 1960, 1963, Box 101, Risø National Laboratory, Executive Committee, Danish National Archives.

33. Danish Atomic Energy Commission to the Danish Ministry of Foreign Affairs, May 20, 1960, UM 105.F.2.b/2, Archive for the Ministry of Foreign Affairs, Danish National Archives.

34. Embassy of the United States of America, N° 334, May 25, 1960, UM 105.F.2.b/2, Archive for the Ministry of Foreign Affairs, Danish National Archives.

35. C. J. Liebe, "Referat. Verbalnote fra den amerikanske ambassade vedrørende spørgsmålet om amerikansk ansvar for eventuelle skader forårsaget af atomreaktoren i Camp Century" [Minutes. Verbatim note from the American embassy concerning the question of American liability for potential damage caused by the atomic reactor in Camp Century], June 14, 1960, UM 105.F.2.b/2, Archive for the Ministry of Foreign Affairs, Danish National Archives.

36. Verbatim note dated July 29, 1960, from the Danish Ministry of Foreign Affairs to the U.S. embassy in Copenhagen, UM 105.F.2.b/2, Archive for the Ministry of Foreign Affairs, Danish National Archives.

37. Minutes of meeting concerning the question of liability for damage caused by the operation of the nuclear reactor (Camp Century), September 12, 1960, UM 105.F.2.b/2, Archive for the Ministry of Foreign Affairs, Danish National Archives.

38. Draft note, September 23, 1960, UM 105.F.2.b/2, Archive for the Ministry of Foreign Affairs, Danish National Archives.

39. Danish Ministry of Justice to the Danish Ministry of Foreign Affairs, October 3, 1960, UM 105.F.2.b/2, Archive for the Ministry of Foreign Affairs, Danish National Archives.

40. N. C. Tillisch, "Minutes. The issue of responsibility concerning the Camp Century nuclear-reactor project," April 11, 1961, UM 105.F.2.b/2, Archive for the Ministry of Foreign Affairs, Danish National Archives.

41. Danish Ministry of Foreign Affairs to the Danish Embassy in Washington, DC, June 23, 1961, UM 105.F.2.b/2, Archive for the Ministry of Foreign Affairs, Danish National Archives.

42. "Lov om nukleare anlæg (Atomanlægsloven)" [Nuclear Installations Act (Atomic Plant Act)], Danish Act no. 170, dated May 16, 1962.

43. Root (American embassy in Copenhagen) to Frellesvig (Danish Ministry of Foreign Affairs), September 18, 1962, UM 105.F.2.b/2, Archive for the Ministry of Foreign Affairs, Danish National Archives. A much later document from the same record series, sent from the Ministry for Greenland to the Ministry of Foreign Affairs (dated April 29, 1968), definitively establishes that the version of paragraph 1 from September 1962 (reproduced in this chapter) was the final rejoinder in the years-long negotiations between Denmark and the United States about permission to construct and operate the reactor at Camp Century.

44. Suid (1990), 64.

45. Clark (1965), 34.

46.   Barnett (1961).
47.   Barnett (1961), 6; Clark (1965), 34.
48.   Suid (1990).
49.   Wager (1960).
50.   Wager (1962).
51.   Wager (1962), 81.
52.   Barnett (1961), 116–20; Suid (1990), 66.
53.   Barnett (1961), 121.
54.   Barnett (1961), 122–26; Suid (1990), 67–68. In 1960, scientists measured the probable detrimental health effects in a unit called "millirem," or "mrem," based on the abbreviation for a "Röntgen Equivalent Man." So one rem, consisting of 1,000 mrem, is defined as an 0.05% higher risk of developing cancer, and levels above 100 rem (or 100,000 mrem) can result in acute radiation damage, also known as radiation sickness. Since 1976, scientists have used the unit "millisievert," abbreviated "mSv," with 1 mrem = 0.01 mSv.
55.   P. Steenberger, "Referat: Atomreaktoren i Camp Century" [Minutes: The atomic reactor in Camp Century", December 17, 1960, UM 105.F.2.b/2, Archive for the Ministry of Foreign Affairs, Danish National Archives.
56.   Danish Ministry of Foreign Affairs to the Danish Embassy in Washington, DC, December 27, 1960, UM 105.F.2.b/2, Archive for the Ministry of Foreign Affairs, Danish National Archives.
57.   E. L. Faust to T. Dahlgaard, Danish Embassy in Washington, DC, January 11, 1961, UM 105.F.2.b/2, Archive for the Ministry of Foreign Affairs, Danish National Archives. The stated figure of 40 r/hour corresponds to 40 mSv/hour. Povl Ølgaard's report from the Danish visit to Washington, DC, in December 1959 shows that the maximum dose permitted for a person working with the reactor or other equipment that emits radiation is 300 mrem/week and 5 rem/year. Danish Atomic Energy Commission (1960), "Referat af møderne."
58.   Faust to Dahlgaard, January 11, 1961.
59.   ALCO Products, "Start-up testing of the PM-2A nuclear power plant," March 31, 1962, tables 4.3 and 4.6, E UD-WW-20, Box 1, Office of the Chief of Engineers, RG 77, National Archives and Records Administration.
60.   Stacy (2000), chap. 16.

4. NEWS FROM GREENLAND

1.   Kinney (2013).
2.   Nielsen and Nielsen (2013).
3.   Notits vedrørende danske og amerikanske journalisters virksomhed på Grønland, [Internal memo relating to the activities of Danish and American journalists on Greenland], May 14, 1952, UM 105.F.179, Archive for the Ministry of Foreign Affairs, Danish National Archives.

4. Memorandum, March 7, 1953, UM 105.F.179, Archive for the Ministry of Foreign Affairs, Danish National Archives.

5. Memorandum, March 7, 1953.

6. Minutes of meeting on November 12, 1953, UM 105.F.10.b, Archive for the Ministry of Foreign Affairs, Danish National Archives.

7. H. Kauffmann to N. Svenningsen, April 12, 1956, UM 105.F.10.b, Archive for the Ministry of Foreign Affairs, Danish National Archives.

8. Draft of agreement dated April 30, 1960, UM 105.F.10.b, Archive for the Ministry of Foreign Affairs, Danish National Archives.

9. Osgood (2006).

10. Nye (2004).

11. Kinney (2013), 349.

12. Bernard (1999), 142–43.

13. United States Army (1953).

14. Kinney (2013).

15. United States Army (1953).

16. Cull (2008).

17. Eisenhower (1953).

18. Chernus (2005).

19. Chernus (2002); Hewlett and Holl (1989).

20. Christensen (2002); Rasmussen (2009).

21. Mechling and Mechling (1995).

22. *AG* (1960). Today, "Narssarssuak" is spelled Narsarsuaq, and "Julianehåb" goes by its Greenlandic name, Qaqortoq.

23. Hammerich (1960).

24. Hammerich (1960).

25. *CBS News* (2016).

26. *CBS News* (2016).

27. "Atom Town," *Peruvian Times* (Peru), October 30, 1959; "'Real Cool' Camp at Seventy Below," *The Observer* (UK), April 17, 1960; "Eine Stadt entsteht unter dem ewigen Eis," *Neue Ruhr Zeitung* (West Germany), August 16, 1960; "Camp Century," *Il Tempo Illustrato* (Italy), November 1960.

28. The following year, Walter Wager expanded on the article he wrote for the *Saturday Evening Post* in a book entitled *Camp Century: City Under the Ice*. Wager would later leave journalism to become a successful writer of science fiction. The year after his article, two more books were published about Camp Century in the United States: Daugherty (1963) and Hamilton (1964), the latter written for children and adolescents. The description in the following pages about the Danish authorities' comments on articles by non-Danish journalists is based on Nielsen and Nielsen (2013) and on Nielsen, Nielsen, and Martin-Nielsen (2015).

29. Handwritten comment dated July 4, 1960 and initialed "HL" in the Ministry for Greenland; found on a letter dated June 22, 1960, from the Danish embassy in Washington, DC, to the Danish Ministry of Foreign Affairs (a copy forwarded to the

Ministry for Greenland), Joint Archive of the Permanent Secretaries (confidential), case files, XLI A II Camp Century, Box 29, Archive of the Ministry for Greenland, National Danish Archives.

30. Walter Wager, "Camp Century—the Army Base Under the Snow," manuscript in the Joint Archive of the Permanent Secretaries (confidential), case files, XLI A II Camp Century, Box 29, Archive of the Ministry for Greenland, National Danish Archives.

31. Wager (1960).

32. Unlike the two other Danish ministries, the Ministry of Defense had no objections to Romersa's manuscript. According to the sources we have been able to access, there was a pattern: the civil servants at the Ministry of Defense did not comment on the wording of the manuscript, whereas those in the Ministry for Greenland were relatively critical. The Danish Ministry of Foreign Affairs played the role of main coordinator, meaning that its civil servants were largely aligned with their counterparts at the Ministry for Greenland when passing on the final comments to the Danish embassy in Washington, DC, whose task it was to forward communications to the journalist in question.

33. Luigi Romersa, "Camp Century," manuscript in the Joint Archive of the Permanent Secretaries (confidential), case files, XLI A II Camp Century, Box 29, Archive of the Ministry for Greenland, National Danish Archives.

34. Ministry for Greenland to the Ministry of Foreign Affairs and Ministry of Defense, December 5, 1960, Joint Archive of the Permanent Secretaries (confidential), case files, XLI A II Camp Century, Box 29, Archive of the Ministry for Greenland, National Danish Archives.

35. Ministry for Greenland to the Ministry of Foreign Affairs and Ministry of Defense, December 5, 1960.

36. Quoted from Nielsen and Nielsen (2015), 345. Colt's original article was published in *Male*, October 1960, 34, 62–67.

37. Johansen (1960a), 106; Johansen (1960b), 229.

38. Danish Ministry of Foreign Affairs to the Danish embassy in Washington, DC, December 13, 1963, UM 105.F.10.b, Archive for the Ministry of Foreign Affairs, Danish National Archives.

39. DIIS (2005), 2:28.

40. *Oxford Dictionaries* (2018).

41. The "containment" metaphor in the context of Camp Century news is discussed in depth in Nielsen and Nielsen (2013).

5. SCOUTING IN THE HIGH ARCTIC

1. Gregersen (1960).

2. *New York Times* (1960).

3. Kinney (2013), 344–45.

4. *Scouting* (1960), 7.

5.   mn. (1960).

6.   *Berlingske Tidende* (1960).

7.   *Berlingske Tidende* (1960).

8.   United States Army (1960), 14.

9.   Unpublished diary, generously made available to Henry Nielsen by Søren Gregersen.

10. Wager (1962), 101–15.

11. United States Information Service (1961).

12. Ueda (2002), 16.

13. The following description of everyday life in Camp Century is especially based on Wager (1962).

14. Gregersen (1960), 12.

15. Wager (1962), 104.

16. Goering (1961).

17. Unless another source is specified, the quotations in this section are from Gregersen's diary.

18. Johansen (1960a, 1960b).

19. Martin-Nielsen (2012), 78.

20. "5 mr" denotes "5 millirem," a unit of measure, now outdated, which designates the probable biological effect of ionized (i.e., radioactive) radiation; see chapter 3, note 54.

21. Suid (1990), 66–68.

22. Herb Ueda was an employee of the U.S. Army Polar Research and Development Center who wintered in Camp Century for the first time the same year the two scouts did. In a 2002 interview, he related the following joke, popular among the Camp Century personnel in the winter of 1960/1961: "If Camp Century was first prize, what the hell did the runner-up get [for] purgatory?" Ueda (2002), 20.

23. Because of various technical difficulties, the drilling did not begin in earnest until 1963. The work was done by Lyle Hansen, Herb Ueda, Chester C. Langway Jr., and their colleagues from the U.S. Army Cold Region Research and Engineering Laboratories, established in 1961 to deliver scientific and engineering support to the U.S. Army Corps of Engineers with a core emphasis on cold environments. The drilling was successfully concluded in 1966. Langway (2008), Ueda and Garfield (1968).

24. Ueda (2002), 17.

25. *Belvoir Castle* (1961).

26. *New York Times* (1961).

27. Hughes (1961).

28. Kinney (2013), 344–57.

29. Herczeg-Konecny (2013), 36.

30. United States Army (1961b).

31. Kinney (2013), 345.

32. United States Army (1961b).

33. The four Danish articles appearing in *Politiken* about "The Scout in the Ice Cap," written by Søren Gregersen and edited by Paul Hammerich, are entitled "Først is-smelteren—så atomreaktoren" [First the ice melter—then the nuclear reactor], November 27, 1960, 12; "Her går det godt, men pigen savnes" [Doing fine, but girl sorely missed], January 15, 1961, 8; "Jeg har været 60 meter nede i indlands-isen" [I've been 60 meters down into the ice sheet], February 19, 1961, 13; and "Anlagde skøjte-bane under indlandsisen" [Built ice-skating rink under the ice sheet], April 9, 1961, 37.

6. U.S. MILITARY R&D ON THE NORTHERN FRONTIER

1. Quoted here after Doel (2003), 636.
2. P. A. Siple to MGEN H. S. Aurand, October 10, 1947, Geographic File 381 Arctic Area, Box 3, Folder Strategic Evaluations of the Arctic and Sub-Arctic Regions, RG 218, National Archives and Records Administration.
3. Doel (2016), 29. The expression was also used in public, for instance in *Time* (1947).
4. Doel (2016), 34–36.
5. Doel (2016), 34–36.
6. From 1962 onward, the American applications for the following year for tests and experiments outside the "defense areas" were presented to and discussed by KVUG (the Commission for Scientific Research in Greenland) before the Danish Ministry of Foreign Affairs sent its response to the United States. The KVUG held its first such meeting on April 12, 1962.
7. Unofficial memorandum, June 16, 1958, UM 105.F.9.a, Archive for the Ministry of Foreign Affairs, Danish National Archives. See also DIIS (1997), 1:241–48.
8. DIIS (1997), 1:306–8.
9. Fristrup (1963), 25.
10. Martin-Nielsen (2012), 72–73.
11. Fleming (2010); Harper (2017).
12. Martin-Nielsen (2012), 74.
13. Martin-Nielsen (2012), 74; Hicks (1965), 1–2.
14. Hicks (1965), 5–11.
15. Hicks (1965), 13–18.
16. Hicks (1965), 19.
17. Martin-Nielsen (2012), 76.
18. Martin-Nielsen (2012), 80.
19. *AG* (1960), 3. We have also used an excerpt of this quotation in chapter 4.
20. Fristrup (1962), 330; Rausch (1957).
21. Report 2 from the Danish scientific adviser Vagn Buchwald to the Danish liaison officer at Thule Air Base, August 25, 1961, p. 6, UM 105.F.8, Archive for the Ministry of Foreign Affairs, Danish National Archives.
22. Martin-Nielsen (2012), 78.

23. United States Army Material Command, "Top of the World Railroad," press release, U.S. Army Material Command, Washington, DC, 1963, Joint Archive of the Permanent Secretaries (confidential), case files, XLI A II Camp Century, Box 29, Ministry for Greenland, Danish National Archives.
24. Fristrup (1963), 181.
25. Martin-Nielsen (2012), 76–78.
26. Quoted after Martin-Nielsen (2012), 78.
27. Gregersen (1961), memorandum dated November 7, 1961.
28. Clark (1965), 37–38.
29. Scientific adviser Valdemar Poulsen to the Danish liaison officer at Thule Air Base, September 23, 1963, UM 105.F.8, Archive for the Ministry of Foreign Affairs, Danish National Archives.
30. Clark (1965), 41.
31. Petersen (2008), 87.

7. THE COLD WAR AND CLIMATE RESEARCH

1. Yamanouchi (2011).
2. Mattox (1973), 116.
3. Callendar (1938); Weart (2008), 2–3. The first scientist to calculate a rise in global temperature as a result of human CO_2 emissions into the atmosphere was the Swedish chemist Svante Arrhenius, in 1896.
4. Quoted after Doel (2016), 37.
5. Doel (2016), 37.
6. Doel (2016), 38.
7. Bader (1949).
8. Bader (1949), 1309.
9. Bader (1949), 1312.
10. SIPRE Report I (1950), 3.
11. The best popular-science source on Willi Dansgaard's life and work is a book he wrote himself: Dansgaard (2000), full version in Danish only; abbreviated English version (2005) downloadable at http://www.iceandclimate.nbi.ku.dk/publications/Frozen Annals.pdf. Lolck (2006), in Danish, also gives a good account of ice-core research in Greenland during the Cold War. Her book is based, among other things, on interviews with Dansgaard and his team. The actual drilling operation at Camp Century and its Cold War context are described in greater detail in Martin-Nielsen (2013).
12. The prevalence of the two isotopes in water at room temperature and standard atmospheric pressure for 1,000 oxygen atoms is approximately 998 light O^{16} atoms and just two heavy O^{18} atoms. Dansgaard was aware that the $O^{18}:O^{16}$ ratio depends on temperature: the warmer the water, the higher the proportion of O^{18} atoms.
13. Dansgaard (1954), 241–60.
14. Dansgaard (2000), 72.

15. Dansgaard (1954), 260.

16. Korsmo (2010).

17. Launius, Fleming, and DeVorkin (2010); Needell (2000).

18. Langway (2008), 9–10; Martin-Nielsen (2013).

19. Langway (2008), 10–16.

20. Langway (1967).

21. Langway (2008), 17–26.

22. The various types of drills and problems involved in the Camp Century drilling operations are described in Ueda and Garfield (1968).

23. V. Buchwald, report dated September 23, 1963, UM 105.F.8, Archive for the Ministry of Foreign Affairs, Danish National Archives.

24. Langway (2008), 20.

25. Ueda and Garfield (1968), 3.

26. Ueda and Garfield (1968), 3–6. See also Langway (2008), 20–22.

27. Langway (2008), 24–26.

28. B. Fristrup and S.E. Almgreen, report dated August 12, 1966, UM 105.F.8, Archive for the Ministry of Foreign Affairs, Danish National Archives.

29. Langway (2008), 24.

30. Bader (1962); U.S. Army Material Command, "Ice Core Drilling, Fact Sheet," September 20, 1966, UM 105.F.2b/2, Archive for the Ministry of Foreign Affairs, Danish National Archives.

31. Langway (1967).

32. Lolck (2006), 80–83.

33. Dansgaard (2000), 149; Lolck (2006), 88–91.

34. Dansgaard et al. (1969).

35. Dansgaard et al. (1969).

36. Weart (2008), 71–72.

37. Dansgaard (2000), 155–242; Langway (2008), 27–37; Lolck (2006), 93–136.

38. Edwards (2012).

39. Edwards (2012), 30.

40. Edwards (2012), 33.

41. Edwards (2012), 34–36.

42. Martin-Nielsen (2013).

8. LEAVING THE ICE SHEET: A LINGERING FAREWELL

1. Sullivan (1964).

2. *Berlingske Tidende* (1963).

3. Danish daily *Aalborg Stiftstidende* (1963).

4. Sullivan (1964).

5. Baldwin (1985), 42–53.

6. Kennedy's "flexible response" doctrine has been treated in detail in Gaddis (2005) and numerous other books.

7. DIIS (1997), 2:314–54. The Ramsey report used "MRBM" (Medium Range Ballistic Missile), which is equivalent to the expression "IRBM" (Intermediate Range Ballistic Missile) used elsewhere in this book.

8. Cover letter for the report on Project Iceworm, DIIS (1997), 2:312–13.

9. DIIS (1997), 2:344.

10. DIIS (1997), 2:344.

11. Petersen (2008), 88–93.

12. *Nucleonics Week*, February 21, 1963.

13. The reports on the Danish inspection visits are found in: Material concerning PM-2A Camp Century, Miscellaneous correspondence, box 101, Risø Nuclear Research Laboratory, Executive Committee, Danish National Archives.

14. In the review article, Jørgen Taagholt—who personally served as scientific adviser to the Danish liaison officer at Thule Air Base from 1967 to 1999—stated that radioactivity measurements were routinely made at 28 measuring points inside and outside the tunnels at distances of up to 800 meters from the nuclear reactor. Taagholt also states that the total value for low-level radioactive liquid waste for all four years did not exceed 2.7 GBq (72 millicuries). Taagholt (2002), 73.

15. V. Buchwald, report dated September 23, 1963, UM 105.F.8, Archive for the Ministry of Foreign Affairs, Danish National Archives.

16. Buchwald, report dated September 23, 1963.

17. Buchwald, report dated September 23, 1963.

18. Letter from the Danish embassy in Washington, DC, to the Danish Ministry of Foreign Affairs in Copenhagen, March 4, 1963, "Summary of operations: PM-2A Power Plant, 1. January 1963–31. December 1963," UM 105.F.2b/2, Archive for the Ministry of Foreign Affairs, Danish National Archives.

19. U.S. Department of Defense to the Danish embassy in Washington, DC, January 22, 1964, UM 105.F.2b/2, Archive for the Ministry of Foreign Affairs, Danish National Archives.

20. Suid (1990), 71.

21. C. F. Jacobsen, "RE: Radiological Clearance of the PM-2A Nuclear Power Plant Facility, Camp Century, Thule Area, Greenland," October 2, 1964, UM 105.F.2b/2, Archive for the Ministry of Foreign Affairs, Danish National Archives.

22. Clark (1965), 51.

23. Jacobsen, "RE: Radiological Clearance."

24. Jacobsen, "RE: Radiological Clearance."

25. Suid (1990), 72.

26. Suid (1990), 72.

27. Kovacs (1970).

9. THE LEGACY OF CAMP CENTURY

1. Colgan et al. (2016), 8091–96.

2. Roszak (1969) is one of the earliest examples of this interpretation.

3.   McCormick (1989), Meadows et al. (1972).

4.   Nissen (2005).

5.   Horton (2005).

6.   The report mentioned here is Clark (1965).

7.   Wilkes (1980), 18–20.

8.   Unlike the PM-2A, which had been built by ALCO, the PM-3A reactor was built by the Martin Company.

9.   Wilkes and Mann (1978), 32.

10.   Wilkes (1980), 20.

11.   -h. (1980).

12.   The Danish Ministry of the Environment, J.nr. D 2702-175, July 3, 1980, Grønlands-udvalget [Greenland Committee] (2016b), attachment.

13.   Danish Ministry of the Environment, July 3, 1980.

14.   Danish Ministry of the Environment, July 3, 1980.

15.   Danish Ministry of the Environment, July 3, 1980.

16.   Claesson (1983), esp. 81, 107–8. Far from being a tourist guide to Greenland, as the title seen in isolation might well indicate, this book was in fact a security policy analysis of Greenland's situation during the Cold War, a period when the huge island's position made it a geopolitical fulcrum in the center of the Arctic Ocean, which, like a northerly Mediterranean Sea, lies between the continents of North America and Eurasia.

17.   Fukuyama (1992).

18.   Atomenergikommissionen [Danish Atomic Energy Commission] (1970), 11.

19.   Sundhedsstyrelsen [Danish Health Authority] (1991).

20.   Sundhedsstyrelsen [Danish Health Authority] (2011).

21.   Brink (1998).

22.   Blüdnikow (2015); Villaume (1997, 2015).

23.   Det Udenrigspolitiske Nævn [Foreign Policy Committee] (1996). See also DIIS (1997), 1:15.

24.   Kanstrup (1995).

25.   DIIS (1997), 1:15.

26.   DIIS (1997), 1:15.

27.   DIIS (1997), 2:315–48.

28.   Andersen and Larsen (1997).

29.   Mylenberg and Rostrup (1997).

30.   Mylenberg and Rostrup (1997).

31.   Faurby (1997). In chapter 4 we also quoted this passage from *Det Bedste*, the Danish version of *Reader's Digest*.

32.   Berthelsen (1995).

33.   Berthelsen (1995). 72 millicuries corresponds to 2.7 GBq in current-day SI units.

34.   M. Lidegaard to A. Hammond, May 26, 2014, Grønlandsudvalget [Greenland Committee] (2016b), attachment.

35.   M. Lidegaard to A. Hammond, August 21, 2014, Grønlandsudvalget [Greenland Committee] (2016b), attachment.

36. C. F. Jacobsen, "RE: Radiological Clearance of the PM-2A Nuclear Power Plant Facility, Camp Century, Thule Area, Greenland," October 2, 1964, UM 105.F.2b/2, Archive for the Ministry of Foreign Affairs, Danish National Archives; Clark (1965).
37. Colgan et al. (2016).
38. American Geophysical Union (2016).
39. Rosen (2016).
40. Hannestad (2016b).
41. Hannestad (2016b).
42. Vestergaard (2016), 7.
43. Colgan et al. (2016), 8092–93.
44. Colgan et al. (2016), 8092–93.
45. Sørensen (2017a, 2017b).
46. Colgan et al. (2016), 8092–93.
47. Colgan et al. (2016), 8094–95.
48. J. S. Nielsen (2016a).
49. J. S. Nielsen (2016a).
50. Friedrich (2016).
51. J. S. Nielsen (2016a).
52. J. S. Nielsen (2016b).
53. J. S. Nielsen (2016b).
54. Grønlandsudvalget [Greenland Committee] (2016a).
55. Grønlandsudvalget [Greenland Committee] (2016a).
56. Udenrigsministeriet [Danish Ministry of Foreign Affairs] (1951); Yale Law School (2008).
57. Qujaukitsoq (2016).
58. Hannestad (2016a).
59. Hannestad (2016a).
60. Turnowsky (2016).
61. Jørgensen (2016b).
62. Hannestad (2016d).
63. Brøns (2016).
64. Hannestad (2016c).
65. Hannestad (2016c).
66. Breum (2016).
67. KNR [Kalaallit Nunaata Radioa—Greenlandic Broadcasting Corporation] (2016).
68. Sørensen (2017c).
69. Veirum and Kristiansen (2017).
70. Breum (2017).
71. Kleist and Lihn (2017).
72. Ritzau (2017a).
73. Ritzau (2017b).
74. DR [Danish Broadcasting Corporation] (2018).
75. DR [Danish Broadcasting Corporation] (2018).

76. DR [Danish Broadcasting Corporation] (2018).

77. Grønlandsudvalget [Greenland Committee] (2018). The underlining is in the original speaker's notes used by the Danish Minister of Foreign Affairs.

78. Grønlandsudvalget [Greenland Committee] (2018).

79. E-mail from the Danish Ministry of Defense to Henry Nielsen, dated September 26, 2018.

80. Author interview with Tuk Erik Jørgen-Jensen, May 14, 2018.

81. "Månedsrapport for tiden 1. juli til 31. juli 1959" [Monthly report for the period July 1 to July 31, 1959], J.nr: FTR 307.01, KA Records for the period 1954–60 (confidential), Greenland Command, Liaison Officers, Thule Air Base, Danish National Archives. Regarding Liaison Officer Edvars, he and six others were killed in a helicopter crash near Thule Air Base on August 26, 1959, just eight days after Jens Otto Krag and Val Peterson met in Copenhagen.

82. "Månedsrapport for tiden 1. juli til 31. juli 1959."

83. "Månedsrapport for tiden 1. juli til 31. juli 1959"; Helge Larsen, "Foreløbig rapport fra den videnskabelige rådgiver til den danske forbindelsesofficer ved Thule Air Base" [Preliminary report from the scientific adviser to the Danish liaison officer at Thule Air Base], July 20, 1959, UM 105.F.8., Archive for the Ministry of Foreign Affairs, Danish National Archives.

84. E-mails from Tuk Erik Jørgen-Jensen to the authors, August 17 and September 8, 2018.

85. E-mails from Tuk Erik Jørgen-Jensen to the authors, August 17 and September 8, 2018; author interview with Tuk Erik Jørgen-Jensen, May 14, 2018.

86. DIIS (1997), 1:313; Oskins and Maggelet (2010).

87. E-mail from Tuk Erik Jørgen-Jensen to the authors, December 8, 2018.

88. E-mail from Tuk Erik Jørgen-Jensen to the authors, December 8, 2018.

89. DIIS (1997), 1:15.

90. Clark (1965), 47–51; E. L. Faust to Tyge Dahlgaard, Danish Embassy, January 11, 1961, UM 105.F.2.b/2, Archive for the Ministry of Foreign Affairs, Danish National Archives.

91. Pengelly (2019).

92. Ritzau (2019).

93. Conley and Melino (2019).

94. DeLillo (1997). See also K. H. Nielsen (2017).

95. Nielsen and Nielsen (2013).

96. Agger and Wolsgård (2001b); DIIS (2005), 1:312.

97. DIIS (1997), 2:314–54.

98. *Berlingske Tidende* (1964).

ARCHIVES

DANISH NATIONAL ARCHIVES

MINISTRY OF FOREIGN AFFAIRS

105.F.2.a. Forsvarsområderne på Grønland [The defense areas in Greenland], 1949–1972.

105.F.2.b/2. Mobil prøvereaktor på Thule [Mobile research reactor at Thule], 1959–1972.

105.F.8. Videnskabelig rådgiver for forbindelsesofficeren i Thule [Scientific adviser to the Danish liaison officer at Thule Air Base], 1954–1972.

105.F.9.a. Amerikansk aktivitet uden for forsvarsområderne [American activity outside the defense areas in Greenland], 1953–1968.

105.F.9.b. Artikler m.v. vedr. amerikansk aktivitet uden for forsvarsområderne på Grønland [Articles etc. concerning American activity outside the defense areas in Greenland], 1957–1964.

105.F.10.b. Press Releases.

105.F.179. Danske og udenlandske pressebesøg i Grønland [Danish and foreign press visits to Greenland], 1952–1972.

105.F.220. Danske ministres og embedsmænds besøg i Grønland [Visits to Greenland by Danish ministers and civil servants], 1958–1972.

MINISTRY FOR GREENLAND

Fælles departementschefsarkiv (fortroligt). Journalsager [Joint Archive of the Permanent Secretaries (confidential). Case files], 1950–1978.

J.nr. XLI A

I: Militærvidenskabelige undersøgelser og Camp Century [Military scientific research and Camp Century].
II: Camp Century.

J.nr. XLI B

I: Militærvidenskabelige undersøgelser [Military scientific research].
II: Amerikanske videnskabelige undersøgelser [American scientific research].
V. Amerikanske militærvidenskabelige undersøgelser [American military scientific research].

ARCHIVES OF RESEARCH CENTER RISØ

Risø National Laboratory, Executive Committee.
Material concerning PM-2A plant maintenance, Camp Century, Thule, 1958–1963.

LABOR MOVEMENT LIBRARY AND ARCHIVE, DENMARK

Archive of Jens Otto Krag, Diaries 1948–1961.

U.S. NATIONAL ARCHIVES AND RECORDS ADMINISTRATION (NARA)

Department of State, RG-59.
Office of the Chief of Engineers, RG-77.
Office of the Chief Signal Officer, RG-111.
U.S. Joint Chiefs of Staff, RG-218.

REFERENCES

Aalborg Stiftstidende. 1963. "Verdens nordligste atomreaktor kold" [World's most northerly nuclear reactor goes cold]. *Aalborg Stiftstidende*, November 16.

AG. 1960. "Atombyen på Indlandsisen vil blive anlagt i løbet af sommeren" [The atomic city on the ice cap will be built during the summer]. *Atuagagdliutit/Grønlandsposten*, April 29.

Agger, Jonathan Søborg, and Lasse Wolsgård. 2001a. "Den størst mulige fleksibilitet: Dansk atomvåbenpolitik, 1956–60" [The greatest possible flexibility: Danish nuclear arms policy, 1956–60]. *Historisk Tidsskrift* 101(1): 76–108.

——. 2001b. "Pro Memoria: Atombomben er vor ven; Den danske regerings stillingtagen til og reaktioner på atomvåbnenes integration i NATOs forsvarsstrategi 1949–1956" [Pro Memoria: The atomic bomb is our friend; The Danish government's position on, and reactions to, the integration of nuclear weapons into NATO's defense strategy, 1949–1956]. *Historisk Tidsskrift* 101(2): 393–434.

American Geophysical Union. 2016. "Melting Ice Sheet Could Release Frozen Cold War-Era Waste." August 4. https://news.agu.org/press-release/melting-ice-sheet-could-release-frozencold-war-era-waste/.

Andersen, Simon, and Jesper Larsen. 1997. "Angreb fra Thule" [Attack from Thule]. *Morgenavisen Jyllands-Posten*, January 18.

Archer, Clive. 1988. "The United States Defence Areas in Greenland." *Cooperation and Conflict* 23(3): 123–44.

Arnold, Henry. 1946. "Air Power for Peace." *National Geographic* 89(2): 170.

Atomenergikommissionen. 1970. *Project Crested Ice: A Joint Danish-American Report on the Crash near Thule Air Base on 21 January 1962 of a B-52 Bomber Carrying Nuclear Weapons. Risø Report 213*. Copenhagen: Atomenergikommissionen [The Danish AEC], Forsøgsanlæg Risø [Risø Nuclear Research Laboratory].

Bader, Henri. 1949. "Trends in Glaciology in Europe." *Bulletin of the Geological Society of America* 60(9): 1309–14.

——. 1962. "Scope, Problems, and Potential Value of Ice Core Drilling in Ice Sheets." *CRREL Special Report 58.* Hanover, NH: Cold Regions Research and Engineering Laboratory.

Baldwin, William C. 1985. *A History of the U.S. Army Engineer Studies Center 1943–1982.* Fort Belvoir, VA: U.S. Army Engineer Studies Center.

Barnett, James W. 1961. *Construction of the Army Nuclear Power Plant PM-2A at Camp Century, Greenland: Final Report.* Hanover, NH: U.S. Cold Regions Research and Engineering Laboratory. https://usace.contentdm.oclc.org/digital/collection/p266001coll1 /id/3968.

Belvoir Castle. 1961. "Boy Scouts Depart Greenland; Helped Army in Research Task." April 7.

Berlingske Tidende. 1959. "Atom-Kraftværk i Grønland overvejes" [Atomic-power plant in Greenland being considered]. *Berlingske Aftenavis,* August 27.

——. 1960. "Udmærkelsesstudent halvt år under isen" [Upper-secondary honors graduate six months under the ice]. October 1.

——. 1963. "Den atomdrevne by under indlandsisen" [The nuclear-powered city under the ice sheet]. April 5.

——. 1964. "Amerika har store planer i Grønland" [America has grand plans in Greenland]. May 2.

Bernard, Nancy E. 1999. *U.S. Television News and Cold War Propaganda, 1947–1960.* Cambridge: Cambridge University Press.

Berthelsen, Anders W. 1995. "Mistanke om radioaktivt spildevand" [Suspicion of radioactive wastewater]. *Berlingske Tidende,* July 14.

Beukel, Erik, Frede Jensen, and Jens Ole Rytter. 2010. *Phasing Out the Colonial Status of Greenland, 1945–54: A Historical Study.* Copenhagen: Museum Tusculanum Press.

Blüdnikow, Bent. 2015. "Journalistiske konspirationsfantasier" [Journalistic imaginings of conspiracy]. *Berlingske Tidende,* April 3.

Breum, Martin. 2016. "Analysis: What a Trump Presidency Means for Denmark and Greenland." *Arctic Deeply,* November 22.

Breum, Martin. 2017. "Grønlands udenrigsminister trækker sig efter heftig magtkamp om Danmark" [Greenland's foreign minister steps down after intense power struggle over Denmark]. *Information,* April 26.

Brink, Poul. 1998. *Thule-sagen—løgnens univers* [The Thule affair: A universe of lies]. Copenhagen: Aschehoug.

Brodie, Bernard. 1959. *Strategy in the Missile Age.* Princeton, NJ: Princeton University Press.

Brøns, Malik. 2016. "Demokraterne rystet over Vittus" [Democrats in shock over Vittus]. *KNR* [Greenlandic Broadcasting Corporation], December 14.

Buderi, Robert. 1996. *The Invention That Changed the World: How a Small Group of Radar Pioneers Won the Second World War and Launched a Technological Revolution.* New York: Simon & Schuster.

Callendar, Guy S. 1938. "The Artificial Production of Carbon Dioxide and Its Influence on Temperature." *Quarterly Journal of the Royal Meteorological Society* 64: 223–40.

CBS News. 2016. "Cronkite Visits City Under the Ice." http://www.cbsnews.com/news/60 -minutes-overtimecronkite-visits-city-under-the-ice/.

Chernus, Ira. 2002. *Eisenhower's Atoms for Peace*. College Station, TX: Texas A&M University Press.

——. 2005. "Operation Candor: Fear, Faith, and Flexibility." *Diplomatic History* 29(5): 779–809.

Christensen, Nikoline Ridder. 2002. "Atoms for Peace & Pax Americana." *Den jyske Historiker* 97: 87–106.

Claesson, Paul, ed. 1983. *Grønland—Middelhavets Perle* [Greenland: Pearl of the Mediterranean]. Copenhagen: Eirene.

Clark, Elmer F. 1965. *Camp Century: Evolution of Concept and History of Design, Construction, and Performance.* Technical Report 174. Hanover, NH: U.S. Cold Regions Research and Engineering Laboratory. https://apps. dtic.mil/dtic/tr/fulltext/u2/477706.pdf.

Colgan, William, Horst Machguth, Mike MacFerrin, Jeff D. Colgan, Dirk van As, and Joseph A. MacGregor. 2016. "The Abandoned Ice-Sheet Base at Camp Century, Greenland, in a Warming Climate." *Geophysical Research Letters* 43(15): 8091–96.

Colt, Ivan. 1960. "Camp Century: America's Fantastic Under-the-Ice Military Base." *Male* 10 (October).

Conley, Heather A., and Matthew Melino. 2019. *The Implications of U.S. Policy Stagnation Toward the Arctic Region*. Washington, DC: Center for Strategic and International Studies. https://csis-prod.s3.amazonaws.com/s3fs-public/publication/191009_ConleyMelino .pdf.

Cull, Nicolas J. 2008. *The Cold War and the United States Information Agency: American Propaganda and Public Diplomacy*. Cambridge: Cambridge University Press.

Danish National Archives. 2017. "Theme: Sale of the Danish West Indian Islands to the USA." The Danish West Indies—Sources of History. https://www.virgin-islands-history .org/en/history/sale-of-the-danish-west-indian-islandsto-the-usa.

Dansgaard, Willi. 1954. "The O^{18}-Abundance in Fresh Water." *Geochimica et Cosmochimica Acta* 5–6: 241–60.

——. 2000. *Grønland—i istid og nutid* [Greenland in the Ice Age and the present]. Copenhagen: Rhodos. Abridged English version (2005) available at http://www.iceandclimate .nbi.ku.dk/publications/FrozenAnnals.pdf.

Dansgaard, Willi, Sigfus T. Johnsen, Jesper Møller, and Chester C. Langway Jr. 1969. "One Thousand Years of Climatic Record from Camp Century on the Greenland Ice Sheet." *Science* 166(3903): 377–81.

Daugherty, Charles M. 1963. *The City Under the Ice*. New York: Macmillan.

DeLillo, Don. 1997. *Underworld*. New York: Scribner.

Det Udenrigspolitiske Nævn [Danish Parliament Foreign Affairs Committee]. 1996. "Beretning om undersøgelsen af regeringens håndtering af Thule-sagen" [Report on the investigation of the government's handling of the Thule Affair], no. 3, 1995–1996, 1. samling. https://www.retsinformation.dk/eli/ft/19951SR00003.

DIIS. 1997. *Grønland under den kolde krig: Dansk og amerikansk sikkerhedspolitik 1945–1968* [Greenland during the Cold War: Danish and American security policy, 1945–1968]. Copenhagen: Dansk Institut for Internationale Studier.

——. 2005. *Danmark under Den Kolde Krig: Den sikkerhedspolitiske situation 1945–1991* [Denmark during the Cold War. The security policy situation, 1945–1991]. Copenhagen: Dansk Institut for Internationale Studier.

Divine, Robert A. 1993. *The Sputnik Challenge: Eisenhower's Response to the Soviet Satellite.* New York: Oxford University Press.

Doel, Ronald E. 2003. "Constituting the Postwar Earth Sciences: The Military's Influence on the Environmental Sciences in the USA After 1945." *Social Studies of Science* 33(5): 635–66.

Doel, Ronald E. 2016. "Defending the North American Continent: Why the Physical Environmental Sciences Mattered in Cold War Greenland." In Doel, Harper, and Heymann (2016), 25–46.

Doel, Ronald E., Kristine C. Harper, and Matthias Heymann, eds. 2016. *Exploring Greenland: Cold War Science and Technology on Ice.* New York: Palgrave Macmillan.

DR. 2018. *Manden uden skygge* [The man without a shadow]. Radio/podcast series. https://www.dr.dk/radio/p1/mandenuden-skygge/manden-uden-skygge-1-3.

Edwards, Paul N. 2012. "Entangled Histories: Climate Science and Nuclear Weapons." *Bulletin of the Atomic Scientists* 68(4): 28–40.

Eisenhower, Dwight D. 1953. "'Atoms for Peace': Address Before the General Assembly of the United Nations on Peaceful Uses of Atomic Energy, New York City." December 8. https://www.eisenhower.archives.gov/all_about_ike/speeches/atoms_for_peace.pdf.

Evans, Thomas C. 1961. *The Construction of Camp Century.* Hanover, NH: U.S. Army Polar Research and Development Center.

Farquhar, John T. 2014. "Arctic Linchpin: The Polar Concept in American Air Atomic Strategy, 1946–1948." *Air Power History* (Winter): 34–45.

Faurby, Ib. 1997. "Missilbase under isen" [Missile base under the ice]. *Politiken*, January 18.

Fleming, James Roger. 2010. *Fixing the Sky: The Checkered History of Weather and Climate History.* New York: Columbia University Press.

Friedrich, Doris. 2016. "The Problems Won't Go Away: Persistent Organic Pollutants (POPs) in the Arctic." *Arctic Institute*, July 1.

Fristrup, Børge. 1962. "Overvintringsstationer på indlandsisen. III. Amerikanske permanente stationer m.v." [Overwintering stations on the ice sheet. III. American permanent stations, etc.]. *Tidsskriftet Grønland* 9: 321–34.

Fristrup, Børge. 1963. *Indlandsisen* [The Greenland ice sheet]. Copenhagen: Rhodos.

Fukuyama, Francis. 1992. *The End of History and the Last Man.* New York: Free Press.

Gaddis, John Lewis. 2005. *Strategies of Containment: A Critical Appraisal of American National Security Policy During the Cold War.* Oxford: Oxford University Press.

Goering, Kent L. 1961. "Eagle Under the Ice." *Boys' Life*, March.

Gregersen, Søren. 1960. "Spejderen under indlandsisen. Først is-smelteren—så atomreaktoren" [The Scout in the ice cap. First the ice-melter—then the nuclear reactor]. *Politiken*, November 27.

——. 1961. *Dagbog fra Camp Century* [Diary from Camp Century].

——. 1961a. "Her går det godt, men pigen savnes" [The Scout in the ice cap. Doing fine, but girl sorely missed]. *Politiken*, January 15.

——. 1961b. "Jeg har været 60 meter nede i indlandsisen" [The Scout in the ice cap. I've been 60 meters down into the ice sheet]. *Politiken*, February 19.

——. 1961c. "Anlagde skøjtebane under indlandsisen" [The Scout in the ice cap. Built ice-skating rink under the ice sheet]. *Politiken*, April 9.

Grønlandskommissionen [Greenland Commission]. 1950. *Grønlandskommissionens betænkning*. Copenhagen: S. L. Møller.

Grønlandsudvalget [Danish Parliament's Greenland Committee]. 2016a. "Alm. del 2015–16: Spørgsmål 57" ["General part 2015–16. Question 57"]. http://www.ft.dk/samling/20151/almdel/gru/spm/57/index.htm.

——. 2016b. "Alm. del 2015–16: Spørgsmål 58" [General part 2015–16. Question 58]. http://www.ft.dk/samling/20151/almdel/gru/spm/58/index.htm.

——. 2018. "Alm. del 2017–18: Spørgsmål 67" [General part 2015–16. Question 67]. https://www.ft.dk/samling/20171/almdel/GRU/spm/67/svar/1496078/index.htm.

-h. 1980. "Vældigt område af indlandsisen svagt radioaktivt" [Huge region of the ice sheet slightly radioactive]. *Atuagagdliutit/Grønlandsposten*, April 24.

Hamilton, Lee David. 1964. *Century: Secret City of the Snows*. New York: Putnam.

Hammerich, Paul. 1960. "Liv under indlandsisen: Camp Century—Aarhundredets by" [Life under the ice sheet: Camp Century—city of the century]. *Politiken*, May 26.

Hannestad, Adam. 2016a. "Grønland truer Danmark og USA: Vil gå til FN om missilbase under isen" [Greenland threatens Denmark and U.S., intends to go to the UN about missile base under the ice]. *Politiken*, November 16.

——. 2016b. "Forbløffet forsker: Vi ville bare advare om klimaforandringerne" [Surprised scientist: We just wanted to warn about climate change]. *Politiken*, November 23.

——. 2016c. "Grønland raser over dansk 'arrogance'" [Greenland irate about Danish "arrogance"]. *Politiken*, December 12.

——. 2016d. "For os er det 75 års opsparet frustration" [For us, this is 75 years of pent-up frustration]. *Politiken*, December 13.

Hansen, Peer Henrik. 2000. *Påskekrisen 1948: Dansk dobbeltspil på randen af Den Kolde Krig* [The Easter Crisis 1948: Danish double-dealing on the brink of the Cold War]. Copenhagen: Høst.

Harper, Kristine. 2017. *Make It Rain: State Control of the Atmosphere in Twentieth-Century America*. Cambridge, MA: MIT Press.

Heefner, Gretchen. 2012. *The Missile Next Door: The Minuteman in the American Heartland*. Cambridge, MA: Harvard University Press.

Herczeg-Konecny, Jessica. 2013. "'We Will Be Prepared': Scouting and Civil Defense in the Early Cold War, 1949–1963." Master's thesis, Indiana University–Purdue University, Indianapolis. https://scholarworks.iupui.edu/handle/1805/4033.

Hewlett, Richard G., and Jack M. Holl. 1989. *Atoms for Peace and War: The Eisenhower Administration and the Atomic Energy Commission*. Berkeley: University of California Press.

Hicks, J. R. 1965. "Summary of Whiteout Studies." CRREL Technical Report 158. Hanover, NH: Cold Regions Research and Engineering Laboratories.

Horton, Murray. 2005. "Obituary: Owen Wilkins." *Peace Researcher* 31 (October).

Hughes, Cindy. 1961. "Even at 64 Below, Two Scouts Like Greenland." *New York World Telegram & Sun*, April 7.

Huntington, Samuel P. 1961. *The Common Defense: Strategic Programs in National Politics.* New York: Columbia University Press.

Jensen, Thomas E., Ann Vibeke Knudsen, and Finn Andersen. 2000. *Bornholm i Krig 1940–1946* [Bornholm at war 1940–1946]. Rønne: Bornholms Museum.

Johansen, Herbert O. 1960a. "Byen under Grønlands Is" [The town under Greenland's ice]. *Det Bedste* 15(7): 104–7.

Johansen, Herbert O. 1960b. "U.S. Army Builds a Fantastic City Under Ice." *Popular Science*, February, 86–89, 229–30.

Jørgensen, Trine Juncher. 2016b. "Sagen er dybt pinlig for Danmark" [The matter is profoundly embarrassing for Denmark]. *Sermitsiaq*, November 18.

Kanstrup, Per. 1995. "Dommedagsbrag i Thulesagen" [Judgment Day boom in the Thule Affair]. *Ekstra Bladet*, June 30.

Kinney, Donald J. 2013. "Selling Greenland: The Big Picture Television Series and the Army's Bid for Relevance During the Early Cold War." *Centaurus* 55(3): 344–57.

Kleist, Bikki, and Anton Gundersen Lihn. 2017. "Grønland klager over Danmark til FN." [Greenland complains about Denmark to UN]. *KNR*, May 16.

KNR. 2016. "Overblik: Sagen om den mistede Pituffik-servicekontrakt" [Overview: The case of the lost Pituffik service contract]. *KNR*, June 24.

Knudsen, Henrik, and Henry Nielsen. 2016. *Uranbjerget: Om forsøgene på at finde og udnytte Grønlands uran fra 1944 til i dag* [Uranium mountain: On the attempts to find and exploit Greenland's uranium from 1944 up to the present]. Copenhagen: Vandkunsten.

Korsmo, Fae L. 2010. "The Genesis of the International Geophysical Year." *Physics Today* 60(7): 38–43.

Kovacs, Austin. 1970. Camp Century Revisited: A Pictorial View 1969." CRREL Special Report 150. Hanover, NH: Cold Regions Research and Engineering Laboratory.

Langway, Chester C. 1967. "Stratigraphic Analysis of a Deep Ice Core from Greenland." CRREL Research Report 77. Hanover, NH: Cold Regions Research and Engineering Laboratory.

——. 2008. "The History of Early Polar Ice Cores." ERDC/CRREL TR-08-01. http://icecores.org/docs/Langway_2008_Early_polar_ice_cores.pdf.

Launius, Roger D., James Roger Fleming, and David H. DeVorkin, eds. 2010. *Globalizing Polar Science: Reconsidering the International Polar and Geophysical Years.* New York: Palgrave Macmillan.

Lidegaard, Bo. 1996. "Nils Svenningsens anfægtelse" [Nils Svenningsen's misgivings]. *Historisk Tidsskrift* 96(1): 184–94.

——. 2001. *Jens Otto Krag 1914–1978.* Vol. 1: *1914–1961.* Copenhagen: Gyldendal.

Lolck, Maiken. 2006. *Klima, kold krig og iskerner* [Climate, Cold War, and ice cores]. Aarhus: Aarhus Universitetsforlag.

m-. 1958a. "Atom-Ubaaden kommer ikke til København—Videnskaben advarer" [Atomic submarine not coming to Copenhagen—science warns]. *Politiken*, August 22.

——. 1958b. "Dramatisk advarsel fra videnskaben mod U-baaden" [Dramatic warning from science against the submarine]. *Politiken*, August 23.

Madsen, Frank. 1994. *Kurt Dunder på Grønland* [Kurt Dunder in Greenland]. Copenhagen: Carlsen Comics.

Mattox, William G. 1973. "Fishing in West Greenland 1910–1966: The Development of a New Native Industry." *Meddelelser om Grønland* 197(1): 1–344.

Martin-Nielsen, Janet. 2012. "The Other Cold War: The United States and Greenland's Ice Sheet Environment, 1948–1966." *Journal of Historical Geography* 38(1): 69–80.

——. 2013. "'The Deepest and Most Rewarding Hole Ever Drilled': Ice Cores and the Cold War in Greenland." *Annals of Science* 70(1): 47–70.

McCormick, John. 1989. *Reclaiming Paradise: The Global Environmental Movement.* Bloomington: Indiana University Press.

Meadows, Donalla H., Dennis L. Meadows, Jørgen Randers, and William W. Behrens III. 1972. *The Limits to Growth: A Report for the Club of Rome's Project on the Predicament of Mankind.* London: Earth Island.

Mechling, Elizabeth Walker, and Jay Mechling. 1995. "The Atom According to Disney." *Quarterly Journal of Speech* 81(4): 436–53.

Mikkelsen, Aksel. 1987. "Eventyret om Blyklippen i Mesters Vig" [The tale of "Lead Mountain" at Mesters Vig]. *Tidsskriftet Grønland* 1: 18–23.

mn. 1960. "Dansk spejder et halvt år under Thules indlands-is" [Danish scout six months under Thule ice sheet]. *Politiken*, September 11.

Mylenberg, Troels, and Ask Rostrup. 1997. "Operation Is-orm" [Operation Iceworm]. *Berlingske Tidende*, January 18.

n-. 1958a. "H. C. Hansen om aflysningen: Ingen politisk forbindelse" [H. C. Hansen on cancellation: No political link]. *Politiken*, August 23.

——. 1958b. "Raket-vaabnene mere almindelige." [Rocket weapons more common]. *Politiken*, November 19.

Needell, Allan A. 2000. *Science, Cold War, and the American State: Lloyd V. Berkner and the Balance of Professional Ideals.* Amsterdam: Harwood Academic.

New York Times. 1960. "Scout to Go to Arctic." June 26.

——. 1961. "2 Scouts Return from Arctic Trip." April 7.

Nielsen, Henrik Karl. 2004. "Den danske Højesterets dom over tvangsflytningen af Thules befolkning" [The Danish Supreme Court's ruling on forced relocation of Thule population]. *Nordisk Tidsskrift for Menneskerettigheder* 22(3): 315–29.

Nielsen, Henry, and Kristian H. Nielsen. 2013. "Inddæmning og tilbagerulning: Om danske myndigheders censur af presseomtale af amerikanske militære aktiviteter i Grønland" [Containment and rollback: On the Danish authorities' censoring of press coverage of American military activities in Greenland]. *temp—tidsskrift for historie* 7: 141–62.

——. 2015. "Camp Century: Koldkrigsbyen i Grønlands indlandsis" [Camp Century: Cold War city in the Greenland ice sheet]. In *Forandringens Vinde—Nye Teknologihistorier,* by Henry Nielsen, Kristian H. Nielsen, Keld Nielsen, and Hans Siggaard Jensen, 314–51. Copenhagen: Praxis—Nyt Teknisk Forlag.

——. 2016. "Camp Century—Cold War City Under the Ice." In Doel, Harper, and Heymann (2016), 195–216.

Nielsen, Jørgen Steen. 2016a. "Camp Century—en iskold gyser om fortidens synder" [Camp Century: A chilling thriller about the sins of the past]. *Information*, August 10.

——. 2016b. "Stor uro i Grønland over USA's affald i indlandsisen" [Great disquiet in Greenland about U.S. waste in the ice sheet]. *Information*, August 11.

Nielsen, Kristian H. 2013. "Transforming Greenland: Imperial Formations in the Cold War." *New Global Studies* 7(2): 129–54.

——. 2017. "Camp Century's Degrees of Coldness: From Cold War Icon to Climate Change–Induced Problem." *Nach Feierabend: Zürcher Jahrbuch für Wissensgeschichte* 13: 17–37.

Nielsen, Kristian H., and Allan Lyngs Kjærgaard. 2015. "At se og fejle som en velfærdsstat: Moderniseringsbestræbelser og -problemer i Grønland efter anden verdenskrig" [Seeing and erring as a welfare state: Modernization efforts and problems in Greenland after World War II]. *temp—tidsskrift for historie* 12: 41–58.

Nielsen, Kristian H., Henry Nielsen, and Janet Martin-Nielsen. 2014. "City Under the Ice: The Closed World of Camp Century in Cold War Culture." *Science as Culture* 23(4): 443–64.

Nissen, Henrik S. 2005. "Kampagnen mod Atomvåben" [The campaign against nuclear weapons]. *Gyldendals og Politikens Danmarkshistorie*. http://denstoredanske.dk/index.php?sideId=306507.

Nye, Joseph S. 2004. *Soft Power: The Means to Success in World Politics*. New York: Public Affairs.

O'Gorman, Ned. 2012. *Spirits of the Cold War: Contesting Worldviews in the Classical Age of American Security Strategy*. East Lansing, MI: Michigan State University Press.

Olesen, Thorsten Borring. 2013. "Between Facts and Fiction: Greenland and the Quest for Sovereignty, 1945–1954." *New Global Studies* 7(2): 117–28.

Olesen, Thorsten Borring, and Poul Villaume. 2005. *Dansk udenrigspolitiks historie, bd. 5: I blokopdelingens tegn 1945–1972* [The history of Danish foreign policy, vol. 5: Under the sign of bloc divisions, 1945–1972]. Copenhagen: Danmarks Nationalleksikon.

Osgood, Kenneth. 2006. *Total Cold War: Eisenhower's Secret Propaganda Battle at Home and Abroad*. Lawrence: University Press of Kansas.

Oskins, James C., and Michael H. Maggelet. 2010. *Broken Arrow*. Vol. 2: *A Disclosure of Significant U.S., Soviet, and British Nuclear Weapon Incidents and Accidents, 1945–2008*. Raleigh, NC: Lulu.com.

Oxford Dictionaries. 2018. "Censorship." https://en.oxforddictionaries.com/definition/censorship.

P. 1958. "Dramatisk advarsel fra videnskaben mod u-baaden" [Dramatic warning from science against the submarine]. *Politiken*, August 23.

Pengelly, Martin. 2019. "Trump Confirms He Is Considering Attempt to Buy Greenland." *The Guardian*, August 18.

Petersen, Nikolaj. 2008. "The Iceman That Never Came: Project Iceworm, the Search for a NATO Deterrent, and Denmark, 1960–62." *Scandinavian Journal of History* 33(1): 88–93.

——. 2011. "SAC at Thule: Greenland in the U.S. Polar Strategy." *Journal of Cold War Studies* 13(2): 90–115.

Politiken. 1959. "Måske får Grønland vort første Atomværk" [Perhaps Greenland will get our first nuclear power plant]. August 28.

Qujaukitsoq, Vittus. 2016. "Der skal ryddes op på de militære anlæg i Grønland" [The military bases in Greenland have to be cleaned up]. *Berlingske*, October 13.

Rasmussen, Søren Hein. 2009. *Den kolde krigs billeder* [Pictures of the Cold War]. Copenhagen: Gyldendal.

Rausch, D. O. 1957. "Interim Report, Ice Tunnel, Tuto Area." SIPRE Technical Report 44. U.S. Army Corps of Engineers.

Ritzau. 2017a. "Grønland presser Løkke for at få fjernet USA's gamle skrald" [Greenland putting pressure on Løkke to have old U.S. garbage removed]. *Politiken*, June 13.

——. 2017b. "Læs hensigtserklæringen om oprydning i Grønland." [Read the statement of intent about cleanup in Greenland]. *Information*, June 14.

——. 2019. "Trump: Frederiksens kommentar om Grønland var væmmelig." [Trump: Frederiksen's comment on Greenland was nasty]. *Politiken*, August 21.

Roman, Peter J. 1995. *Eisenhower and the Missile Gap*. Ithaca, NY: Cornell University Press.

Rosen, Julia. 2016. "Mysterious, Ice-Buried Cold War Military Base May Be Unearthed by Climate Change." *Science News*, August 4.

Ross, Fredric S., and Poul Ancker. 1977. "Thule Air Base." *Tidsskriftet Grønland* 9: 268–78.

Roszak, Theodore. 1969. *The Making of a Counter-Culture: Reflections on the Technocratic Society and Its Youthful Opposition*. Berkeley: University of California Press.

Scouting. 1960. "Deepfreeze Explorer." *Scouting* 48 (November 7).

Sermitsiaq. 2016. "Lyt til advarslen" [Listen to the warning]. December 16.

SIPRE. 1950. "Interim Report to Snow, Ice, and Permafrost Research Establishment." SIPRE Report 1. Minneapolis: University of Minnesota.

Sørensen, Axel Kjær. 2006. *Denmark-Greenland in the Twentieth Century*. Copenhagen: Danish Polar Center.

——. 2015. "Grønland" [Greenland]. Danmarkshistorien.dk. August 11. http://danmarkshistorien.dk/leksikon-og-kilder/vis/materiale/groenland.

Sørensen, Helle Nørrelund. 2017a. "Camp Century: Skrappe krav til atomaffald beroliger ekspert" [Camp Century: Stringent requirements to nuclear waste reassure expert]. *KNR*, February 21.

——. 2017b. "Risø-ekspert: Spildevand på Camp Century er ufarlig" [Risø expert: Wastewater at Camp Century is harmless]. *KNR*, June 1.

——. 2017c. "Camp Century: Nu går undersøgelse i gang" [Camp Century: Investigation now getting underway]. *KNR*, June 20.

Spinardi, Graham. 1994. *From Polaris to Trident: The Development of U.S. Fleet Ballistic Missile Technology*. Cambridge: Cambridge University Press.

——. 2007. "Golfballs on the Moor: Building the Fyllingdales Ballistic Missile Early Warning System." *Contemporary British History* 21(1): 87–110.

Stacy, Susan M. 2000. *A History of the Idaho National Engineering and Environmental Laboratory, 1949–1999*. Idaho Falls: Idaho Operations Office of the Department of Energy.

Suid, L. H. 1990. *The Army's Nuclear Power Program*. Contributions in Military History 98. New York: Greenwood.

Sullivan, Walter. 1964. "U.S. Will Remove Reactor in Arctic." *New York Times*, June 7.

Sundhedsstyrelsen [Danish Health Authority]. 1991. *Undersøgelse af danske statsborgere, der opholdt sig på Thule Air Base i perioden 21/1–17/9 1968* [Examination of Danish citizens who were present at Thule Air Base during the period January 21–September 17, 1968]. Copenhagen: Sundhedsstyrelsen.

——. 2011. *Thule-ulykken: Vurdering af stråledoser fra radioaktiv forurening af landjorden* [The Thule Incident: Assessment of radiation doses from radioactive contamination of the ground]. Copenhagen: Sundhedsstyrelsen.

Taagholt, Jørgen. 2002. "Thule Air Base." *Tidsskriftet Grønland* 2: 42–112.

Time. 1947. "Deepfreeze Defense." *Time*, Atlantic Overseas Edition, January 27.

Turnowsky, Walter. 2016. "Aaja skuffet efter Camp Century-samråd" [Aaja disappointed after Camp Century consultation meeting]. *Sermitsiaq*, November 3.

Udenrigsministeriet [Danish Ministry of Foreign Affairs]. 1951. "Forsvarsaftalen af 1951. Bekendtgørelse om den i København den 27. april 1951 undertegnede overenskomst i henhold til Den nordatlantiske Traktat mellem Regeringerne i Kongeriget Danmark og Amerikas Forenede Stater om forsvaret af Grønland" [The Defense Agreement of 1951. Statutory Order on the agreement signed in Copenhagen on April 27, 1951, pursuant to the North Atlantic Treaty, between the governments in the Kingdom of Denmark and the United States of America on the defense of Greenland]. http://www.stm.dk/index.dsp?page=5562.

——. 1968. *Dansk sikkerhedspolitik 1948–1966* [Danish security policy, 1948–1966]. Copenhagen: Udenrigsministeriet.

Ueda, Herbert T. 2002. Oral interview conducted by Brian Shoemaker, October 23. https://kb.osu.edu/dspace/bit-stream/handle/1811/44677/1/Uedatranscript1.pdf.

Ueda, Herbert T., and Donald E. Garfield. 1968. "Drilling Through the Greenland Ice Sheet." CRREL Special Report 126. Hanover, NH: Cold Regions Research and Engineering Laboratory.

United States Army. 1953. "Operation Blue Jay." https://archive.org/details/gov.archives.arc.2569497.

——. 1960. "Trail Blazed by Renowned Explorer Leads Danish, U.S. Scouts to Arctic Adventure." *Army Research and Development* 1 (December): 14. https://asc.army.mil/docs/pubs/alt/archives/1960/Dec_1960.PDF.

——. 1961a. *The Story of Camp Century: The City Under the Ice*. http://archive.org/details/gov.arc.2569752.

——. 1961b. *U.S. Army and the Boy Scouts*. https://www.youtube.com/watch?v=bRynW4i1iCo.

United States Information Service. 1961. "Søren Spejder i lejr under Grønlands is" [Søren Scout in camp under Greenland's ice]. *U.S.A. i dag* [USA today]. Copenhagen: United States Information Service.

U.S. Army Polar Research and Development Center. 1958. "Design and Construction of an Undersnow Camp on the Greenland Icecap." USA Polar R&D Center Report 1. Fort Belvoir, VA: Corps of Engineers.

Veirum, Thomas Munk, and Ivik Kristiansen. 2017. "Danmark vil undersøge forurening ved Camp Century" [Denmark will investigate contamination at Camp Century]. *KNR*, February 15.

Vestergård, Gunver Lystbæk. 2016. "Camp Century og Frøken Tø" [Camp Century and Miss Thaw]. *Weekendavisen*, sektion 4 (Ideer), August 12.

Villaume, Poul. 1995. *Allieret med forbehold: Danmark, NATO og Den Kolde Krig. Et studie i dansk sikkerhedspolitik 1949–1961* [Ally with reservations: Denmark, NATO, and the Cold War: A study of Danish security policy, 1949–1961]. Copenhagen: Eirene.

——. 1997. "Thule—en sag" [Thule—an affair]. *Information*, November 10.

——. 2015. "'Idealisten' fortegner danmarkshistorien" ["The Idealist" distorts Danish history]. *Politiken*, April 23.

Wager, Walter. 1960. "Life Inside a Glacier." *Saturday Evening Post*, September 10.

——. 1962. *Camp Century: The City Under the Ice*. Philadelphia: Chilton.

Walsøe, Per. 2003. *Thule farvel: Tvangsflytningen i 1953* [Farewell to Thule: The forced relocation in 1953]. Copenhagen: Tiderne Skifter.

Weart, Spencer. 2008. *The Discovery of Global Warming*. Cambridge, MA: Harvard University Press.

Weiss, Eric D. 2001. "Cold War Under the Ice: The Army's Bid for a Long-Range Nuclear Role, 1953–1963." *Journal of Cold War Studies* 3(3): 31–58.

Wikipedia. 2017. "History of the Boy Scouts of America." https://en.wikipedia.org/wiki/History_of_the_Boy_Scouts_of_America.

Wilkes, Owen. 1980. "Hvad indlandsisen gemmer" [What's hidden in the (Greenland) ice sheet]. *Forsvar* 1: 18–20.

Wilkes, Owen, and Robert Mann. 1978. "The Story of Nukey Poo." *Bulletin of Atomic Scientists*, October.

Wright, Edmund A. 1986. "CRREL's First 25 Years, 1961–1986." Hanover, NH: Cold Regions Research and Engineering Laboratory. http://www.dtic.mil/dtic/tr/fulltext/u2/a637200.pdf.

Yale Law School. 2008. "Defense of Greenland: Agreement Between the United States and the Kingdom of Denmark, April 27, 1951." Avalon Project: Documents in Law, History, and Diplomacy. http://avalon.law.yale.edu/20th_century/den001.asp.

Yamanouchi, Takashi. 2011. "Early 20th Century Warming in the Arctic: A Review." *Polar Science* 5(1): 53–71.

IMAGE AND PHOTO CREDITS

The images in this book originate from a wide variety of sources. The editorial team has done their utmost to identify and contact all copyright holders, which may not have been possible in every instance. Any copyright holder unintentionally omitted is welcome to contact the publishers, who will honor valid copyright claims with compensation as though a prior standard agreement had existed.

Figure 0.1: Frank Madsen, *Kurt Dunder i Grønland* [Kurt Dunder in Greenland], Carlsen Comics.
Figure 1.1: R. M. Chapin Jr., *Time*, January 27, 1947.
Figure 1.2: Keystone/Ritzau Scanpix, Image ID 20170814-145548-4.
Figure 1.3: C.-H.K. Zakrisson/Narayana Press.
Figure 1.4: Time & Life Pictures/Getty Images, Image ID 92302856.
Figure 1.5: DIIS (formerly DUPI) (1997), 245.
Figure 1.6: NARA-111-SC-592972, box 1359, no. 12.
Figure 2.1: Dørge/The Worker's Museum, Copenhagen.
Figure 2.2: Keystone Press/Alamy Stock Photo, Image ID E0R936.
Figure 2.3: Robert Hardin/Ritzau Scanpix, Image ID 19981110-020600-mf.
Figure 2.4: NARA-111-SC-586767, box 1337, no. 8.
Figure 3.1: George Burns, *Saturday Evening Post*, 1959.
Figure 3.2: U.S. Army.
Figure 3.3: U.S. Army.
Figure 3.4: Robert C. Magis/*National Geographic*, May 1962, 714–15.
Figure P.1: U.S. Army.
Figure P.2: U.S. Army.
Figure P.3: *National Geographic*, May 1962, 720–21.
Figure P.4: NARA-111-SC-566769, box 1265, no. 6.

Figure P.5: NARA-111-SC-566774, box 1265, no. 11.

Figure P.6: NARA-111-C-16148, box 13, no. 2.

Figure P.7: NARA-111-SC-566789, box 1265, no. 16.

Figure P.8: NARA-111-SC-566794, box 1265, no. 21.

Figure P.9: NARA-111-SC-566796, box 1265, no. 23.

Figure P.10: NARA-111-SC-566797, box 1265, no. 24.

Figure P.11: Pictorial Parade/Staff/Getty Images, Image ID 179671174.

Figure P.12: NARA-111-C-16163, box 13.

Figure P.13: NARA-111-C-17385, box 13.

Figure P.14: W. Robert Moore/National Geographic/Getty Images.

Figure P.15: W. Robert Moore/National Geographic/Getty Images.

Figure P.16: NARA-111-SC-586790, box 1337, no. 11.

Figure P.17: NARA-111-SC-586833, box 1337, no. 54.

Figure P.18: U.S. Army.

Figure P.19: NARA-111-SC-586804, box 1337, no. 25.

Figure P.20: NARA-111-SC-586825, box 1337, no. 46.

Figure P.21: NARA-111-SC-576913, box 1301, no. 3.

Figure P.22: NARA-111-SC-586820, box 1337, no. 41.

Figure P.23: W. Robert Moore/National Geographic/Getty Images.

Figure P.24: W. Robert Moore/National Geographic/Getty Images.

Figure P.25: W. Robert Moore/National Geographic/Getty Images.

Figure P.26: NARA-111-SC-592975, box 1359, no. 16.

Figure P.27: NARA-111-SC-586846, box 1337, no. 66.

Figure P.28: NARA-111-SC-586844, box 1337, no. 64.

Figure P.29: NARA-111-SC-586839, Box 1337, N° 59.

Figure P.30: Private photo collection of Tuk Erik Jørgen-Jensen.

Figure P.31: NARA-111-SC-592989, box 1359, no. 32.

Figure P.32: NARA-111-SC-592995, box 1359, no. 38.

Figure 4.1: Christen Hansen/The Royal Danish Library.

Figure 4.2: Chilton Books, 1962.

Figure 4.3: The Macmillan Company, 1963.

Figure 4.4: Putnam, 1964.

Figure 4.5: McCall Studios/*Popular Science*, February 1960.

Figure 5.1: *Scouting* 48, no. 8 (November 1960): 7.

Figure 5.2: Erik Gleie/Ritzau Scanpix, Image ID 59975639.

Figure 5.3: *Army Research and Development* 1, no. 1 (December 1960): 14.

Figure 5.4: W. Robert Moore/National Geographic/Getty Images.

Figure 5.5: Henrik Storgaard/*Politiken*, November 27, 1960.

Figure 5.6: NARA-111-SC-577981, box 1305, no. 7.

Figure 5.7: *National Geographic*, May 1962.

Figure 5.8: Ritzau Scanpix, Image ID 2486974.

Figure 5.9: Private photo collection of Søren Gregersen.

Figure 5.10: Private photo collection of Søren Gregersen.

Figure 5.11: Private photo collection of Søren Gregersen.

Figure 6.1: Technical Report 158, 1965, 12, CRREL.

Figure 6.2: Technical Report 72, 1961, 10, CRREL.

Figure 6.3: Special Report 150, 1970, 9, CRREL.

Figure 6.4: "Top of the World Railroad," Press Release, U.S. Army Material Command, Washington, DC, 1963.

Figure 6.5: Special Report 34, July 1959, 4, SIPRE.

Figure 6.6: Special report 150, 1970, CRREL.

Figure 7.1: Willi Dansgaard.

Figure 7.2: Willi Dansgaard.

Figure 7.3: NARA-111-C-36225, box 13, no. 1.

Figure 7.4: NARA-111-SC-633230, box 1502, no. 4.

Figure 7.5: DeWikiMan/Wikimedia Commons.

Figure 7.6: Dansgaard et al., *Science* 166, no. 3903 (October 17, 1969): 380.

Figure 7.7: J. Murray Mitchell, courtesy AIP Emilio Segrè Visual Archives/Gift of Chester C. Langway Jr.

Figure 7.8: Lars Krabbe/Ritzau Scanpix, Image ID 9896562.

Figure 8.1: Al Fenn/Getty Images, Image ID 50398019.

Figure 8.2: Donald Uhrbrock/Getty Images, Image ID 50561211.

Figure 8.3: Technical Report 174, 1965, 50, CRREL.

Figure 8.4: Jon Fresch, Copyright by Steffen Winther, The Thuleforum.

Figure 8.5: Jon Fresch, Copyright by Steffen Winther, The Thuleforum.

Figure 9.1: Henrik Storgaard/*Berlingske Tidende*, January 18, 1997.

Figure 9.2: William Colgan, GEUS.

Figure 9.3: Colgan (2016), 8093.

Figure 9.4: Colgan (2016), 8094.

Figure 9.5: Evan Vucci/Ritzau Scanpix, Nº 20160617-205736-L.

Figure 9.6: William Colgan, GEUS.

Figure 9.7: Private photo collection of Tuk Erik Jørgen-Jensen.

Figure 9.8: Private photo collection of Tuk Erik Jørgen-Jensen.

Figure 9.9: Private photo collection of Tuk Erik Jørgen-Jensen.

INDEX